Christian
Political
Theology

Christian
Political
Theology
A Marxian Guide

Joseph M. Petulla

Foreword by George A. Mueller, M.M.

ORBIS
BOOKS
MARYKNOLL.
NEW YORK

Copyright © 1972 Orbis Books, Maryknoll, New York 10545
Library of Congress Catalog Card Number: 77-190167

ISBN 0-88344-0601

Second Printing

Manufactured in the United States of America

Contents

Foreword

Political theology is assuming growing importance in Christian thinking. Books and articles are being written to explore the roots, work out the implications, and develop the possibilities of this "new" theology.

Just another fad? Hardly. A solidly grounded and balanced political theology is capable of presenting, in a more useful context, the best insights such as those of the Death of God, the theology of hope, and the theology of liberation.

In addition to this synthesizing function, political theology is forcing a new look at Scripture, encouraging the debate in philosophy over theory and praxis, integrating social sciences into a practical (should we say "moral"?) theology, and examining the historical evolution of structures which it aims both to criticize and to open up to new possibilities. Most important, it is helping Christians to become involved as Christians in the world about them; it is sensitizing them to issues that call for social change through effective action.

Since Vatican II the Catholic Church has become conscious of the need for new relationships with men of all political positions. Specifically, John XXIII wanted new relationships with the Marxist world and shifted official Catholic attitudes toward an openness and desire for contact at all levels. The dialogue that has resulted has compelled theologians to take a fresh look at Marxian thought and the power it has generated around the world.

Christian Political Theology is an expression of this new Christian eagerness to listen to others. It is a search for guidelines along which to develop a political theology. The author, a Roman Catholic theologian, focuses on the central issue. He does not use the biblical ánd missionary term "conversion" but rather "transformation of man and his society," an expression which best places a Christian footing on contemporary thresholds. It puts Christians into a much larger world where they are but a minority working for social change.

Unfortunately, Christians have not had easy acćess to the people whom they formerly considered as most unfriendly if not hostile—people who were more committed to radical social and political change than were traditional Christians. The author now places the interested Christian reader in direct contact with radical socialists, revealing their experience, methods, and insights. He thereby enables the reader to discover how his deepest concerns for integral human development can be translated into Christian social action—action that is relevant only when the issues have been exposed to a forceful Marxian analysis.

By design, then, this book becomes "A Marxian Guide." In no way is it a guide to Marxism or Marxist ideas. Such books exist elsewhere. The author is interested in keys to action, not to socialist ideology. That is why he avoided the subtitle "A *Marxist* Guide." He wants the reader to examine the social and political realities facing the world today and to come up with a rigorous method of analysis. He also provides some working tools to help the reader discern in a more scientific manner the mainsprings of processes shaping society for better or for worse.

The author is therefore quite selective in order to offer only what is of direct value. This selectivity eliminates the need for negative critique, and enables both author and reader to focus on man and his task rather than on Marxism. The author is guided throughout this well-researched synthesis by his Christian heritage and its original perspectives. His work thus becomes a starting point from which Christians can once more discover the unique contributions they can make to our global society—if they are willing to face the questions which this book opens for them.

George A. Mueller, M.M.

Acknowledgments

The author gratefully acknowledges the permissions granted by publishers to quote from books and articles.

KARL MARX: *Capital*, Vol. I (© 1967); *Capital*, Vol. III (© 1967); *The Poverty of Philosophy* (© 1963); *Pre-Capitalist Economic Formations* (© 1963); *Wage-Labour and Capital* (© 1933). KARL MARX and FREDERICK ENGELS: *German Ideology* (© 1966). FREDERICK ENGELS: *Socialism: Utopian and Scientific* (© 1935). I. V. LENIN: *Imperialism: The Highest Stage of Capitalism* (© 1939); *Left-Wing Communism* (© 1940); *State and Revolution* (© 1943); *War and the Workers* (© 1940); *What Is To Be Done* (© 1969). [Reprinted by permission of International Publishers.]

Karl Marx Early Writings, translated by T. B. Bottomore, © 1963 by T. B. Bottomore. [Used by permission of McGraw-Hill Book Company.]

CHE GUEVARA: "Notes on Man and Socialism in Cuba," in *Che Guevara Speaks*, © 1967 by Merit Publishers. [Reprinted by permission of Pathfinder Press.]

HARVEY COX: "The Marxist-Christian Dialogue," in *Marxism and Christianity*, edited by Herbert Aptheker, © 1968 by Humanities Press, Inc.

NORMAN GOTTWALD: *The Church Unbound*, © 1967 by
Norman Gottwald. [Reprinted by permission of J. B. Lippincot
Company.]

H. RICHARD NIEBUHR: *The Meaning of Revelation*, © 1941
by The Macmillan Company, renewed by Florence Niebuhr,
Cynthia Niebuhr, and Richard H. Niebuhr.

FRIEDRICH GOGARTEN: *Despair and Hope for Our Time*,
translated by Thomas Weiser (Philadelphia: Pilgrim Press), ©
1970 by United Church Press. [Reprinted by permission.]

Sincere appreciation is also expressed to Mrs. Charlotte
Petulla for reading and typing the manuscript; to Norman
Gottwald and Charles McCoy of the Graduate Theological
Union, Berkeley, for their continued encouragement and
helpful suggestions; and to Leszek Kolakowski and Richard
Lichtman, whose lectures on Marxism at the University of
California, Berkeley, afforded valuable guidance to the author's
own Marxian studies.

Christian
Political
Theology

Introduction

During an address at a large theological gathering a few years ago, the Roman Catholic theologian Yves Congar commented on a familiar objection to Christian preaching in recent times—that there is too much talk about social issues and not enough about traditional Christian spiritual themes.[1] Congar did not believe the accusation could be supported by sufficient evidence to make it credible; but even if it were, he said, the problem lies in the presentation of social questions in pious generalities rather than in carefully worked-out analytical studies.

Congar's discourse included a few suggestions for broadening the present "task of theology." One of his models was Vatican II's *Gaudium et spes*, the Pastoral Constitution on the Church in the Modern World.[2] He noted that a classical, deductive theological method was inadequate when the Council Fathers had to come to terms with social and ethical matters in the world. For examining the world's institutions and human interaction, an analytical, investigative, descriptive theological approach is needed. This construct has theological validity because its foundation "is the elaboration of an ethics of the social and historic man viewed precisely in the historic and social conditions of his actions and duties. The man of our current moral treatises is the individual subject loaded with obligations towards God and his neighbors; he is not the man engaged in the construction of the world and called to take a position in the causes of justice, of peace, of progress and organization."[3]

Congar is arguing for a formal theological discipline as a branch of the larger theological program "dealing with the Christian engaged in the social and political movements which serve the construction of a *human* world, a world tailored to the measure of the whole man and of all men."[4] Johannes Metz calls this branch of theology "political theology." It is the springboard of my own investigations.

Metz and Moltmann, two popular exponents of the theology of hope who have furnished a strong beginning in the elaboration of a political theology, are considered in Chapter One. Here I show why I prefer a Marxian approach, taking leads from Ernst Bloch and of course from Marx himself. I present background material leading to a methodology for political theology, a methodology which requires an analytical instrument for grappling with the social processes of the world. Marxism provides such a powerful analytical tool.

But when a theologian decides to utilize a particular analytical instrument, he has to justify it by showing a basic agreement between the religious foundation and its analytical superstructure. Not every philosophy or religion can support a Marxian conceptual apparatus, a fact clarified in recent years by the discussions about the compatability of Marxism and existentialism and similarly of Marxism and Christianity. The difficulty with these discussions, or even with a discussion about the compatability between Marxism and Buddhism or Hinduism, lies in the possibility of most philosophies and religions being validly interpreted in more than one way, depending on the criteria the interpreter prefers. All religions have inspired mystic, eremitic cultists as well as political visionaries. One can even consider ascetic Hindu retreat houses, Buddhist temples, or medieval Catholic monasteries in terms of their protest against the oppressive structures of the larger society rather than as antiworldly, nonpolitical, sectarian communities.

At any rate, the political theologian has to establish fundamental connections between any two systems he wants to relate. My contention is that Christianity and Marxism share a basic "onlook" (Donald Evans' term, discussed in Chapter One), or commitment perspective, on the question of man's alienation and liberation, which justifies the theologian's use of a Marxian analysis. A univocal onlook exists neither in Christianity nor in Marxism; in fact, the same symbols, myths, teachings often have different meanings for different people. Marx "looked on" the social, political, and economic processes of history and developed a theory which he believed most accurately described them. Alienated relationships within the state and civil society, struggles among the classes, the emergence of the proletariat, the changing character of labor, technological economic developments which foreshadowed socialistic institutions, a changing consciousness in the working class—these are some of the historical categories which shaped Marx's theoretical understanding of reality and "onlook." Just as Marx's onlook was derived from an analysis of historical processes, early Christianity's onlook was formed from an appreciation of its Old Testament roots and beginning history. I try to uncover some historical evidence which shows that Christianity has reason to look at the world in a manner compatible with a Marxian worldview, although a Christian onlook on alienation and liberation lacks precisely the "scientific" social analysis which is present in a Marxian onlook. Furthermore, although the onlook of Marx and the Marxists rests on an historical base, it is indistinguishable from their social analyses; therefore I do not separate the Marxian onlook from its analytical application to the world.

A primary purpose of this book is the presentation of a Marxian conceptual device as a contribution to an understanding of economic, political, and social processes from within a Christian theological perspective. My feeling is that this intention can best be accomplished by the selection of significant passages on alienation and liberation from Marxist theoreticians—Marx himself, Engels, Lenin, Mao Tse-Tung, Fidel Castro, and Che Guevara—with minimal commentary. I present these passages in Chapter Two and Chapter Three in a way that allows Marx and the Marxists to speak for themselves. My hope is that the selections not only offer conceptual units which may be absorbed by political theology, but also give a glimpse into the personality of each author. To accomplish these ends it has been necessary to include a few rather long passages, but I think their inclusion is warranted on the basis of importance and interest. Lenin, Mao, Castro, and Guevara put new vitality and realism into Marxian thinking. Their contributions form an important part of these chapters. This is not because the men agreed with Marx on every point, or understood the alienating institutions of their societies in the same way. Neither is it because they confronted identical problems when they came to power, or even because they exert enormous influence around the world today. Rather, this set of Marxist thinkers is notable because each handled Marx's theology and method in a practical way. Each looked upon Marx's writings as a guide to action and sought to apply one of Marx's basic dictums—"To overthrow all conditions in which man is an oppressed, enslaved, forsaken and wretched being"—to the conditions of his own society. Recent history, unfortunately, has shown that the full liberation of their people has not easily been achieved, as much for reasons of economic underdevelopment as because of the struggle to establish themselves as world powers. This fact should not lead to total neglect of their theories or efforts any more than democratic theory and practice should be discounted because large segments of the American population have not been able to fully exercise their democratic prerogatives.

It is not my intent in Chapters Two and Three to compare Marxian and Christian theory in detail. The purpose of these chapters is the systemization of an analytical conceptual instrument, something beyond the scope of traditional Christianity. The Marxian analysis in several historic forms is presented first. Then a contemporary Marxian viewpoint is offered to illustrate how Marxian conceptual units may be employed in the context of an advanced industrial capitalist society. Finally, a brief survey of the origins of Christianity indicates some points of similarity between Marxian and Christian onlooks. A glance at the two chapters might lead one to suspect they are unduly weighted in favor of the Marxian analysis. Indeed they are, because their aim is not the elucidation of Christian revolutionary theory, but the outline of a conceptual device with which political theologians might gain a practical approach to economic, political, and social processes.

The Christian onlook is an important but secondary consideration.

The project is a neutral one in the sense that it would be
counterproductive to offer a total critique of the Marxian
account. However, I have highlighted those aspects which I
consider to be most valuable and played down or eliminated
facets of Marxian theory with which I do not agree or which I
do not believe to be applicable to political theology. It would
be impossible to list all these areas of disagreement or
inapplicability, but there are a few examples which can be
mentioned: Marx's optimistic view that history necessarily is
going in the direction of ultimate socialization and therefore
humanization, or his economic materialism which tended to
make the economic base of society the lone determinative
factor for change in all social institutions—legal, religious,
educational, etc. Marx's handling of religion is another case in
point. Looking at nineteenth-century Christianity, he concluded
that religion hindered the free development of man and the
world and therefore is a source of alienation. I omit extensive
coverage of the religion question because I believe that religion
can be a progressive rather than a reactionary force. In my final
chapter I give some of my reasons for this belief. This procedure
may be considered indirectly critical of Marxism, but it in no
way pretends to be a rounded evaluation of Marxist theory.

Marx thought that it should be the purpose of philosophy
to change the world; I contend that political theology should
adopt this intention. My assumption is that the theory
developed by political theologians will have the power to induce
self-awareness and emotional involvement in the process of
social change. The implications of this assumption are that
political theologians will break the shackles of didactic abstractions and formulate their conclusions more artistically, more
popularly, more innovatively, in the milieu of the people they
are serving, and that they will work actively for social change.
That is, political theology must be developed out of active
praxis within the social structures that are being described. An
analysis of the alienating quality of economic, political, or
social life must carry a personal bite or flavor with it; the
theologian must understand the personal measure of alienating

harm or liberating change. Both experiences are facilitated in
small ecclesial communities that help to mediate the meaning of
alienation and liberation. The praxis of these ecclesial communities represents the content of Chapter Four.

The reader will observe a shifting of gears in this chapter; I
cover the historical Christian tradition first, then offer texts
from Lenin and Mao on specific strategies and tactics which
might be applicable to ecclesial communities. Here I do not
view the Marxists from the standpoint of their analytical social
theory, but rather I am interested in their practical guidelines
on the relationship of the Party to society. Thus the specific
Christian character of ecclesial groups is discussed first, and
afterward the concrete, adaptable political features are taken
from the Marxists.

A question which might repeatedly arise in the mind of the
reader is what does all this have to do with Christianity. If a
simplistic comparison between Marxism and Christianity is not
possible and if traditional Christianity has often been asocial or
even antisocial, why not simply adopt a Marxian analysis and
drop the question of Christianity? The fact is that the
theologian's Christian faith informs his selection of Marxian
data, and his faith also is responsible for a unique understanding
of political activity. In Chapter Five I consider the Christian
teachings that seem to me to directly affect the style of political
theology. Although the focus of political theology is directed at
society, it rests on fundamental notions about God, man, and
community.

Many Americans will object to the presentation of the
works of Marx and his communist followers in this enterprise.
We remember the Stalin purges, Hungary, Czechoslovakia. The
word *communism* conjures up images of bloodbaths, oppression, censorship, fear, elitist bureaucracies, and the crushing of
the individual to advance the causes of the state. Even the New
Left in America and abroad have been outspoken in their
denunciations of Soviet repression and economic imperialism. It
is not difficult to find weaknesses in the political life of
communist nations. Of course, the inhabitants of communist
countries experience the same negative feelings about capitalist
liberal democracies, which they see as perpetrators of impe-

rialist wars, police repression of demonstrations, racist domestic policies, unequal distribution of wealth, etc.

This book was not prepared to offer a critique of either liberal democracies or communist states. Its implications apply to both societies, for the value of any social order must be measured according to the "value it places upon man's relation to man. It is not just a question of knowing what the liberals have in mind but what in reality is done by the liberal state within and beyond its frontiers. Where it is clear that the purity of its principles is not put into practice, it merits condemnation rather than absolution."[5] With the communist state as with the capitalist liberal state, condemnation, and, more important, change are in order.

Political theology must take up this new task.

Notes

1. Yves Congar, "Theology's Task after Vatican II" in *Theology of Renewal*, Vol. I (Montreal: Palm, 1968), pp. 61-62.
2. *Ibid.*, pp. 57-58.
3. *Ibid.*, p. 61.
4. *Ibid.*, p. 58.
5. Maurice Merleau-Ponty, *Humanism and Terror* (Boston: Beacon, 1969), p. xiv.

The Contours of Political Theology

THE ROOTS OF POLITICAL THEOLOGY

Political theology is not the result of completely new enterprises. Its roots reach deep into ancient Middle Eastern civilizations, where religion played a major role in stabilizing political and social institutions. The monarch was regarded as a sacred person, one who enjoyed the prerogative of understanding the unchanging truths of a divinely governed cosmos. Through him stability and harmony were assured, as well as an immutable social order. Religion guaranteed the continuance of his political realm by its sacred rites, which were performed to protect an unchanging harmony in man's relations with nature. Any kind of change threatened society's fall back into primordial chaos. Van Leeuwen shows that religion and rule were joined in virtually every ancient civilization of the Near and Far East, though superficial external differences between them existed.[1]

Hellenistic society utilized this notion of the universe, but added some philosophical sophistication. By the fourth century B.C. Plato provided a model for Greek society that served to unite philosophy, religion, and politics in a static conception of the world. Since the world is finite and everything in it transitory, society must participate in an infinite, permanent, immutable source of reality to maintain itself in existence. The

8

world soul, or being, has a divine character that lends this permanence, unity, and goodness to the universe. The worship of seasons in ancient societies became joined with emperor worship in Hellenistic and, later, in Roman social systems. The unity of being was preserved in the political order through the emperor.

Aristotle's ontocratic model, which followed Plato's conception, was applied consciously and unconsciously for many centuries; it took hold rather firmly in the Christian West at the time of Constantine. Origen laid the the foundation for Christianity's new "divine right of kings" theory with a notion of God provided by Greek philosophy—the Supreme Being.[2] Transition from the Greek philosophical concept of being to the Christian theological notion of Supreme Being carried political overtones with it. The emperor enjoyed primary access to that Being and protected the sacred order of the Christian empire, the unity of which became necessarily identified with religious uniformity. Heresy was a public offense against truth, order, and harmony in the realm; centuries earlier Plato propounded a similar view regarding atheists in his *Laws*.[3] Ontocratic remnants linger in variegated areas of contemporary society: hierarchical prerogatives of established churches and "princes" of the church, the state church, religion as a sanction of static political systems.

As the theory of an ontocratic society was failing to live up to its expectations, St. Augustine introduced an alternative view of society and the church. According to his conception, spelled out in *The City of God*, the coming of Jesus Christ into the world has radically re-ordered all of history. In Christ mankind is redeemed, fulfilled, brought to perfection; henceforth nothing can happen in history that has not already happened in Christ. It remains only for individual men to accept Christ in faith and re-live his life in their own personal histories. Thus men can exist in an earthly city and a heavenly city simultaneously. The focus of Augustinian theory was directed at Christ in contrast to the earlier emphasis on a Supreme Being; Augustine was interested in explaining the world's unstable conditions (notably the fall of Rome to Alaric in 410) in different terms. Since the earthly and heavenly orders of existence are irreconcilable, tension between them will always create problems for believers in a sinful and fallen world. Individual men can be saved from the corruption of earthly society by casting their lot with the heavenly realm, which exists in the world within the hearts and souls of men. The history of the earthly city will never improve. It is the task of the church to preach the gospel to all men so that everyone may have the opportunity to enter the heavenly city by baptism and gain salvation at the consummation of the world.[4]

In contrast to earlier Christian theologians, Augustine moved the emphasis from "God in the world through an established order of life" to "Christ in the believer by faith." His theory entailed a different ontology, one in which the individual is specified and becomes the center of the world. Man's belief, his subjectivity, transcends the world. The seeds were sown for a new metaphysics and a different conception of God and the church. The practical effect of the theory in the political order was the stifling of the possibility of change. If only the heavenly remains important, all change is fruitless and unnecessary. The course of history is therefore removed from the intentional activity of men. History's final end alone concerns the believer; that will be the time of his deliverance from society's injustices.

The Augustinian tradition was embraced by Luther and enshrined in his doctrine of the separation of the two realms—the worldly and the spiritual. Lutheran teaching generally has regarded the spiritual realm as subject to the Lordship of Christ while the world is given an independent history, only indirectly accountable to Christ. Modern variants of the theory of two realms place all societies and nations under Christ's Kingship, but even this approach fails to include provision for social change in the temporal order. Until very recently Christian theology has vacillated between an ontocratic view of society and a theory based on the doctrine of the two realms, with the scattered historical exceptions of a sectarian Christian underground whose primary emphasis was temporal and "this-worldly."

KARL MARX'S CRITIQUE

The unworldly, unrevolutionary, superstitious approach of Christianity is precisely what Marx opposed in the Christianity of his day. Marx's interest in religion stemmed from his concern for man. Taking Feuerbach's lead, he developed a theory of religious alienation—that man projects his own perfections into the supernatural and calls the sum of these qualities "God." This process alienates man from himself. Marx went beyond Feuerbach in asserting that economic and social forces drive man to create illusions such as religion. It does no good to recognize that man is alienated from himself in religion as long as man is not emancipated from the underlying causes of alienation found in the economic order. He furthermore insisted that religion inhibits genuine revolutionary movements towards social change. "Religion is the opium of the people" means both that religion is a protest against inhuman social structures and also that religion is a safety valve for people who would otherwise engage in revolutionary activity. Religion, according to Marx, always manages to offer divine legitimacy for unjust structures and profits from the arrangement. The proper role of man is the creation of new, liberated structures.

According to Marx, Hegel was also unworldly and unrevolutionary, but in a different way. Although Hegel attempted to bridge the gap between Spirit and history, he ended up, says Marx, with an "Idea" outside actual men's lives. Hegel placed history under the logical, abstract control of Spirit and its self-realization in the world. He speaks of Spirit as "manifesting, developing, and perfecting its powers in every direction which its manifold nature can follow . . . . What powers it inherently possesses, we can learn from the variety of products and formations which it originates."[5] That is, history is the external object of the work of Spirit.

The opposite is true from Marx's viewpoint. Instead of starting with Spirit or Reason or Idea, he begins with man as maker of history, as creative producer of his world. It is man's activity, praxis, labor, that transforms nature, not a Spirit objectifying itself. Neither is man a mere reflection of history's social institutions, as the nineteenth-century French materialists claimed. Marx dealt with this problem in the *German Ideology*: "circumstances make men as much as men make circumstances."[6] The circumstances that influence men today were created by men yesterday, and today men are creating circumstances that will influence other men tomorrow. "History is nothing but the succession of the separate generations, each of which exploits the materials, deposits the productive forces handed down to it by all preceding ones, and thus, on the one hand, continues the traditional activity in completely changed circumstances and, on the other hand, modifies the old circumstances with a completely changed activity."[7]

All economic, political, and social relationships are the result of man's praxis. This is the reason Marx will insist against Proudhon that it is not enough to describe economic relationships in a given society, but one has to understand how men have created these very relationships. Men are responsible for even the dehumanized aspects of their world, but this alienation contains the seed of a liberated future.

The dynamism of man's praxis is its unconscious effort to liberate itself from various forms of dehumanization, "the positive supersession of all alienation."[8] Such a notion presupposes a teleological conception of history, which Marx learned from Hegel, and a vague preconception of what man could become in a nonalienated life situation. Marx's anthropology, made clear in his 1844 manuscripts, also assumes that man will not be able to fulfill himself as a free creative being in isolation from his fellow men. The free development of every individual is the condition of free development for all, and social cooperation is the fulfillment of all of man's human potentialities.

Marx's idea of praxis is at the same time a critique of a society that harbors and necessitates alienation. Man alienates his material and spiritual activity from himself as he builds a society that becomes oppressively hostile to its creator. In one of his 1844 manuscripts, "Alienated Labor," Marx speaks of the four sides of alienation.[9] Each of these concerns man's labor, his everyday praxis.

Alienation first of all refers to the objects which man produces in his labor. These works represent social man's creative labor, but they are taken from him and eventually enslave him in an exchange economy. Next, the productive activity itself is alienated from human labor, since it does not affirm man's inmost creative needs. Third, because his activity is alienated from him, man is in fact alienating himself from his essence, which consists of creative activity. Finally, the result of alienated labor is the alienation of men from other men. They do not work with one another as they fulfill themselves in a community of human labor; instead men are separated from each other at the very source of this same life activity.

For Marx the alienated man is not truly a man and won't become one until his labor becomes nonalienated. When man's actual daily existence, his praxis, fully exhibits his social essence as realized creative freedom, then man will become what he should be. Such praxis cannot be forced from the outside by the artificial construction of an ideal social system. It can only be developed by men in the context of their own labor and social struggle. As man is the sum of his own historically created possibilities, so society is the historical creation of human activity. The difference between Marx and Hegel does not lie in the notion of activity since man is an active being for Hegel as well as Marx. Hegel, however, saw man's activity as mainly derived from his activity of self-consciousness, the final goal of which is absolute knowledge of reality, the end of human history. For Marx man's activity is directed to the creation of a de-alienated world. His evaluation of history and society is far from either the ontocratic or Augustinian tradition, both static and nonrevolutionary views of history.

ERNST BLOCH

If the Christian theologians of hope have recently begun to reinterpret their heritage, a major stimulus for their work has come from a contemporary Marxist, Ernst Bloch, who also happens to be Jewish and an atheist. It is not difficult to understand why Bloch has exercised such a profound influence on modern theologians, despite the disparity in both background and belief. His principal sourcebook is the Bible, which he secularizes radically.

Bloch highlights two ideas in his work: the quality of man's hope and the consequences of a completely open future. Hope means possibility. It is the foundation of a future that is not-yet-being, something not-yet-conscious, and something that is not-yet-come-into-being. Man lives in a preconscious hope and through hope creates a new society. Bloch sees the two ideas linked in the preaching of Jesus in a way that distinguishes his teaching from all other religions of ancient civilizations: the motions of a new kingdom and a new life. "The preaching of Jesus, being eschatological in nature, was the least conciliatory toward the 'existing aeon,' which was why it caused the greatest sensitivity to mere lip service and ecclesiastic compromise. Presenting a contrast was vital to it, far more than other religions, since it began as a thoroughly social movement among the laboring and heavily laden; at the same time it gave to those who labored and were heavily laden an impulse, a sense of values, and a hope they could never have found in the mere fact of their oppression—or have not found there, at least, in four thousand years."[10]

Bloch credited Christianity as the one religion that emerged from its mythical predecessors, "not a static and thus apologetic mythus, but a human-eschatological and thus explosively posited messianism"; it should become "total hope, and an explosive one."[11] But Christianity must shake off its illusion, eliminate the divine hypostasis, the Supreme Being that is a supreme obstacle to a completely open future. God, the *ens perfectissimum*, defines the present along with the future by his very being: "where there is a great master of the world there is no room for freedom, not even for the freedom of God's children."[12]

It is the eschatology of the Bible that excites Bloch. He sees a secularized kingdom as the solution to the problems of religious projection and superstition. God is done away with and redefined as "the supreme utopian problem," the problem of the end.

In his place is left no vacuum. Into the space, the field in which religious projections and myths of perfection have dwelled, Bloch places his concept of the not-yet-being, in religious terms, the kingdom. Yet, this kingdom is not one identified with a transcendent, other-worldly, divine order. It exists in the real world of possibility: "that we shall be saved, that there can be a kingdom of heaven, that an evident insight into dream contents establishes them for the human soul, that correlatively confronting them is a sphere of reality, no matter how we define it—this is not only conceivable, that is, formally possible; it is downright necessary, far removed from all or real indications, proofs, allowances, and premises of its existence."[13]

The not-yet-being harbors an open future, and thus the possibility of chaos as well as kingdom; either the threat of nothingness or the promise of all, either heaven or hell. Satan, the Prince of Darkness, is the myth in the space of religious projection that envisages horror, destructiveness, evil, pain. When this religious projection is demythologized, the not-yet-being space in man enables him to see demonic possibilities in history's future as well as divine ones. Bloch sees utopian space problems, problems of the end, as questions that are anthropocentric, not theocentric, and immanent in history, not transcendent. They do not deal with the *Above*, or *Other*, or *Mystery*, or the *Ineffable*. The not-yet-being requires no final leap. It is not a separate supernatural sphere of existence.

Bloch believes that the concept of the kingdom requires atheism because it must be something attainable, not a wishful void: "the kingdom remains a messianic frontal space without any theism . . ., without atheism there is no room for messianism."[14] Rather than look for a will in heaven, which is for Bloch nowhere, a religious people should create the future towards which their true instincts of hope propel them. Messianism, the quest for emancipation, lies deep within the hopeful hearts of all men. "Messianism is the salt of the earth—and that of heaven, lest not only the earth lose its savor but the intended heaven too."[15] The social mission of hope can only be unleashed in the world when the God hypostasis is gone once and for all. There is no doubt about Bloch's Marxian belief that religion interferes with radical social change.

THEOLOGY OF HOPE

The theologians of hope who have followed Bloch's lead take their name from the title of his principal work, *Das Prinzip Hoffnung*. Jürgen Moltmann, the pioneer spokesman of the school, author of *The Theology of Hope*, which started the discussion, shares with Bloch the view that man is a "hopeful" being, and that the future must be open. He believes especially that the eschatalogical perspective of the Bible offers the key to authentic Christianity. Moltmann's biblical theology reverses all Platonic ontocratic models and their variants. His system is based on change rather than the permanence which "being" implies; in fact, his approach is not a theological system at all because this tradition necessitates rules, laws, or doctrines with the underpinnings of permanence.

Moltmann differs from Bloch's position that a theory of change demands atheism. The eschatological promises of the God of Abraham and Father of Jesus Christ relate the kingdom to God himself. God is not the Ground of Being in the world, who interferes with man's freedom and through whom all things derive their being and existence, but the God of the coming kingdom. God is not "above us" or "within us" but ahead of us, hidden in the radically "new," the *novum* accessible only by his promises. He has nothing in common with the Greek preoccupation with the eternal present. He is a "God of hope" (Rom.15:13), "YHWH, as the name of God who first of all promises his presence and his kingdom and makes them prospects for the future, is a God 'with future as his essential nature,' a God of promise and of leaving the present to face the future, a God whose freedom is the source of new things that are to come."[16]

Moltmann's contribution lies in his acceptance of Bloch's challenge to Christian theology. He attempts to pull theology away from its quest for truth within the Greek categories of the eternal present or timeless being. He introduces the category of the "new" in his imperative that an eschatological faith demands the transformation of the world: "It is not concerned with an event that took place at the beginning of time nor with explaining why the world exists and why it is as it is. It is oriented towards the future, and hence its object is to change the world rather than explain it, to alter human existence rather than elucidate it. This eschatological attitude towards the world is concerned more with making history than with interpreting nature."[17]

In Moltmann's scheme the promise of God's coming in the kingdom of righteousness and truth constantly challenges the institutions of the world. Hope theology leads to a commitment of social change through the freedom of human existence in an open future. Moltmann exhorts Christians to enter the political arena, criticize the weaknesses of industrial society and inject the revolutionary spirit of hope into society. The promise of the kingdom offers the inspiration for Christianity's mission, the transformation of the world. Present historical structures have not been canonized with any divine performance. With Bloch, Moltmann considers world history an open process with salvation or destruction at stake. But for Moltmann, like Jesus' resurrection and his return, the coming kingdom is a certainty of faith and a reality beyond any earthly possibility; its arrival and existence in no way depend on man's efforts.

When Moltmann says the object of eschatological faith is "to change the world rather than explain it," he is stating more than an oblique reference to Marx's eleventh thesis against Feuerbach. With Marx it was *philosophy's* purpose to change the world; with Moltmann the task demands *eschatological faith;* Johannes Metz places at least part of the burden on *political theology*, a term he introduced into the discussion.

Metz constructs his political theology with the same eschatological foundation used by Bloch and Moltmann. Like the latter he views hope as a fundamental theological category. He takes an additional step when he attacks the privatized quality of contemporary theology and advocates militant action as the single avenue to the *novum* of the future: "The relationship to such a future cannot be purely contemplative and cannot remain in the order of representation, since representations and pure contemplation refer to what has already come into existence or what still is. Rather, the relationship to the future is an operative one and the theory of this relationship is directed to effective action."[18] Metz wants to blend theory and practice in his new-style political theology. We can get to the future not by representational ideas, but only by activity; theory must always find fulfillment in action. Christian hope is the dynamism that powers the Christian's "being for others" in the world. Like Moltmann, Metz attests to God's future as beyond man's plans, works, and enterprises, but its "newness corresponds to a promise which originally set in motion our search and our creative and active drive to the future."[19]

He defines political theology as the attempt to become "a critical correction of present-day theology inasmuch as this theology shows an extreme privatizing tendency . . . and a positive attempt to formulate the eschatological message under conditions of our present society."[20] According to Metz, political theology is a reaction to the extreme privatizing influence that existentialism and personalism have exercised on contemporary biblical interpretation and theology. The eschatological promises of the Bible—peace, justice, reconciliation—cannot be privatized. They are *social* values emerging from life in the kingdom. When political theology "formulates the eschatological message under conditions of our present society," it is assuming a critical function. It uses the normative values of life in the kingdom to judge contemporary society.

It is primarily the church's task, Metz claims, to be concerned with political theology in that the church is an institution within society whose main function lies in criticizing the dehumanizing aspects of the world by word and action. All classes, groups, societies, nations, institutions fall under the eschatological proviso—nothing created is permanent; with the eschatological horizon as a guide the church can exercise a critical, liberating role. With its eschatological consciousness the church has a right to judge other institutions as long as it is willing to submit itself to the same proviso: admitting that Christian institutions also have a provisional existence relative to what they proclaim, the kingdom of God.

For Metz racism, war, the oppression of impoverished peoples of the world, etc. stand in stark contrast to the normative promises of the kingdom.[21] The church's critical theory stems from an operative, creative, militant work in an alienated world. Truth must be "done"; although the future will always be shrouded in mystery, and although it is never certain what the future will bring, Christian hope must entail creative responsibility for the future.

THE LIMITATIONS OF HOPE THEOLOGY

"A new heaven and a new earth." With the help of this eschatological rubric, contemporary Christian theology has received revitalization. The *novum* is a revolutionary concept because the hope it inspires promises a qualitatively new future. It is the resurrection of Jesus that offers believers a hope for the resurrection of all. With a "hope and faith active in love" and an expectation of a final transformation of the world, Christians are to engage themselves in the process of changing society's structures in accordance with their image of that promise. The hope theologians' attempts to move away from ontocratic models of the universe are based on the permanence of being, contemplation of the past, and privatization of life styles into new future-oriented, active, socialized categories.

However attractive this theological stance appears, even its proponents admit that the position carries a number of problems with it. The primary difficulty deals with the transcendence of the absolute future, equated with God and his kingdom. There can be no empirical relationship between the hard experience of the present and such a future since eschatological promises require a qualitatively different order, a transcendent level of existence. The Christian kingdom represents a reality in which the God of hope fulfills his promises; for a' skeptic this hope is utopian, that is, *u-topos*, "no place" in the real world. Christians believe that "with God all things are possible" but a transcendent kingdom cannot serve as an empirical model for the world today. One need not subscribe to a Marxian ideology to ask what methodological connection exists between the present society and the eschatological kingdom.

This methodological question leads to a further criticism of hope theology. Simply because Moltmann substitutes an open future for a shadowy past or reified present, has he truly rejected an ontocratic model? What is meant by a "qualitatively new" future which relies on eschatological images for its existence if not a new ontology springing from utopian considerations? That is, so long as the mental models of either the future or the past are not rooted in present historical movements, can we say that the hope theologians' program is really revolutionary? Or is it not simply another ontocratic model that happens to be justified by the eschatological tradition of the Bible?

Perhaps Ernst Bloch himself offered the best critique of the position of hope theology. He places a reality-base in preconscious hope. It looks forward to a "new heaven and a new earth" *in this world—diesseits*, as Marx said, "on this side."

Critical theory cannot be separated from the struggles and contradictions within society: "The dialectic has to be set up as a critical method, as a bitingly critical method of upheaval: first, so that *something* happens, so that something is going on not merely in the head under the sleeping cap; second, so that one knows *what sort* of contradictions are taking place, so that the Utopia-making, the chasing after things in advance which have never existed, has a foot to stand on, so that it becomes concrete and mediates with the world. Only in this way, in this important self-analytical process of mediation, is there openness toward the future, a genuine future which amounts to more than simply being before us. Only in this way can concrete changes be made."[22] Bloch discounts a critical theology that constructs its norms from transcendental, unempirical eschatology as well as a hope that looks for fulfillment beyond this world's boundaries. Hope is determined by practical knowledge of concrete human events. If hope tries to move out of these limits, it becomes mythical, unreal, consoling but not effective for the work of changing society.

Both Moltmann and Metz try to deal with this criticism by distinguishing between hoping and planning.[23] Hoping offers a stimulus for planning and thrives on a deeper level of consciousness but both are directed towards the future. Planning refers to the "advance disposition for the future"; it utilizes scientific-technological possibilities and probabilistic systems. Hope is more subjective, psychological, religious; it is an active partner of the planning mentality. Planning constructs the societies of tomorrow but it is not sufficient in itself. Hope adds a necessary transcendent dimension lacking in planning, Moltmann maintains, as he quotes social scientist Raymond Aron with approval: "As long as socialism is being erected it can preserve the magic of a genuine transcendence. To the extent that it is created, it loses this spell. But can a man live without any transcendence after the transcendence of the future, after the transcendence of God has been eliminated?"[24] Marxists like Bloch and Roger Garaudy admit a need for a qualitatively new future but do not think that such a view necessitates a divine hypostasis separated from the historical process.

A distinction between hoping and planning merely takes the problem a step in the direction away from a possible solution. It ignores the paramount questions. How does the concept of a transcendent kingdom necessarily induce a militantly operative faith? If Christian faith does become active, how can it distinguish between historically helpful and harmful modes of "being for others"? Is a transcendental norm necessary for a critical political theology? Where can a standard of criticism and self-criticism be found, and by what methodology can it be put into operation?

THE METHOD OF POLITICAL THEOLOGY

In this essay we are affirming, among other things, that Marxism and Christianity share a basic secular symbolic "onlook" and because they hold this "onlook" in common, Christian political theology may utilize a method derived from Marxian critical theory. Donald Evans coined the word "onlook" because "no existing word is quite appropriate. The word 'view' would be misleading, since it is so close to 'opinion,' especially in its plural form—my views concerning x.' The word 'conception' is a little too intellectual, and like 'outlook' and 'perspective,' it lacks the element of commitment and is too vague."[25] Evans indicates that "onlooks" include the elements of commitment, personal involvement, behavior, perspectives, feelings, stance, and schematics. Onlooks are derived from feelings and conceptual symbols by which a person "looks on" reality.

Marx developed his onlook from presuppositions inherited from Fichte and Rousseau: that man's generic nature is social and that one cannot find personal fulfillment by himself outside of community with other men and the world. For Marx the basic social problem lay in the contradictory assumptions of liberal capitalist society, whose energy was directed to creating political, economic, and social conditions that demanded the privatization of life. The keystone of liberal society is the right to the private pursuit of wealth. The contradiction according to Marxian theory rests in the violation of the social nature of man and the social base of natural goods when individuals are compelled or encouraged independently to build their own little—or magnificent—castles. As long as a society exists on premises that do not recognize the social character of human life and of all wealth, the members of that society will necessarily become more and more estranged from each other.

Marx was convinced that this estrangement or alienation is the root cause of dehumanization. Mankind will be on the road to humanization only when men can regain control of the products of their labor in a way that satisfies their creative needs, when they begin to relate to each other cooperatively and equally rather than competitively in unequal classes, when man's actual social existence coincides with his social essence, when the privatization of the institutional structures of society gives way to communal social relationships, and when the mystified consciousness of men is gradually transformed into true consciousness that is able to understand its own real social needs in a classless society. True human history will begin at this point, according to Marx.

Marx's philosophy of praxis is tied in with his presupposition about the social character of man's existence. For him man always "does" the truth, which evolves throughout history in the process of men working together. By his productive activity man creates his own essence in common with other men; at the same time he creates society. One generation after another contributes its own gift to the preceding period in science, technology, culture, language. The subsequent generation builds on the activity of its fathers. At the time of the capitalist era, according to Marx, all the creative work of centuries was appropriated and controlled by private individuals in an institutionalized system of private property.

Marx's critical theory begins with his philosophy of praxis. When he speaks of "revolutionary," i.e., humanizing, "practical-critical," praxis in his first thesis against Feuerbach, he is simply saying that critical theory is found in the activity of men: some activity is humanizing, some is alienating; the humanizing praxis is "revolutionary" and therefore critical. His second thesis, and indeed all eleven theses, confirms the first: "In practice man must prove the truth." Truth, for Marx, is anthropocentric. It is expressed by the human praxis that affirms the human potential. Whenever man's social activity leads to a progressive de-alienation of his existence, that activity is true, or revolutionary, and critical of alienated activity.

Again in the third thesis, "the coincidence of the changing

of circumstances and of human activity can be conceived and rationally understood only as revolutionizing practice." Certain human activity serves to de-alienate circumstances that are dehumanizing; this is "revolutionary," practical-critical activity. The praxis can range from manual labor to political agitation, but its locus will always be found in the proletarian class. As the proletariat becomes conscious of its dehumanized life, as its "praxis comes to thought," it will perceive the true nature of the historical process and become the revolutionary force in society. Only the proletariat, then, can become the educator and emancipator of all mankind.[26] Only the proletariat can embody revolutionary praxis, consciousness, critical theory.

The eleventh thesis against Feuerbach becomes more illuminating in this context: "The philosophers have only interpreted the world; the point is to change it." Ernst Bloch includes an extensive commentary on this thesis in *Das Prinzip Hoffnung*, in which he indicates Marx's concern to place philosophy in its true role of changing history.[27]According to Bloch, Marx wanted philosophy to become the theoretical reflection of revolutionary praxis, a critical theory reserved for authentic philosophizing. Marx did not look upon philosophy as an isolated science beside the other sciences. Philosophy is to be the awareness of the whole human experience. Bloch asserts that Marx's most original contribution to philosophy is his understanding of the philosophy of praxis, that the present is potentially revolutionary. Philosophy before Marx gave precedence to the interpretation of the past, a most nonrevolutionary occupation.

Marx called his critical theory "scientific socialism" against the utopian socialists because he believed his philosophy was rooted in the objective behavior of men. The utopians, he thought, simply dreamed up beautiful ideas and expected society to conform to their moral intentions. Marx claimed that his theory conformed to historical circumstances based on actual economic praxis and social relationships in society.

However, Marx's critical theory of revolutionary praxis fails to specify which proletarian praxis is "revolutionary" and which is not. His normative bias is found on a deeper level than the data he examined. All of Marx's anthropocentric presuppositions about alienation and liberation indicate the locus of his commitment. Marx started with a profound personal belief that certain forms of human activity dehumanized men and that their liberation would come when their actual social praxis, not their mental activity, became "the definitive resolution of the antagonism between man and nature, and between man and man . . . [and] is the true solution of the conflict between essence and existence, between objectification and self-affirmation, between freedom and necessity, between individual and species."[28] Dehumanized man restored to his own essence, to his productive activity, to other men, to nature—this is the hidden yardstick Marx applies to economic praxis and class relationships. This is also where his commitment is uncovered.

Of course, the first step of Marx's methodology always articulated an analysis of some concrete aspect of existing praxis. His critical theory selectively isolated the varieties of dehumanized, alienated labor and its historical genesis. The theory furthermore explained why such praxis was alienated and how the alienation contained the seeds of its own liberation. That is, Marx "scientifically" substantiated a hunch or tacit hypothesis about bourgeois society.

Marx cannot be criticized, however, for a procedure that is common to every methodology, scientific or otherwise. Science and philosophy alike work out of their own interpretative frameworks, often without any clear knowledge of the presuppositions by which their assertions are arrived at. Certain presuppositions become so much a part of our mental apparatus and accepted as truth that we identify ourselves with them and rely on them for an integrated view of the world: "This reliance is a personal commitment which is involved in all acts of intelligence by which we integrate some things subsidiarily to the center of our focal attention."[29] Although Marx's critical method seems at times to beg the question about alienation and liberation, it is internally consistent in its selectivity.

THE ROLE OF ONLOOK

Michael Polanyi calls attention to the faith dimension of our consciousness. Under the surface of all rational demonstrability lie tacit powers, which demand an implicit faith in a particular view of reality. Although the faith dimension is personal, it is not merely subjective. Faith commitments seek universal meaning in their surroundings: "The fiduciary passions which induce a confident utterance about the facts are personal, because they submit to the facts as universally valid."[30] The actual facts Marx saw in the capitalist society of his day were seen within the structure of his own life commitment, his "onlook." His analytical concepts, or units, were selected because they best conformed to this commitment—"To overthrow all conditions in which man is an oppressed, enslaved, forsaken, and wretched being."

The advantage of the Marxian methodology for political theology lies in its analysis of the economic and social praxis of society rather than the application of predetermined norms or codes. But the coincidence of Marxism and Christianity comes at the commitment level, the onlook, in their common selective perception of alienating or liberating sides of society. Where Marxism sees alienation, Christianity finds demonic influences in the world. What Marxism sees as the seeds of liberation, Christianity views as redemption, glimpses of the coming kingdom, or the communal fellowship of men.

The onlook of a Christian stems from the community in which he was nurtured, formed, taught values and roles: "Tacit assent and intellectual passions, the sharing of an idiom and of a cultural heritage, affiliation to a like-minded community: such are the impulses which shape our vision of the nature of things on which we rely for our mastery of things. No intelligence, however critical or original can operate outside such a fiduciary framework."[31] The "fiduciary framework" of the Christian calls into play centuries of beliefs, stories, symbols, myths, and tradition. All focus on Jesus Christ and the meaning men have found for their lives through him. The gospel stories and the thousands of testimonies of belief since Jesus lived have produced a rich tradition exhibiting a variety of patterns and expressions.

The political theologian doesn't claim that his commitment represents the whole of Christian tradition. The symbols that underlie his concern pertain to the alienation-liberation schema. Neither need he employ exclusively eschatological categories, however helpful the notion of the coming kingdom

might be in its signification of man's freedom and the content
of his hope. What matters is the content of the faith
commitment which is inspiring him in the present, *at this
moment*, in a way that moves him to engage in revolutionary
praxis from which historical awareness results. The sources that
nourish this commitment are manifold: gospel stories and
parables, Christian hero models or friends, key words in the
Bible, the personality of Jesus—however revolutionary—and his
sayings, meaningful doctrines developed throughout Christian
history, and all the events associated with the experience of the
Christian faith in a man's lifetime.

Those symbols, beliefs, myths, and experiences are not
necessarily an articulated aspect of political theology. Its
essential aspect is critical analysis of class and group relationships and an understanding of these relationships. The personal
Christian vision and knowledge lies below the surface and is
responsible for the selectivity of the analysis. The dedicated
conviction of personal knowledge demands a praxis that injects
a revolutionary hope into the world. Metz is quite correct when
he concludes that the way into the future is operative activity,
not theoretical contemplation. Political theology aids this praxis
by developing self-awareness and involvement through its
historical analysis, which already presupposes personal knowledge and praxis. It does not begin with a set of eschatological
norms, then aim for them by activity in the world, using
appropriate means to attain the designated end, because all
classes and ideologies have utilized these same utopian norms to
justify their behavior. The theory of political theology, inspired
by Christian conviction, has its source in praxis and leads to
further praxis. Political theology is a unity of theory and praxis.

GUIDELINES FOR A POLITICAL THEOLOGY

Political theology needs some guidelines to protect its conclusions from a utopian fate despite the fact that procedural rules
are difficult to formulate for an analysis that deals with the
interpretation of experience and consciousness. Although political theologians are "scientific" in a Marxian sense, they admit
their own confessional selective perception as they look at

society, participate in its struggles, and attempt to understand conflicting consciousness. These guidelines are suggested as a beginning in the work of political theology: [32]

1. *Actual economic, political, and social praxis with corresponding social consciousness, rather than normative models or utopian preconceptions, represents the starting point of political theology.*

Political theology is not done in a vacuum or even in a laboratory. It "returns again and again to the living it wants to serve . . . Multidimensional concepts are required which permit the consideration of the wide range of relationships that may emerge within any environment. As life is accepted on the terms it exhibits, old patterns of men's minds can be stretched."[33] Political theology must try to understand the category of the "new" as it emerges in dialectical relationships with old patterns and institutional arrangements. Man's praxis creates liberating new counter-environments within alienating old environments; political theology has to provide an awareness of this phenomenon.

The political theologian will always have to cope with the problem of methodology. What kind of instrument will best serve the cause of uncovering man's daily praxis, dialectical-conceptual or atomistic-empirical? Marx himself used conceptual tools because he was interested in grasping the praxis of his society in a global perspective in a way that no empirical instrument could effectively grasp it. His concepts and units were taken from a variety of sources—German philosophers (alienation, man's self-creation), French socialists (exploitation, communism), French historians (class, class conflict), English economists (commodity, labor theory of value), etc. His conceptual tools were chosen according to their ability to present an accurate picture of society at large, the "totality," and at the same time faithfully represent the smallest microcosm of that society.[34] The units Marx used—alienated labor, division of labor, class, surplus value, etc.—can be, for many reasons, eminently helpful in the work of political theology as long as the concepts are carefully defined for use in our own age.

Marx's method stands in marked contrast to the approach of the atomistic-empirical school, which narrows its field of inquiry in the interests of exactitude. The problem with a limited view of social praxis is that the analysis becomes reified and difficult to relate to the dynamics of the whole society. George Lukács, one of the foremost Marxist theoreticians of this century, was especially sensitive to this danger. He maintained the superiority of the Marxian method because it takes the dialectical quality of social situations into account. History can move in many directions as social, economic, and political institutions change in an ongoing process. Units of analysis must be flexible and related to the "totality." When facts are ripped out of their historical context and converted into "laws," much in the way the facts of liberal economics were and are formulated, research fails to account for the inherent dynamics in history. Lukács is following Marx's method closely when he indicates that social research by segments is deceptive and misleading.

The notion of "totality" that Lukács repeats so frequently refers to both negative and positive elements in social analysis. Negatively, the research must avoid categorizing isolated phenomena in a linear cause-effect mechanism as though they were removed from the rest of society. Positively, analysis must include social data in its relationship to the alienating or liberating tendencies of the rest of society. It furthermore includes a vision towards which the present moment could progress. Of course, research has to isolate and analyze certain data, but "the decisive point is whether or not the isolating abstraction maintains a relationship to the whole or whether it makes itself into a goal in itself autonomously."[35] The reason that this book is presented as a "Marxian Guide" to Christian political theology is that we have accepted a Marxian methodology in our model of societal analysis.

2. *Political theology attempts in particular to articulate the equal or unequal interactional praxis of social groups, institutions, and movements, and their respective ideologies.*

Every mode of research rests on some form of selective perception, an "onlook." Polish philosopher Leszek Kolakowski indicates a characteristic of a Marxian methodology that is appropriate for the work of political theology: "Another typical trait is Marx's practical orientation in the social sicences. He selected problems to be dealt with according to whether they served the cause of an egalitarian society, the cause of abolishing class divisions and of emancipating the exploited and oppressed."[36] No research can truly be labeled completely "objective," because the researcher is dependent on his language, cultural background, national heritage, and religious or ideological onlook. The onlook of the Marxian-Christian methodology selectively analyzes the relationships of social groups.

Relationships among classes and groups are in a continuous process of communication and control, which in today's world are reflected more often indirectly and obliquely than directly and clearly. Class conflict, class domination and subordination, class politics, or revolutionary class praxis are rarely clearly defined. Since interactional praxis consists primarily of the use of power, it is important to uncover the positions of power in a community or nation to determine how power is exercised institutionally, and to discover whether or not a system of privilege is in operation. At the same time it is necessary to clarify these relationships, especially since oppressed groups often cannot or will not communicate among themselves.

Closely connected with the task of determining the interactional praxis of social groups is the task of understanding the ideologies or value systems that justify these groups' programs. Very often ideologies are perpetrated in society to neutralize any possibility of change and to keep a privileged group in power. At times ideologies are constructed for out-groups, using slogans and programs to gain their attention. Ideologies always exhibit value assertions and usually attempt to educate or convince their own communities as well as outside groups. Ideologies intend to knit social groups together and to act as blueprints in times of social unrest. The problem for social analysis lies in sifting conflicting ideologies, some of which control the resources that can most easily propagate their view. Neo-imperialism, racism, nationalism, male chauvinism, and social authoritarianism all are justified by ideologies that political theology must be concerned with.

3. *Political theology assumes that no single model of reality or mode of analysis provides a total explanation of social praxis.*

Social processes appear and disappear; interaction changes social patterns; contradictions arise, are resolved, and recur in new forms, etc. Yet, political theologians have to strive to make global connections out of the innumerable varieties of interaction. Marxism unifies its vision of society by looking at economic influences and class relationships. Such an analysis is extremely beneficial for basic insights. Other models will give further glimpses of social reality: i.e., from technological developments, linguistic and cultural anthropology, ideological analysis, political structures, etc. "Reference points are arbitrary descriptions logically determined with an eye to the power they give to explain a desired realm . . . They are tools an observer uses to establish his power to interpret concretely. Their power should not be dismissed easily, however, for only in terms of the reference they provide can the observer modify his functionally perceived world."[37]

Praxis is "functionally perceived" in an effort to grasp meaning here and now. A functional approach is tentative and relative, in contrast to the more absolute norms of eschatological categories. Although the referent points of a political theology based on social praxis are relative, they are the only reality from which theoretical historical or social awareness can be derived. This theoretical awareness has the power to induce self-awareness or emotionally involved social awareness.

Of course, emotionally involved awareness can be induced by means other than those from the social sciences. Political theology can be undertaken through literature, art, drama, worship, philosophy, or any activity or cultural medium that may bring about historical and self-awareness.[38] Political theology preaches, celebrates, meditates, dialogues, demonstrates, protests, worships, confronts, listens, and looks. Its content is revolutionary, its methodology is multidimensional, its voice is the voice of protest.

It is apparent that many plays, films, communal "happenings," and cultural celebrations have the power to raise, at least temporarily, men's awareness. The connection drawn between the city and the heroes of *Midnight Cowboy* makes one wonder whether or not capitalism itself is not ultimately to blame for the privatization and competitiveness of society. Peter Weiss's *Marat-Sade* grapples with the problems of social reform through revolution. The inmates of an asylum, playing revolutionaries, profess that only such a revolution as occurred in 1789 in

France would have solved the inequities of the day, but they moan that "now" in 1793 their social condition remains the same:

Marat, we're poor and the poor stay poor
Marat, don't make us wait any more
We want our rights and we don't care how
We want our revolution NOW . . .

The theory of political theology need not be explicitly "religious." It does aim towards developing new levels of awareness. Therefore,

4. *Philosophers have only interpreted the world; the point of political theology is to change it.*

Political theology can be defined as a mode of analysis that acknowledges its reliance on Christian symbols and commitment as it attempts to develop theoretical and self-awareness of economic, political, and social relationships. The commitment is operative particularly when the political theologian engages in the praxis of the world, and from his involvement selects data and develops conclusions. In short, the work of political theology is social change, and in the long run, radical social change.

Political theologians cannot do their work apart from other men. It is difficult to understand social relationships outside of social or communal praxis. The importance of ecclesial or commitment groups looms large for political theology since they represent communities, Christian or otherwise, that are engaging in communal praxis which is a catalytic agent of social change. This activity can take many shapes but must be done within the economic, political, and social structures that determine the quality of men's lives. Political theologians lose their credibility when they spin off theories in the sacred tombs of the churches, universities, or suburbs.

Christianity's ecclesial praxis should joyfully wrestle with experimental styles of life, of work, and of celebration because such praxis tends to effect humanizing social change; a strong case can be made that experimentation was the rule in the early Pauline churches. Once again the Marxist leaders of this century have had abundant experience, successful and unsuccessful, in both political experimentation and in developing strategies and tactics leading to radical social change. Other subcultures and the Christian heritage itself provide rich complements in the development of humanizing life styles.

These guidelines are more like suggestions than rules or even general norms. They are meant to give Christians who are increasingly aware of Christianity's revolutionary potential a solid base from which to spur the process of social change. To those whose stake in the system is so great that they fear any change, or to those who identify the words "Marxist" or "Communist" with conspiracy, sabotage, violence, and evil, the work of political theology so described will appear threatening. In subsequent chapters I hope the threat will disappear as it becomes apparent that Marxists and Christians can share a responsible concern for humanity's condition and future.

Notes

1. A. Th. Van Leeuwen, *Christianity in World History* (London: Edinburgh House, 1964), p. 173.
2. *Cf.* Hugh T. Kerr, *The First Systematic Theologian: Origen of Alexandria* (Princeton: Princeton Theological Seminary, 1958), pp. 21-24, 34-37, and Eugene DeFaye, *Origen and His Work* (New York: Columbia University Press, 1929), pp. 55-74.
3. *The Laws of Plato*, trans. A. E. Taylor (London: Dent and Sons, 1934), pp. 302-304.
4. St. Augustine, *City of God* (Garden City: Doubleday, 1958), pp. 483-493.
5. *The Philosophy of History*, trans. J. Sibree (New York: Dover, 1956), p. 73.
6. New York, 1960, p. 29.
7. *Ibid.*, p. 38.
8. *Karl Marx: Early Writings*, trans. T. B. Bottomore (New York: McGraw-Hill, 1964), p. 156.
9. *Ibid.*, pp. 120-134.
10. *Man on His Own* (New York: Herder and Herder, 1970), p. 152. The brief sketch of Bloch's thought here is taken from

this volume and from *Das Prinzip Hoffnung*, three sections of which are translated in *Man on His Own.*

11. *Ibid.*
12. *Man on His Own,* p. 161.
13. *Ibid.*, p. 70.
14. *Ibid.*, p. 161-162.
15. *Ibid.*, p. 163.
16. *Theology of Hope* (New York: Harper and Row, 1967), p. 30.
17. "The Category of the New in Theology" in *The Future as the Presence of Shared Hope*, ed. Maryellen Muckenhirn (New York: Sheed and Ward, 1968), p. 12.
18. "Created Hope" in *New Theology No. 5*, ed. Martin E. Marty and Dean G. Peerman (New York: Macmillan, 1968), p. 131.
19. *Ibid.*, p. 137.
20. *Theology of the World* (New York: Herder and Herder, 1969), p. 107.
21. See "The Return of J. B. Metz," *New Book Review*, December 1968, pp. 10-13.
22. "Creative Possibility," *Cross Currents*, XVIII, No. 3, (Summer 1968), p. 279.
23. Moltmann, "Hoping and Planning," *Cross Currents*, XVIII, No. 3, (Summer 1968), 279; Metz, *Theology of the World*, pp. 141-155.
24. Moltmann, *Ibid.*, p. 315.
25. *The Logic of Self Involvement* (London: SCM Press, 1963), p. 125.
26. *Cf.* "Critique of Hegel's Philosophy of Right" in *Karl Marx: Early Writings*, pp. 55-56.
27. *Das Prinzip Hoffnung*, Erster Band (Frankfurt: Suhrkamp Verlag, 1959), pp. 319-334.
28. "Private Property and Communism" in *Karl Marx: Early Writings*, p. 155.
29. Michael Polanyi, *Personal Knowledge* (New York: Harper and Row, 1964), p. 61.
30. *Ibid.*, p. 303.
31. *Ibid.*, p. 266.
32. The content of the four guidelines is taken primarily from Georg Lukács, "Was Ist Orthodoxer Marximus" in *Ges-*

chichte und Klassenbewusstsein (Berlin: Malik, 1923), pp. 13 ff.; an unpublished paper, "Historicity and Empirical Method" by David S. Steward, Graduate Theological Union, Berkeley; and Paul Watzlawick et al., *The Pragmatics of Human Communication* (New York: Norton, 1967).

33. Steward, "Historicity and Empirical Method," pp. 4-5.
34. *Cf.* "Preface to the First German Edition of the First Volume of Capital,'" *Selected Works* (Moscow: Foreign Languages, 1962), p. 449.
35. Lukács, "Rosa Luxembourg als Marxist," *Geschichte und Klassenbewusstsein* p. 40.
36. *Toward a Marxist Humanism (New York: Grove Press,* 1969), p. 180.
37. Steward, *op. cit.*, pp. 6-7.
38. *Cf.* Herbert Marcuse, *Negations* (Boston: Beacon, 1969), pp. 88-133 for an elucidation of culture's role in unconscious protest in society.

CHAPTER TWO

Theory: Alienation

In this chapter we will examine the fundamental perspective by which Marx and a few of his followers viewed man in an alienated world. Within the development of the onlook of Marxian theory are contained basic conceptual units which may be utilized in the work of political theology because, as we will demonstrate, Christianity shares a similar onlook towards alienation. Therefore, for this specific exercise in political theology we will borrow the Marxian analytical instrument. We will perceive the world through the window of a Marxian analysis, examine it with Marxian concepts, measure it with Marxian tools, and judge it with Marxian norms. At the end of the chapter we will justify this route by indicating how Christianity came to its onlook towards alienation.

MARX AND ENGELS

For Marx,[1] man defines himself by creative praxis. Man is a producing artist. This is what makes the difference between men and animals: animals simply extract what they need for survival from nature while men realize themselves in and through nature. Man creates the world, transforms nature, makes his own civilization. The image of a society of free, creative praxis is the presupposition of the notion of alienation.

35

There are other hints of life in a liberated society that recur in the writings of Marx. One of them can be seen in his definition of wealth:

> *In fact, however, when the narrow bourgeois form has been peeled away, what is wealth, if not the universality of needs, capacities, enjoyments, productive powers, etc., of individuals, produced in universal exchange? What, if not the full development of human control over the forces of nature—those of his own nature as well as those of so-called "nature"? What, if not the absolute elaboration of his creative dispositions, without any preconditions other than antecedent historical evolution which makes the totality of this evolution—i.e. the evolution of all human powers as such, unmeasured by any previously established yardstick—an end in itself? What is this, if not a situation where man does not reproduce himself in any determined form, but produces his totality? Where he does not seek to remain something formed by the past, but is in the absolute movement of becoming? In bourgeois political economy—and in the epoch of production to which it corresponds—this complete elaboration of what lies within man, appears as the total alienation and the destruction of all fixed, one-sided purposes, as the sacrifice of the end in itself to a wholly external compulsion.* [2]

In this passage Marx is describing primitive Asiatic property relations in which "the individual does not become independent of the community; the circle of production is a self-sustaining unity of agriculture and craft manufacture, etc." [3] The individual fulfilling himself in community is the Marxian archetypal symbol of life in a Communist society, i.e., without alienation. Because of alienation man is dehumanized in increasing intensity through the course of history and the alienation reaches its climax in capitalist society. For Marx the survivals of alienation in our age include alienated labor, class division and exploitation, ideological domination, intensified privatization, and competition and monopoly capital.

Alienated Labor

The story of man's alienation and dehumanization in a Marxian account is long and complicated. As Marx indicates in the passage quoted above, the alienation of contemporary society reverses the ideal social order: where human mutuality and free exchange of capacities, needs, and productive powers prevail rather than the domination of one class by another, the freedom to grow and develop on one's own terms, rather than on terms dictated by a society mobilized for production, is present. The ability to interact with nature is the norm, rather than man's control by nature. The free expression of one's creativity is enhanced rather than expropriated for the marketplace. This theory grows mainly out of Marx's understanding of history. So long as food or other needs of survival did not exceed what could be utilized by the tribe day by day, so long as no social surplus needed to be divided, alienation was kept to a minimum in primitive societies. Each worked for all, and all protected the common goods of the group. Production and consumption were equalized. The economy was self-sufficient and self-contained within a natural work cycle.

However, at a very early period of history, impossible to fix precisely, economic surplus appeared and with it the problem of how to distribute the social excess. Some groups or elites began to exercise power over others, and the class division of society was born. The social surplus was divided unequally, and the resultant social stratification enabled upper ranks of society to control the lives of lower echelons. The common denominator Marx found in history was the production of new values and wealth by the working classes and the appropriation of these values by nonworking classes. According to Marx, elites have always used their wealth to maintain their privileged position in society: an armed lord would seize the greater portion of a tiller's produce; a slaveowner would force a slave into productive activity and provide only a subsistence level of existence for the slave; a feudal lord would appropriate the products of the free labor that the serfs were forced to furnish in the form of the corvée. As society developed, surplus value became simply the difference between the wealth created by the laborer and the cost of his maintenance. The economics of

ancient Greece and Rome as well as feudal society remained
self-sufficient and self-contained.

What about capitalist society? The self-contained connections became broken into new economic relations among cities,
provinces, and nations. Division of labor emerged as the new
tradition. Although men became more interdependent because
of technological advances, laborers still turned over the new
values they created to the owners of the means of production.
In a capitalist society laborers are forced to sell their labor-
power as a commodity:

Consequently, labour-power is a commodity which its
possessor, the wage-worker, sells to the capitalist. Why
does he sell it? It is in order to live.

But the putting of labour-power into action, i.e., the
work, is the active expression of the labourer's own life.
And this life activity he sells to another person in order to
secure the necessary means of life. His life activity,
therefore, is but a means of securing his own existence. He
works that he may keep alive. He does not count the
labour itself as a part of his life; it is rather a sacrifice of
his life. It is a commodity that he has auctioned off to
another. The product of his activity, therefore, is not the
aim of his activity. What he produces for himself is not the
silk that he weaves, not the gold that he draws up the
mining shaft, not the palace that he builds. What he
produces for himself is wages; and the silk, the gold, and
the palace are resolved for him into a certain quantity of
necessaries of life, perhaps into a cotton jacket, into
copper coins, and into a basement dwelling. And the
labourer who for twelve hours long, weaves, spins, bores,
turns, builds, shovels, breaks stone, carries hods, and so
on—is this twelve hours' weaving, spinning, boring,
turning, building, shovelling, stone-breaking, regarded by
him as a manifestation of life, as life? Quite the contrary.
Life for him begins where this activity ceases, at the table,
at the tavern seat, in bed. The twelve hours' work, on the
other hand, has no meaning for him as weaving, spinning,
boring, and so on, but only as earnings, which enable him
to sit down at a table, to take his seat in the tavern, and to

lie down in a bed. If the silk-worm's object in spinning were to prolong its existence as caterpillar, it would be a perfect example of a wage-worker.[4]

Marx here not only indicates the alienated quality of work in industrial society and the motivations of the average worker but also introduces the concept of labor-power. The connection between capitalism and former economic systems lies in an understanding of this process, according to Marx, whereby the employer buys labor-power at a price much lower than the new value a laborer will create. The surplus goes into the pocket of the capitalist, now "surplus value."

The laborer cannot work at the kind of labor he might prefer. "In order to live," he sells his labor to the highest bidder; his labor power has become a commodity in the marketplace. Furthermore, the working class is dominated by commodity exchange. A laborer cannot produce what he thinks he or his community needs but only what is demanded in an exchange economy, where priorities are determined by the degree of profit a product brings.

Abstraction and rationalization characterize an exchange economy.[5] The reasons Marx outlines are simple. First of all, labor-power is reduced to a common denominator; men sell abstract labor-power to other men who expropriate the newly created value. Next, men's products of labor become separated from their makers as mere commodities and sometimes hostile objects. Both necessities and luxuries dominate their makers because in a consumer society people need or are conditioned to desire these items and yet never can fully attain what they are expected to attain. Goods are not naturally produced by a community to fulfill human needs. Goods become commodities and are worshiped from afar. Marx termed this process "the fetishism of commodities," i.e., commodities have become fetishes, out of the reach of the men who created them. All things become alienated and objects of exchange, even man's most personal qualities:

There was a time, as in the Middle Ages, when only the superfluous, the excess of production over consumption, was exchanged.

> *There was again a time, when not only the super-fluous, but all products, all industrial existence, had passed into commerce, when the whole of production depended on exchange. How are we to explain this second phase of exchange—marketable value at its second power? . . .*
>
> *Finally, there came a time when everything that men had considered as inalienable became an object of exchange, of traffic and could be alienated. This is the time when the very things which till then had been communicated, but never exchanged; given, but never sold; acquired, but never bought—virtue, love, conviction, knowledge, conscience, etc.—when everything, in short, passed into commerce. It is the time of general corruption, of universal venality, or, to speak in terms of political economy, the time when everything, moral or physical, having become a marketable value, is brought to the market to be assessed at its truest value.*[6]

The abstraction of labor-power depends on the rationalized activity of the world. Rationalization indicates that human interaction is reduced to a common denominator—money and exchange. Men enjoy direct ties with one another less and less. They interrelate only indirectly through the intermediary of an exchange economy. Commodities and objects are the main concern of human relationships. At the same time a dependence on money is built into a capitalist society as individuals manufacture new needs for mutual exploitation. Men become increasingly separated from one another in their individual efforts to acquire money, the universal abstract medium of exchange. Marx often tries to explode the myth that the accumulation of money for extra goods would satisfy human needs:

> *Within the system of private property . . . every man speculates upon creating a new need in another in order to force him to a new sacrifice, to place him in a new dependence, and to entice him into a new kind of pleasure and thereby into economic ruin. Everyone tries to establish over others an alien power in order to find there the satisfaction of his own egoistic need. With the increasing*

mass of objects, therefore, the realm of alien entities to which man is subjected also increases. Every new product is a new potentiality of mutual deceit and robbery. Man becomes increasingly poor as a man; he has increasing need of money in order to take possession of the hostile being. The power of his money diminishes directly with the growth of the quantity of production, i.e. his need increases with the increasing power of money. The need for money is, therefore, the real need created by the modern economic system, and the only need which it creates. The quantity of money becomes increasingly its only important quality. Just as it reduces every entity to an abstraction, so it reduces itself in its own development to a quantitative entity. Excess and immoderation become its true standard. This is shown subjectively, partly in the fact that the expansion of production and of needs becomes an ingenious and always calculating subservience to inhuman, depraved, unnatural and imaginary appetites. Private property does not know how to change crude need into human need; its idealism is fantasy, caprice and fancy. No eunuch flatters his tyrant more shamefully or seeks by more infamous means to stimulate his jaded appetite, in order to gain some favour, than does the eunuch of industry, the entrepreneur, in order to acquire a few silver coins or to charm the gold from the purse of his dearly beloved neighbour. (Every product is a bait by means of which the individual tries to entice the essence of the other person, his money. Every real or potential need is a weakness which will draw the bird into the lime. Universal exploitation of human communal life. Just as every imperfection of man is a bond with heaven, a point from which his heart is accessible to the priest, so every want is an opportunity for approaching one's neighbour, in simulated friendship, and saying, "Dear friend, I will give you what you need, but you know the conditio sine qua non. You know what ink you must use in signing yourself over to me. I shall swindle you while providing your enjoyment.") The entrepreneur accedes to the most depraved fancies of his neighbour, plays the role of pander between him and his needs, awakens unhealthy appetites in him,

*and watches for every weakness so that later on he may
claim the remuneration for his labour of love.* [7]

Here Marx wants to drive home the point that the entrepreneur's goods will not contribute to man's creative development.
Man's true needs are satisfied by a communal creative praxis,
from which his real wealth stems. False needs are generated by
isolated, competitive individuals who accumulate more and
more money to satisfy the very false needs they created. In this
never-ending cycle man becomes ever more dependent on
material objects and on a false standard of affluence for a sense
of identity and self-esteem. Capitalist culture not only creates
dependence on material items to satisfy physical needs but also
establishes implicit psychological criteria as conditions that
must be met to attain success in the culture. Both the physical
and the psychological needs that are nurtured in a capitalist
society are felt to be real needs, but their satisfaction is always
beyond the reach of the working class. The capitalist must
expand his markets, excite additional demands for money so
that the labor force will purchase the new commodities they
produced. Again the rub is in the division of the social surplus.
Marx shows that because of the relativity of affluence,
expanding capital is not equally profitable to the capitalist and
worker alike:

> *To say that the interests of capital and the interests of the
> workers are identical, signifies only this, that capital and
> wage-labour are two sides of one and the same relation.
> The one conditions the other in the same way that the
> usurer and the borrower condition each other.*
>
> *As long as the wage-labourer remains a wage-labourer,
> his lot is dependent upon capital. That is what the boasted
> community of interests between worker and capitalists
> amounts to.*
>
> *If capital grows, the mass of wage-labour grows, the
> number of wage-workers increases; in a word, the sway of
> capital extends over a greater mass of individuals.*
>
> *Let us suppose the most favourable case: if productive capital grows, the demand for labour grows. It
> therefore increases the price of labour-power, wages.*

A house may be large or small; as long as the neighbouring houses are likewise small, it satisfies all social requirements for a residence. But let there arise next to the little house a palace, and the little house shrinks into a hut. The little house now makes it clear that its inmate has no social position at all to maintain, or but a very insignificant one; and however high it may shoot up in the course of civilisation, if the neighbouring palace rises in equal or even in greater measure, the occupant of the relatively little house will always find himself more uncomfortable, more dissatisfied, more cramped within his four walls.

An appreciable rise in wages presupposes a rapid growth of productive capital. Rapid growth of productive capital calls forth just as rapid a growth of wealth, of luxury, of social needs and social pleasures. Therefore, although the pleasures of the labourer have increased, the social gratification which they afford has fallen in comparison with the increased pleasures of the capitalist, which are inaccessible to the worker, in comparison with the stage of development of society in general. Our wants and pleasures have their origin in society; we therefore measure them in relation to society; we do not measure them in relation to the objects which serve for their gratification. Since they are of a social nature, they are of a relative nature. [8]

For Marx the entire process of capitalist accumulation and societal rationalization amounts to universal dehumanization. Men sell their labor-power at a price far below the value of the wealth they create. Their labor becomes a commodity in the marketplace as they become assimilated into the market economy. The products which they create return to oppress them in the form of "necessities of life." The work process does not affirm their human need for active creativity; men work passively, often grudgingly, only to stay alive rather than to fulfill their human creative essence. They become gradually degraded to an animal-like existence. While human dignity demands a collective effort in the creation of a new world, capitalist society pits men against each other in the eternal quest for money. Throughout his life Marx pointed to these aspects of alienation: alienation from the product, alienation in the productive process, and alienation within the human community:

Political economy conceals the alienation in the nature of labour in so far as it does not examine the direct relationship between the worker (work) and production. Labour certainly produces marvels for the rich but it produces privation for the worker. It produces palaces, but hovels for the worker. It produces beauty, but deformity for the worker. It replaces labour by machinery, but it casts some of the workers back into a barbarous kind of work and turns the others into machines. It produces intelligence, but also stupidity and cretinism for the workers. . . .

What constitutes the alienation of labour? First, that the work is external to the worker, that it is not part of his nature; and that, consequently, he does not fulfill himself in his work but denies himself, has a feeling of misery rather than well-being, does not develop freely his mental and physical energies but is physically exhausted and mentally debased. The worker, therefore, feels himself at home only during his leisure time, whereas at work he feels homeless. His work is not voluntary but imposed, forced labour. It is not the satisfaction of a need, but only a means for satisfying other needs. Its alien character is clearly shown by the fact that as soon as there is no physical or other compulsion it is avoided like the plague. External labour, labour in which man alienates himself, is a labour of self-sacrifice, of mortification. Finally, the external character of work for the worker is shown by the fact that it is not his own work but work for someone else, that in work he does not belong to himself but to another person. . . .

We arrive at the result that man (the worker) feels himself to be freely active only in his animal functions— eating, drinking, and procreating, or at most also in his dwelling and in personal adornment—while in his human functions he is reduced to an animal. The animal becomes human and the human becomes animal.

> *Eating, drinking and procreating are of course also genuine human functions. But abstractly considered, apart from the environment of human activities, and turned into final and sole ends, they are animal functions.* [9]

Alienation means that man has lost touch with nature, himself, and other men. The three aspects of alienation are related since man cannot shape the world if he is alienated from nature; when the man-made world dominates its maker, man is separated from his free, creative essence; finally, the common quality of the human species lies in its ability to cooperate in creative activity, an ability frustrated in capitalist society. The final result of alienation is a dehumanized human creature:

> *Production does not only produce man as a commodity, the human commodity, man in the form of a commodity; in conformity with this situation it produces him as a mentally and physically dehumanized being. . . . Immorality, miscarriage, helotism of workers and capitalists . . . Its product is the self-conscious and self-acting commodity . . . The human commodity . . . It is a great step forward by Ricardo, Mill, et al., as against Smith and Say, to declare the existence of human beings—the greater or lesser human productivity of the commodity—as indifferent or indeed harmful. The true end of production is not the number of workers a given capital maintains, but the amount of interest it earns, the total annual saving.* [10]

Class Division

Class division has its source in the alienation of labor. The working class depends on the capitalist class for the instruments of labor. Class relationships are anonymous and abstract, not corresponding to the individual dependency, say, that a serf had on his lord in feudal times. Because of the universality of class relationships, Marx could speak of an "average wage" and determine a social average as the abstract, normative rule of human relationships:

> *But the worker, whose only source of income is the sale of his labour-power, cannot leave the whole class of buyers, i.e., the capitalist class, unless he gives up his own*

*existence. He does not belong to this or to that capitalist,
but to the capitalist class; and it is for him to find his man,
i.e., to find a buyer in this capitalist class. . . .*

*This minimum wage, like the determination of the
price of commodities in general by cost of production,
does not hold good for the single individual, but only for
the race. Individual workers, indeed, millions of workers,
do not receive enough to be able to exist and to propagate
themselves; but the wages of the whole working class
adjust themselves, within the limits of their fluctuations,
to this minimum.*[11]

Because labor is a commodity and capital wants to buy labor as
cheaply as possible, the two classes become polarized and
alienated from one another. According to Marx, capitalist
relations to labor necessitate an irreconcilable conflict of interest between the two classes, not only because the capitalist class
appropriates the surplus value which is created by the laboring
class but also because the amount of surplus value comes to
double or triple the amount of the worker's wage. Within
such a societal arrangement the worker's lot can never lead to a
satisfying life.[12] Since Marx assumes that the whole of society
belongs to the collective body of history's social labor, his
invective increases when he writes about the private appropriation of mankind's public enterprise. He links the phenomenon
with alienation:

*Alienation is apparent not only in the fact that my means
of life belong to someone else, that my desires are the
unattainable possession of someone else, but that everything is something different from itself, that my activity is
something else, and finally (and this is also the case for the
capitalist) that an inhuman power rules over everything.
There is a kind of wealth which is inactive, prodigal and
devoted to pleasure, the beneficiary of which behaves as an
ephemeral, aimlessly active individual who regards the
slave labour of others, human blood and sweat, as a
sacrificial and superfluous being. Thus he acquires a
contempt for mankind, expressed in the form of arrogance
and the squandering of resources which would support a
hundred human lives, and also in the form of the infamous*

illusion that his unbridled extravagance and endless unpro-
ductive consumption is a condition for the labour and
subsistence of others. He regards the realization of the
essential powers of man only as the realization of his own
disorderly life, his whims and his capricious, bizarre
ideas. [13]

This theme, that the affluence of an elite class is bought at the
expense of the labor and poverty of the working class is pursued
at length in *The Poverty of Philosophy*. Since there is only a
given amount of surplus (which may fluctuate at any single
moment to keep labor compliant), increase for one class takes
place at the expense of the other. Marx has no illusions about
the capitalist class's willingness to share the increased value of
the production process. The notion of class struggle, then, stems
from Marx's conception of class division:

The bourgeoisie begins with a proletariat which is itself a
relic of the proletariat of feudal times. In the course of its
historical development, the bourgeoisie necessarily
develops its antagonistic character, which at first is more
or less disguised, existing only in a latent state. As the
bourgeoisie develops, there develops in its bosom a new
proletariat, a modern proletariat; there develops a struggle
between the proletarian class and the bourgeois class, a
struggle which, before being felt, perceived, appreciated,
understood, avowed and proclaimed aloud by both sides,
expresses itself, to start with, merely in partial and
momentary conflicts, in subversive acts. On the other
hand, if all the members of the modern bourgeoisie have
the same interests inasmuch as they form a class as against
another class, they have opposite, antagonistic interests
inasmuch as they stand face to face with one another. This
opposition of interests results from the economic condi-
tions of their bourgeois life. From day to day it thus
becomes clearer that the production relations in which the
bourgeoisie moves have not a simple, uniform character,
but a dual character; that in the selfsame relations in which
wealth is produced, poverty is produced also; that in the
selfsame relations in which there is a development of the

productive forces, there is also a force producing repression; that these relations produce bourgeois wealth, i.e., the wealth of the bourgeois class, only by continually annihilating the wealth of the individual members of this class and by producing an evergrowing proletariat.[14]

Wealth tends to concentrate itself into the hands of fewer people. Even many members of the bourgeois are thrown into the ranks of the proletariat and subordinated to more powerful interests.

Class struggle is the inherent result of class domination. The dominative class is driven by a law inherent in the capitalist system to bring more and more of the world's geography, labor, goods, and markets within its orbit. Marx and Engels provide a brief history of the phenomenon:

The history of all hitherto existing society is the history of class struggle.

Free man and slave, patrician and plebian, lord and serf, guild master and journeyman, in a word, oppressor and oppressed, stood in constant opposition to one another, carried on an uninterrupted, now hidden, now open fight, a fight that each time ended either in a revolutionary reconstitution of society at large or in the common ruin of the contending classes.

In earlier epochs of history we find almost everywhere a complicated arrangement of society into various orders, a manifold gradation of social rank. In ancient Rome we have patricians, knights, plebeians, slaves; in the Middle Ages, feudal lords, vassals, guild masters, journeymen, apprentices, serfs; in almost all of these classes, again, subordinate gradations.

The modern bourgeois society that has sprouted from the ruins of feudal society has not done away with class antagonisms. It has but established new classes, new conditions of oppression, new forms of struggle in place of the old ones. . . .

The feudal system of industry, under which industrial production was monopolized by closed guilds, now no longer sufficed for the growing wants of the new markets.

The manufacturing system took its place. The guild masters were pushed on one side by the manufacturing middle class; division of labor between the different corporate guilds vanished in the face of division of labor in each single workshop.

Meantime the markets kept ever growing, the demand ever rising. Even manufacture no longer sufficed. Thereupon steam and machinery revolutionized industrial production. The place of manufacture was taken by the giant, modern industry, the place of the industrial middle by industrial millionaires, the leaders of the whole industrial armies, the modern bourgeois. . . .

The bourgeoisie cannot exist without constantly revolutionizing the instruments of production, and thereby the relations of production, and with them the whole relations of society. Conservation of the old modes of production in unaltered form was, on the contrary, the first condition of existence for all earlier industrial classes. Constant revolutionizing of production, uninterrupted disturbance of all social conditions, everlasting uncertainty and agitation distinguish the bourgeois epoch from all earlier ones. All fixed, fast-frozen relations, with their train of ancient and venerable prejudices and opinions, are swept away; all new-formed ones become antiquated before they can ossify. All that is solid melts into air, all that is holy is profaned, and man is at last compelled to face with sober senses his real conditions of life and his relations with his kind.

The need of a constantly expanding market for its products chases the bourgeoisie over the whole surface of the globe. It must nestle everywhere, settle everywhere, establish connections everywhere. . . .

The bourgeoisie, by the rapid improvement of all instruments of production, by the immensely facilitated means of communication, draws all, even the most barbarian, nations into civilization. The cheap prices of its commodities are the heavy artillery with which it batters down all Chinese walls, with which it forces the barbarians' intensely obstinate hatred of foreigners to capitulate. It compels all nations, on pain of extinction, to adopt the bourgeois mode of production; it compels them to introduce what it calls civilization into their midst, i.e., to become bourgeois themselves. In one word, it creates a world after its own image.

The bourgeoisie has subjected the country to the rule of the towns. It has created enormous cities, has greatly increased the urban population as compared with the rural, and has thus rescued a considerable part of the population from the idiocy of rural life. Just as it has made the country dependent on the towns, so it has made barbarian and semi-barbarian countries dependent on civilized ones, nations of peasants on nations of bourgeois, the East on the West.[15]

Class struggle is the struggle over how the surplus of production will be divided. History reveals that the laborer rarely, if ever, comes out ahead in this struggle. The basic economic feature of class domination rests in the privileged class's ownership of the means of production, as well as their control over the product and the process of production. Class division and domination follow logically in the Marxian scheme of alienation. For Marx social position and psychological dependency are integral parts of an objective economic fact. The person who owns the surplus produce controls everything else in society through his financial power, at least indirectly, including the state, the church, the courts, and even the arts. The capitalist and working classes occupy antagonistic economic relationships, and therefore all society suffers from a fundamentally alienated structure.

Ideological Domination

In Marx's sense the term "ideology" refers to the false consciousness of a society that is not aware of the material forces of production that influence its consciousness. Social and economic conditions are the basis of philosophical ideas. If a philosopher believes that he can change the world by simply changing the ideas of society, he is mystified, Marx and Engels wrote to the "German ideologists."[16] Mystification occurs in history when a division of labor takes place between intellectual and physical activity, when men lose sight of the fact that their ideas have a foundation in social relationships. False consciousness follows alienated social praxis:

The fact is, therefore, that definite individuals who are productively active in a definite way enter into these definite social and political relations. Empirical observation must in each separate instance bring out empirically, and without any mystification and speculation, the connection of the social and political structure with production. The social structure and the State are continually evolving out of the life-process of definite individuals, but of individuals, not as they may appear in their own or other people's imagination, but as they really are; i.e., as they are effective, produce materially, and are active under definite material limits, presuppositions, and conditions independent of their will.

The production of ideas, of conceptions, of consciousness, is at first directly interwoven with the material activity and the material intercourse of men, the language of real life. Conceiving, thinking, the mental intercourse of men, appear at this stage as the direct efflux of their material behaviour. The same applies to mental production as expressed in the language of the politics, laws, morality, religion, metaphysics of a people. Men are the producers of their conceptions, ideas, etc.—real, active men, as they are conditioned by a definite development of their productive forces and of the intercourse corresponding to these, up to its furthest forms. Consciousness can never be anything else than conscious existence, and the existence of men is their actual life-process. If in all ideology men and their circumstances appear upside down as in a camera obscura, this phenomenon arises just as much from their historical life-process as the inversion of objects on the retina does from their physical life-process.

The Real Order

In direct contrast to German philosophy which descends from heaven to earth, here we ascend from earth to heaven. That is to say, we do not set out from what men say, imagine, conceive, nor from men as narrated, thought of, imagined, conceived, in order to arrive at men in the flesh. We set out from real, active men, and on the basis of their real life-process we demonstrate the development of the ideological reflexes and echoes of this life-process. The phantoms formed in the human brain are also, necessarily, sublimates of their material life-process, which is empirically verifiable and bound to material premises. Morality, religion, metaphysics, all the rest of ideology and their corresponding forms of consciousness, thus no longer retain the semblance of independence. They have no history, no development; but men, developing their material production and their material intercourse, alter, along with this their real existence, their thinking and the products of their thinking. Life is not determined by consciousness, but consciousness by life. In the first method of approach the starting-point is consciousness taken as the living individual; in the second it is the real living individuals themselves, as they are in actual life, and consciousness is considered solely as their consciousness.

This method of approach is not devoid of premises. It starts out from the real premises and does not abandon them for a moment. Its premises are men, not in any fantastic isolation or abstract definition, but in their actual, empirically perceptible process of development under definite conditions. As soon as this active life-process is described, history ceases to be a collection of dead facts as it is with the empiricists (themselves still abstract), or an imagined activity of imagined subjects, as with the idealists.

Relation and Consciousness

Only now do we find that man also possesses "consciousness"; but, even so, not inherent, not "pure" consciousness. From the start the "spirit" is afflicted with the curse of being "burdened" with matter, which here makes its appearance in the form of agitated layers of air, sounds, in short of language. Language is as old as consciousness; language is practical consciousness, as it exists for other men, and for that reason is really beginning to exist for me personally as well; for language, like consciousness, only arises from the need, the necessity, of intercourse with other men. Where there exists a relationship, it exists for me: the animal has no "relations" with anything, cannot have any. For the animal, its relation to others does not exist as a relation. Consciousness is therefore from the very beginning a social product, and remains so as long as men exist at all. Consciousness is at first, of course, merely consciousness concerning the immediate sensuous environment and consciousness of the limited connection with other persons and things outside the individual who is growing self-conscious. At the same time it is consciousness of nature, which first appears to men as a completely alien, all-powerful and unassailable force, with which men's relations are purely animal and by which they are overawed like beasts; it is thus a purely animal consciousness of nature (natural religion). . . . But even if this theory, theology, philosophy, ethics, etc. comes into contradiction with the existing relations, this can only occur as a result of the fact that existing social relations have come into contradiction with existing forces of production; this, moreover, can also occur in a particular national sphere of relations through the appearance of the contradiction, not within the national orbit, but between this national consciousness and the practice of other nations, i.e. between the national and the general consciousness of a nation. . . . Communism is for us not a stable state which is to be established, an ideal to which reality will have to adjust itself. We call communism the real movement which abolishes the present state of things. The conditions of this movement result from the premises now in existence. [17]

When Marx returns to this theme in his writing, he tries to walk the narrow line between a determinist position that all of man's consciousness depends on his day-to-day materialist, empirical, historical praxis, and a voluntarist one that maintains a complete separation between man's consciousness and his work. A number of consequences can be drawn from his argument. First, he offers the insight that men tend to develop a psychological stake in the economic system that is supporting their existence. Even though people are alienated by capitalist production and culture, they find it difficult to attack a way of life that is supporting a comfortable existence. Then, Marx advances a theory of contradictions. Because the actual forces of production, the accumulated technology of historical development, are socially integrating and at the same time the social relations of men are alienated from this technology, contradictions arise in the consciousness of men. Men begin to question the validity of the established economic and political structures. Therefore, the ruling capitalist class has to attempt to convince all men in the society that no contradictions exist in their life praxis. The privileged class carries out this mission with the help of the state, the national culture, educational institutions, and the mass media. Ideological domination strengthens and supports economic domination. Since the capitalist class exercises a financial monopoly over the sources of ideological activity, including political life, it tends to control national policy, education, leisure time, the media, etc. Of course, legal, religious, aesthetic, and social traditions develop their own autonomous force in a society and curb the power of the ruling class to a certain degree; this development again pushes the elite to sell their own private interests as ideals for the whole society. Marx and Engels do not argue simplistically on this matter but their strongest emphasis falls on ideological domination:

> The ideas of the ruling class are in every epoch the ruling ideas: i.e. the class, which is the ruling material force of society, is at the same time its ruling intellectual force. The class which has the means of material production at its disposal, has control at the same time over the means of mental production, so that thereby, generally speaking, the ideas of those who lack the means of mental production are subject to it. The ruling ideas are nothing more than the ideal expression of the dominant material relationships, the dominant material relationships grasped as ideas; hence of the relationships which make the one class the ruling one; therefore the ideas of its dominance. The individuals composing the ruling class possess among other things consciousness, and therefore think. In so far, therefore, as they rule as a class and determine the extent and compass of an epoch, it is self-evident that they do this in their whole range, hence among other things rule also as thinkers, as producers of ideas, and regulate the

production and distribution of the ideas of their age: thus their ideas are the ruling ideas of the epoch. For instance, in an age and in a country where royal power, aristocracy and bourgeoisie are contending for mastery and where, therefore, mastery is shared, the doctrine of the separation of powers proves to be the dominant idea and is expressed as an "eternal law." The division of labour, which we saw above as one of the chief forces of history up till now, manifests itself also in the ruling class as the division of mental and material labour, so that inside this class one part appears as the thinkers of the class (its active, conceptive ideologists, who make the perfecting of the illusion of the class about itself their chief source of livelihood), while the others' attitude to these ideas and illusions is more passive and receptive, because they are in reality the active members of this class and have less time to make up illusions and ideas about themselves. Within this class their cleavage can even develop into a certain opposition and hostility between the two parts, however, in the case of a practical collision, in which the class itself is endangered, automatically comes to nothing, in which case there also vanishes the semblance that the ruling ideas were not the ideas of the ruling class and had a power distinct from the power of this class. The existence of revolutionary ideas in a particular period presupposes the existence of a revolutionary class; about the premises for the latter sufficient has already been said above.[18]

Technology and Competition

Technological development is not, in a Marxian account, an unambiguous blessing. In fact, Marx considers its immediate effects alienating, not in the sense that laborers lose their jobs because of new machinery, but because machines crush the workers' creative potential. The laborer withers to a mere "appendage of a machine":

All means for the development of production transform themselves into means of domination over, and exploitation of, the producers; they mutilate the labourer into a

*fragment of a man, degrade him to the level of an
appendage of a machine, destroy every remnant of charm
in his work and turn it into a hated toil; they estrange him
from the intellectual potentialities of the labour-process in
the same proportion as science is incorporated in it as an
independent power; they distort the conditions under
which he works, subject him during the labour-process to a
despotism more hateful for its meanness. . . . It follows
therefore that in proportion as capital accumulates, the lot
of the labourer, be his payment high or low, must grow
worse.*[19]

Although technology adds to the surplus value of the production process, creativity is stifled. Marx argues that technology
itself can never reduce exploitation; furthermore, human labor
is responsible for technological achievement. Technology multiplies wealth that in no way accrues to the benefit of the worker,
another contradiction of capitalism in the Marxian model:

*There is one great fact, characteristic of this, our nine-
teenth century, a fact which no party dares deny. On the
one hand, there have started into life industrial and
scientific forces, which no epoch of the former human
history had ever suspected. On the other hand, there exist
symptoms of decay, far surpassing the horrors recorded of
the latter times of the Roman empire. In our days
everything seems pregnant with its contrary; machinery
gifted with the wonderful power of shortening and
fructifying human labour, we behold starving and over-
working it. The new-fangled sources of wealth, by some
strange weird spell, are turned into sources of want. The
victories of art seem bought by the loss of character. At
the same pace that mankind masters nature, man seems to
become enslaved to other men or to his own infamy. Even
the pure light of science seems unable to shine but on the
dark background of ignorance. All our invention and
progress seem to result in endowing material forces with
intellectual life, and in stultifying human life into material
force. This antagonism between modern industry and
science on the one hand, modern misery and dissolution*

> *on the other hand; this antagonism between the productive powers, and the social relations of our epoch is a fact, palpable, overwhelming, and not to be controverted. Some parties may wail over it; others may wish to get rid of modern arts in order to get rid of modern conflicts. Or they may imagiñe that so signal a progress in industry wants to be completed by as signal a regress in politics. On our part, we do not mistake the shape of the shrewd spirit that continues to mark all these contradictions. We know that to work well the new-fangled forces of society, they only want to be mastered by new-fangled men—and such are the working men. They are as much the invention of modern time as machinery itself. . . .*[20]

Technology is necessary in capitalistic society primarily because competition drives the capitalist to lower costs in order to increase surplus value. Growth, accumulation, expansion—this is the supreme law of capitalism, and it has little regard for human priorities, Marx tells us:

> *We thus see how the method of production and the means of production are constantly enlarged, revolutionised, how division of labour necessarily draws after it greater division of labour, the employment of machinery greater employment of machinery, work upon a large scale work upon a still greater scale. This is the law that continually throws capitalist production out of its old ruts and compels capital to strain ever more the productive forces of labour for the very reason that it has already strained them—the law that grants it no respite, and constantly shouts in its ear: March! march! This is no other law than that which, within the periodical fluctuations of commerce, necessarily adjusts the price of a commodity to its cost of production.*
>   *No matter how powerful the means of production which a capitalist may bring into the field, competition will make their adoption general; and from the moment that they have been generally adopted, the sole result of the greater productiveness of his capital will be that he must furnish at the same price, ten, twenty, one hundred times as much as before. But since he must find a market for, perhaps, a thousand times as much, in order to*

*outweigh the lower selling price by the greater quantity of
the sales; since now a more extensive sale is necessary not
only to gain a greater profit, but also in order to replace
the cost of production (the instrument of production itself
grows always more costly, as we have seen), and since this
more extensive sale has become a question of life and
death not only for him, but also for his rivals, the old
struggle must begin again, and it is all the'more violent the
more powerful the means of production already invented
are. The division of labour and the application of
machinery will therefore take a fresh start, and upon an
even greater scale.*

*Whatever be the power of the means of production
which are employed, competition seeks to rob capital of
the golden fruits of this power by reducing the price of
commodities to the cost of production; in the same
measure in which production is cheapened, i.e., in the
same measure in which more can be produced with the
same amount of labour, it compels by a law which is
irresistible a still greater cheapening of production, the sale
of ever greater masses of product for smaller prices. Thus
the capitalist will have gained nothing more by his efforts
than the obligation to furnish a greater product in the
same labour-time; in a word, more difficult conditions for
the profitable employment of his capital. While competition, therefore, constantly pursues him with its law of the
cost of production and turns against himself every weapon
that he forges against his rivals, the capitalist continually
seeks to get the best of competition by restlessly introducing further subdivision of labour and new machines, which,
though more expensive, enable him to produce more
cheaply, instead of waiting until the new machines shall
have been rendered obsolete by competition.*

*If we now conceive this feverish agitation as it
operates in the market of the whole world, we shall be in a
position to comprehend how the growth, accumulation,
and concentration of capital bring in their train an ever
more detailed subdivision of labour, an ever greater
improvement of old machines, and a constant application
of new machines—a process which goes on uninter-*

ruptedly, with feverish haste, and upon an ever more gigantic scale.[21]

Competition and privatization are the results of capitalist expansion. Not only do capitalists have to compete for markets but workers are forced to compete for jobs. Rather than a cooperative creative praxis, the labor process becomes a private struggle to build individual kingdoms within both capitalist and working classes. Owners solve the problem of competition by forming monopolies, which establish regard for each other's domains, but this phenomenon multiplies the problem for workers, small businessmen, and consumers. Even monopolies can never rest secure, though, for more monopolies spring up in other lands. It is in the nature of capitalism to breed antagonistic groups:

> *In practical life we find not only competition, monopoly and the antagonism between them, but also the synthesis of the two, which is not a formula, but a movement. Monopoly produces competition, competition produces monopoly. Monopolists are made from competition, competitors become monopolists. If the monopolists restrict their mutual competition by means of partial associations, competition increases among the workers; and the more the mass of the proletarians grows as against the monopolists of one nation, the more desperate competition becomes between the monopolists of different nations. The synthesis is of such a character that monopoly can only maintain itself by continually entering into the struggle of competition.*[22]

The argument in favor of capitalism, Marx realizes, is that this is the only system that seems to promote technology, expansion, and growth of capital. But nonetheless Marx sees the process as destructive for the workers, the small manufacturer, and the consumer for whom the capitalist enlists working-class support to generate new false needs:

> *The most favorable condition for the workingman is the growth of capital. This must be admitted: when capital*

remains stationary, commerce and manufacture are not merely stationary but decline, and in this case the workman is the first victim. He will suffer before the capitalist. And in the case of the growth of capital, under the circumstances, which, as we have said, are the best for the workingman, what will be his lot? He will suffer just the same. The growth of capital implies the accumulation and the concentration of capital. This centralisation involves a greater division of labor and a greater use of machinery. The greater division of labor destroys the especial skill of the laborer; and by putting in the place of this skilled work labor which anyone can perform it increases competition among the workers.

This competition becomes more fierce as the division of labor enables a single man to do the work of three. Machinery accomplishes the same result on a much larger scale. The accumulation of productive capital forces the industrial capitalist to work with constantly increasing means of production, ruins the small manufacturer, and throws him into the ranks of the proletariat. Then, the rate of interest falling in proportion as capital accumulates, the people of small means and retired tradespeople, who can no longer live upon their small incomes, will be forced to look out for some business again and ultimately to swell the number of proletarians. Finally, the more productive capital grows, the more it is compelled to produce for a market whose requirements it does not know—the more supply tries to force demand, and consequently crises increase in frequency and in intensity But every crisis in turn hastens the concentration of capital, adds to the proletariat. Thus, as productive capital grows, competition among the workers grows too, and grows in a far greater proportion. The reward of labor is less for all, and the burden of labor is increased for at least some of them.[23]

Marx and Engels foresaw the world-wide consequences of capitalist expansion. International trade, new trade routes, new continents with rich supplies of raw materials all intensified the productive process and technology. Marx's contention was that the workers were responsible for the initial surplus value and communal wealth that capitalists expropriated and then multiplied in new world markets. Marx believed that capitalism would not reach its limits until every patch of the globe fell under its organizational sway. "The particular task of bourgeois society is the establishment of the world market, at least in outline, and of production based upon the world market," Marx wrote to Engels on October 8, 1858.[24] Engels summarized the "vicious circle" of production, expansion, competition, and further expansion:

> But with the extension of the production of commodities, and especially with the introduction of the capitalist mode of production, the laws of commodity production, hitherto latent, came into action more openly and with greater force. The old bonds were loosened, the old exclusive limits broken through, the producers were more and more turned into independent, isolated producers of commodities. It became apparent that the production of society at large was ruled by absence of plan, by accident, by anarchy; and this anarchy grew to greater and greater height. But the chief means of aid of which the capitalist mode of production intensified this anarchy of socialised production was the exact opposite of anarchy. It was the increasing organisation of production, upon a social basis, in every individual productive establishment. By this, the old, peaceful, stable condition of things was ended. Wherever this organisation of production was introduced into a branch of industry, it brooked no other method of production by its side. The field of labour became a battle ground. The great geographical discoveries, and colonisation following upon them, multiplied markets and quickened the transformation of handicraft into manufacture. The war did not simply break out between the individual producers of particular localities. The local struggles begat, in their turn national conflicts, the commercial wars of the seventeenth and the eighteenth centuries.
>
> Finally, modern industry and the opening of the world market made the struggle universal, and at the same time gave it an unheard-of virulence. Advantages in natural or artificial conditions of production now decide the

existence or non-existence of individual capitalists, as well as of whole industries and countries. He that falls is remorsely cast aside. It is the Darwinian struggle of the individual for existence transferred from nature to society with intensified violence. The conditions of existence natural to the ẵnimal appear as the final term of human development. The contradiction between socialised production and capitalistic appropriation now presents itself as an antagonism between the organisation of production in the individual workshop and the anarchy of production in society generally. . . .

We have seen that the ever-increasing perfectibility of modern machinery is, by the anarchy of social production, turned into a compulsory law that forces the individual industrial capitalist always to improve his machinery, always to increase its productive force. The base possibility of extending the field of production is transformed for him into a similar compulsory law. The enormous expansive force of modern industry, compared with which that of gases is mere child's play, appears to us now as a necessity for expansion, both qualitative and quantitative, that laughs at all resistance. Such resistance is offered by consumption, by sales, by the markets for the products of modern industry. But the capacity for extension, extensive and intensive, of the markets is primarily governed by quite different laws, that work much less energetically. The extension of the markets cannot keep pace with the extension of production. The collision becomes inevitable, and as this cannot produce any real solution so long as it does not break in pieces the capitalist mode of production, the collisions become periodic. Capitalist production has begotten another "vicious circle."[25]

LENIN

Besides introducing his own style of revolutionary theory to the corpus of Marxian literature, Vladimir Ilich Lenin contributed greatly to the development of a Marxian theory of imperialism. He took up where Marx left off in his analysis of the monopolies of capitalist countries. He offered an explanation of international relations in the capitalist world, both among capitalist countries themselves and between capitalist and economically underdeveloped countries. In summary, Lenin highlighted the unequal relationships between the economically developed and underdeveloped lands in trade agreements, colonial arrangements, etc. Imperialism is the name Lenin applies to the process of transferring wealth from poor to rich countries.[26] The notion has maximum importance in its contemporary implications:

> On the threshold of the twentieth century, we see a new type of monopoly coming into existence. Firstly, there are monopolist capitalist combines in all advanced capitalist countries; secondly, a few rich countries, in which the accumulation of capital reaches gigantic proportions, occupy a monopolist position. An enormous "superabundance of capital" has accumulated in the advanced countries.
>
> It goes without saying that if capitalism could develop agriculture, which today lags far behind industry everywhere, if it could raise the standard of living of the masses, who are everywhere still poverty-stricken and underfed, in spite of the amazing advance in technical knowledge, there could be no talk of a superabundance of capital. This "argument" the petty-bourgeois critics of capitalism advance on every occasion. But if capitalism did these things it would not be capitalism; for uneven development and wretched conditions of the masses are fundamental and inevitable conditions and premises of this mode of production. As long as capitalism remains what it is, surplus capital will never be utilised for the purpose of raising the standard of living of the masses in a given country, for this would mean a decline in profits for the capitalists; it will be used for the purpose of increasing those profits by exporting capital abroad to the backward countries. In these backward countries profits are usually high, for capital is scarce, the price of land is relatively low, wages are low, raw materials are cheap. . . .

Monopolist Methods

Finance capital has created the epoch of monopolies, and monopolies introduce everywhere monopolist methods: the utilisation of "connection" for profitable transactions takes the place of competition on the open market. The most usual thing is to stipulate that part of the loan that is granted shall be spent on purchases in the country of issue, particularly on orders for war materials, or for ships, etc. . . .

The capital exporting countries have divided the world among themselves in the figurative sense of the term. But finance capital has also led to the actual division of the world. . . .

The capitalists divide the world, not out of any particular malice, but because the degree of concentration which has been reached forces them to adopt this method in order to get profits. And they divide it in proportion to "capital," in proportion to "strength," because there cannot be any other system of division under commodity production and capitalism. But strength varies with the degree of economic and political development. . . .

The "semi-colonial states" provide an example of the transitional forms which are to be found in all spheres of nature and society. Finance capital is such a great, it may be said, such a decisive force in all economic and international relations, that it is capable of subordinating to itself, and actually does subordinate to itself, even states enjoying complete political independence. . . .

The bourgeois reformists, and among them particularly the present-day adherents of Kautsky, of course, try to belittle the importance of facts of this kind by arguing that it "would be possible" to obtain raw materials in the open market without a "costly and dangerous" colonial policy; and that it would be "possible" to increase the supply of raw materials to an enormous extent "simply" by improving agriculture. But these arguments are merely an apology for imperialism, an attempt to embellish it, because they ignore the principal feature of modern capitalism: monopoly. Free markets are becoming more and more a thing of the past; monopolist syndicates and trusts are restricting them more and more everyday, and "simply" improving agriculture reduces itself to improving the conditions of the masses, to raising wages and reducing profits. Where, except in the imagination of the sentimental reformists, are there any trusts capable of interesting themselves in the condition of the masses instead of the conquest of colonies? . . .

Imperialism

If it were necessary to give the briefest possible definition of imperialism we should have to say that imperialism is the monopoly stage of capitalism. Such a definition would include what is most important, for, on the one hand, finance capital is the bank capital of a few big monopolist banks, merged with the capital of the monopolist combines of manufacturers; and, on the other hand, the division of the world is the transition from a colonial policy which has extended without hindrance to territories unoccupied by any capitalist power, to a colonial policy of monopolistic possession of the territory of the world which has been completely divided up. . . .

The imperialism of the beginning of the twentieth century completed the division of the world among a handful of states, each of which today exploits (i.e., draws super-profits from) a part of the world only a little smaller than that which England exploited in 1858. Each of them, by means of trusts, cartels, finance capital, and debtor and creditor relations, occupies a monopoly position in the world market. Each of them enjoys to some degree a colonial monopoly. . . .

The distinctive feature of the present situation is the prevalence of economic and political conditions which could not but increase the irreconcilability between opportunism and the general and vital interests of the working class movement. Embryonic imperialism has grown into a dominant system; capitalist monopolies occupy first place in economics and politics; the division of the world has been completed.[27]

Lenin links finance-capital and imperialism with war, as the following account referring to World War I indicates. His position on this question was not new since classical British imperialism rested on the ideology of the "white man's burden" to civilize all the peoples of the world and on the military tactics of foreign occupation. For Lenin the war was simply an extension of foreign plunder into continental lands for the right to foreign property. President Theodore Roosevelt, his contemporary, did not hesitate to fight for "rights" to the Philippines and the Caribbean with the help of a growing American navy. Trade, investment, and raw materials were the reward of these "enlightened and philanthropic" gestures. Lenin is not so sophisticated with his language:

> This war is a continuation of the politics of conquest, of shooting down whole nationalities, of incredible atrocities perpetrated by the Germans and the English in Africa, by the English and Russians in Persia—I don't know who did most—for which the German capitalists regarded them as enemies. They said in effect: You are strong because you are rich? But we are stronger than you; therefore we have the same "sacred" right to rob as you have. This is what the real history of British and German finance capital for decades preceding the war amounts to. This is what the history of Russo-German, Russo-English and Anglo-German relations amount to. This provides the key to an understanding of what the war is about. This is why the story that is being circulated about the causes of the war is a fraud and deception. Forgetting this history of finance-capital, the history of how this war for redivision matured, they try to make it appear as if two nations had lived in peace, and suddenly one attacked and the other defended itself. All science is forgotten; the banks are forgotten; the nations are called to arms; the peasants who know nothing about politics are called to arms. You must defend—that is all there is to it! If we are going to argue in this way, it would be more logical to suppress all newspapers, burn all books, and prohibit all discussion about annexations in the press—in this way justification of such an attitude towards annexations could be obtained. . . . In every resolution

that is passed—the scores of them are passed and published in, say, the newspaper Zemlya i Volva—*you will find the badly expressed reply: We do not want war for supremacy over other nations; we are fighting for our freedom—this is what all the workers and peasants say, and by this they express the workers' opinion, the workingman's conception of the war. Thus, they say in effect: If the war were in the interests of the working people and against the exploiters, we would be in favour of it. We, too, would be in favour of it; and no revolutionary party could oppose such a war. But the authors of these numerous resolutions are wrong, because they imagine that they are conducting the war. We soldiers, we workers, we peasants are fighting for our freedom. I will never forget the question that one of them put to me after a meeting: "Why do you talk about capitalists all the time? Am I a capitalist? We workers are defending our freedom." It is not true—you are fighting because you are obeying your capitalist government; the war is not being conducted by the people, but by the governments. I am not surprised when a worker, or a peasant who has not studied politics, who has not had the good fortune, or misfortune, to study secret diplomacy, to see this picture of financial plunder (this oppression of Persia by Russia and England for example) forgets this history and naively asks: what have capitalists got to do with it? I am fighting. He does not see the connection between the war and the government; he does not see that the government is conducting the war, and that he is a tool in the hands of the government.*[28]

In another passage Lenin adds a footnote that expresses an important dimension of the theory of alienation, although it is a dimension less and less present in his country after the success of his revolution. Exploitation and class division either on a national or on an international scale alienate exploiter and oppressed alike. All men and classes need each other for true human fulfillment. Lenin summarizes it this way:

"No nation can be free if it oppresses other nations," said Marx and Engels, the greatest representatives of

consistent nineteenth-century democracy, who became the teachers of the revolutionary proletariat. And, full of a sense of national pride, we Great-Russian workers want, come what may, a free and independent, a democratic, republican and proud Great Russia, one that will base its relations with its neighbours on the human principle of equality, and not on the feudalist principle of privilege, which is so degrading to a great nation. Just because we want that, we say: it is impossible, in the twentieth century and in Europe (even in the far east of Europe), to "defend the fatherland" otherwise than by using every revolutionary means to combat the monarchy, the land-owners, and the capitalists of one's own fatherland, i.e., the worst enemies of our country. We say that the Great Russians cannot "defend the fatherland" otherwise than by desiring the defeat of tsarism in any war; this is the lesser evil to nine-tenths of the inhabitants of Great Russia. For tsarism not only oppresses those nine-tenths eco-nomically and politically, but also demoralises, degrades, dishonours and prostitutes them by teaching them to oppress other nations and to cover up this shame with hypocritical and quasi-patriotic phrases.[29]

CASTRO AND GUEVARA

Alienation signifies that people or nations possess little or no control over their own destinies. Marxists, and many non-Marxists, maintain that imperialism is a major cause of contemporary alienation. Cuban leaders, for example, con-tinually point to imperialism as the source of alienation in their country before their 1959 revolution.

At that time there was no hard industry or technological development to speak of in Cuba. Sugar, controlled by American interests, dominated life on the island and accounted for about 80 percent of its exports. Cuba's economy was agrarian and unstable, a situation not unlike that of other Third World countries today. A peasant living in the countryside existed on less than $100.00 a year. Because of widespread unemployment most peasants could work only a few months

during the harvest, a situation handy for the growers who
needed a large labor force for a short period of time.
Imperialism for Cuba meant that outside interests preempted its
best land, mineral resources, and raw materials; it further meant
domination of its internal market, preventing the growth of a
national market. Imperialism meant chronic unemployment
leading to malnutrition, disease, illiteracy, and a cleavage of
classes.

When Fidel Castro addressed the United Nations General
Assembly not long after his revolution, he probably did not
realize the Marxian implications of his remarks. He was aware,
however, of the problems spawned by imperialism. He speaks
for dozens of other Third World countries today:

*Colonies do not speak. Colonies are not recognized in the
world. Colonies are not allowed to express their opinions
until they are granted permission to do so. That is why our
colony and its problems were unknown to the rest of the
world. In geography books there appeared one more flag,
one more coat of arms. There was another color on the
maps. But there was no independent republic on the maps
where the word "Cuba" appeared. Let everyone realize
that by allowing ourselves to be mistaken in this respect
we only play the parts of fools. Let no one be mistaken.
There was no independent republic. It was a colony where
orders were given by the Ambassador of the United States
of America. We are not ashamed of proclaiming this from
the rooftops. On the contrary: we are proud that we can
say that today no embassy rules our people; our people are
governed by Cuba's people.*

*Once again, the Cuban people had to turn and fight
to achieve independence and that independence was finally
attained after seven bloody years of tyranny. What
tyranny? The tyranny of those who in our country were
nothing but the cat's-paws of those who dominated our
country economically.*

*How can any unpopular system, inimical to the
interests of the people, stay in power unless it be by force?
Will we have to explain to the representatives of our sister
republics of Latin America what military tyrannies are?*

*Will we have to outline to them how these tyrannies have
kept themselves in power? Will we have to draw a
blueprint of the history of many of those tyrannies that
are already classical? Will we have to show them what kept
them in power? Will we have to say what national and
international interests kept them at the helm?*

*The military group that tyrannized over our country
was built upon the most reactionary sectors of the nation
and, over and above all, was based upon the foreign
interests that dominated the economy of our country.
Everybody here knows, and we understand that even the
Government of the United States recognizes, that that was
the type of government that was preferred by the
monopolies. Why? Because, with power, you can repress
any claims upon the part of the people. With power, you
repress strikes that seek better conditions of work and of
life. With power, you can quash the most deeply felt
aspirations of the nation. . . .*

*This was the situation that confronted us. Yet it
should not surprise many of the countries represented in
this Assembly, because, when all is said and done, what we
have said about Cuba is, one may say, an X-ray that could
be superimposed and applied to many of the countries
here represented in the Assembly. . . .*

Money Demands

*[After our revolution] the question of payments and
of indemnities came up. Notes from the State Department
rained on Cuba. They never asked us about our problems,
not even out of a desire to express condolence or
commiseration, or because of the hand that they had had
in creating the problems. They never asked us how many
died of starvation in our country, how many were
suffering from tuberculosis, how many were unemployed.
No, they did not ask about that. The feeling of solidarity
regarding our needs was never expressed. The conversa-
tions of the representative of the United States Government were concerned with the telephone company and
with the problem of the lands owned by American
companies. How were we going to pay?*

Naturally, the first thing that should have been asked was, "What with?," not "How?"

Can you gentlemen conceive how a poor, undeveloped country carrying the onus of 600,000 unemployed, with such a high number of sick and illiterate, whose reserves have been sapped, that has contributed to the economy of a powerful country to the tune of one billion dollars in ten years, can have the wherewithal to pay for the lands that are going to be affected by the agrarian reform, or at least pay for them on the conditions on which the North American State Department wanted to be paid in compensation for their affected interests?

They demanded three things: speedy, efficient and just payment. Do you understand that language? Speedy, efficient and just payment? That means, "Pay right now, in dollars and whatever we may ask for our lands."

We were not 150 per cent communists at that time. We just appeared slightly pink. We were not confiscating lands. We simply proposed to pay for them in twenty years, and the only way in which we could pay for them was by bonds—bonds which would mature in twenty years—at 4.5 per cent interest, which would be amortized yearly. How were we to be able to pay for these lands in dollars? How were we going to pay cash, on the spot, and how could we pay for them what they asked? It was ludicrous. . . .

Logic of Power

The attitude of the Revolutionary Government already had been too bold. It had clashed with the interests of the international electric trust; it had clashed with the interests of the international telephone trust; it had clashed with the interests of the international mining trusts; it had clashed with the interests of the United Fruit Company and it had clashed, virtually, with the most powerful interests of the United States, which, as you know, are very closely linked one with the other. And that was more than the Government of the United States could tolerate—that is, the representatives of the United States monopolies.

Then there began a new stage of punishment meted out to our revolution. Can anyone who objectively analyses the facts, who is ready to think honestly and not as the UPI and the AP tell him, to think with his head and to draw conclusions from the logic of his own thinking, to see the facts without prejudice, sincerely and honestly— can anyone who does this consider that the things which the Revolutionary Government did were such as to decree the destruction of the Cuban Revolution? No.

But the interests which were affected by the Cuban Revolution were not concerned over the case of Cuba; they were not being ruined by the measures of the Cuban Revolutionary Government. That was not the problem. The problem lay in the fact that those same interests owned the natural wealth and resources of the greater part of the peoples of the world.

So then the attitude of the Cuban Revolution had to receive its punishment. Punitive actions of every type— even the destruction of those foolhardy people—had to be carried out against the audacity of the Revolutionary Government. On our honor we swear that up to that time we had not had the opportunity even to exchange letters with the distinguished Prime Minister of the Soviet Union, Nikita Khrushchev. That is to say that, when for the North American press and the international news agencies who supply information to the world Cuba was already a Communist Government, a Red peril ninety miles from the United States, with a government dominated by Communists, the Revolutionary Government had not even had the opportunity of establishing diplomatic or commercial relations with the Soviet Union. But hysteria can go to any length; hysteria is capable of making the most unlikely and absurd claims. But of course, let no one for one moment think that we are going to intone here a mea culpa. *There will be no* mea culpa. *We do not have to ask anyone's pardon. What we have done we have done with our eyes wide open and, above all, fully convinced of our right to do it. . . .*

World Picture

*The problems which we have been describing in
relation to Cuba apply perfectly well to all of Latin
America. The control of Latin American economic
resources is exercised by the monopolies which, when they
do not directly own the mines and take charge of the
working of them, as in the case of copper in Chile, Peru
and Mexico and in the case of zinc in Peru and Mexico, as
well as in the case of oil in Venezuela, they are the owners
of the public-service companies, which is the case with the
electric services in Argentina, Brazil, Chile, Peru, Ecuador
and Colombia, or of the telephonic services, which is the
case in Chile, Brazil, Peru, Venezuela, Paraguay and
Bolivia. Or, they exploit commercially our products, as is
the case with coffee in Brazil, Colombia, El Salvador,
Costa Rica and Guatemala, or with the exploitation,
marketing and transportation of bananas by the United
Fruit Company in Guatemala, Costa Rica and Honduras,
or with cotton in Mexico and Brazil. That economic
control is exercised by North American monopolies of the
most important industries of the country, industries which
are dependent completely on the monopolies.*

*Woe betide them on the day when they too shall wish
to carry out agrarian reform! They will be asked for
immediate, efficient, and just payment. . . .*

*The problems of Latin America are like the problems
of the rest of the world: Africa and Asia. The world is
divided up among the monopolies; those same monopolies
that we see in Latin America are also seen in the Middle
East. There the oil is in the hands of monopolistic
companies that are controlled by the financial interests of
the United States, the United Kingdom, the Netherlands,
France, in Iran, in Iraq, in Saudi Arabia, in Kuwait, in
Qatar and, finally, in all corners of the world. The same
thing happens, for example, in the Philippines. The same
thing happens in Africa.*

*The world has been divided among the monopolistic
interests. Who would dare deny this historic truth? The*

monopolistic interests do not want to see the development of peoples. What they want is to exploit the natural resources of the countries and to exploit the people in the bargain, and the sooner they amortize their investments or get them back, the better it is for them.

The problems that the Cuban people have suffered from the imperialist Government of the United States are the same problems that Saudi Arabia would have if it decided to nationalize its oil fields, or if Iran or Iraq decided to do so; the same problems that Egypt had when it quite justifiably and correctly nationalized the Suez Canal; the very same problems that Indonesia had when it wanted to become independent; the same surprise attack that was made against Egypt and on the Congo. Has there ever been a lack of pretexts for the colonialists or imperialists when they wanted to invade a country? They have never lacked pretexts; somehow they have always managed to pull out of the hat the pretext that they wanted. Which are the colonialist countries? Which are the imperialist countries? There are not four or five countries but four or five groups of monopolies which possess the world's wealth.

If a person from outer space were to come to this Assembly, someone who had read neither the Communist Manifesto of Karl Marx nor the cables of the UP or the AP or the other publications of a monopolistic character, and if he were to ask how the world was divided and if he saw on a map of the world that its riches were divided among the monopolies of four or five countries, he would say: "The world has been badly divided up, the world has been exploited." Here in this Assembly, where there is a majority of the under-developed countries, he would say that the great majority of the people you represent are being exploited, that they have been exploited for a long time; the forms of exploitation may have varied, but they are still being exploited. That would be the verdict.[30]

Soon after this speech the United States enforced an economic blockade that has deterred economic growth in Cuba greatly.

Eight years later Castro reflected on the concept of development and imperialism at an International Cultural Conference held in Havana:

There is not a single people, there is not a single contemporary problem where the activities of imperialism are not clearly seen and felt; there is not a single infamous cause in today's world that is not supported by imperialism, as there is not a single just cause in the world that is not opposed by imperialism.

It is no longer just the case of imperialism aiming at and attacking what is called the Third World or the underdeveloped world—or developing world, as others call it. This term, "developing world," is a misnomer, and incorrectly applied concept, because, if we go by the reality of that world, we could call it, rather than a "developing" world—from an economic and technical standpoint, and as a result of the conditions imposed by imperialism on that part of the world—a "world of retrogression." The voracious actions of imperialism are not limited to this part of the world; the actions of that imperialism are directed, ever more seriously, against the interests of the so-called developed countries as well.

There are discrepancies of terminology in this concept of "developed" and "underdeveloped" countries, since it is said that at times a country which is highly developed industrially and economically is at the same time politically and socially underdeveloped, and that a country that is economically underdeveloped is politically and socially more developed. We do not feel in the least offended if we are included among the underdeveloped countries. Because development of awareness, our social as well as our general culture development, is steadily becoming a prerequisite to our economic and industrial development. In this country—as must occur in any other country where conditions are similar to ours—the development of a political as well as social awareness among the people becomes a sine qua non *requisite for winning the battle against economic underdevelopment.*

*Imperialism as a world phenomenon, as a world evil,
as a wolf at large in the world, can exist only if it acts in
this wolflike manner all over the world, if it acts against
the interest of the entire world. And that imperialism
behaves identically toward the rest of the so-called
developed world, the industrialized world.*

One Imperialism

*Nowadays it is common, in political terminology, to
speak of imperialism headed by the United States. The fact
is that in today's world there is only one truly powerful
imperialism, in today's world the mainstay of imperialism,
imperialism in essence, is U.S. imperialism. The powerful
imperialisms of yesteryear are today extraordinarily weak
in comparison with Yankee imperialism. That is the reason
why—and this is becoming understood more and more
clearly by the whole world—the effort, the struggle, is
being concentrated against Yankee imperialism, the mainstay of every reactionary government, of every evil cause
in the world. That imperialism even threatens to devour—
and is actually, to a certain extent, devouring—the other
imperialist powers. It is needless to dwell on this point. It
was discussed in the Congress: brilliant ideas were
expressed and proposals made in this sense. A paper
presented to the Congress examined, and substantiated
with statistics, the phenomenon of Yankee imperialist
penetration in Europe, the drain of capital—it is no longer
a question of the exportation of capital but of the drain of
capital—which Yankee imperialism is carrying out in the
underdeveloped world. An insight was given into the
mechanism of the brain drain which Yankee imperialism
perpetrates all over the world, and facts showing the
phenomenon today of a monopoly over science and
technology, showing how the imperialists utilize the great
advances in science and modern technology. All of this was
brilliantly set forth at the Congress, as was the explanation
of how, at present, when the Yankee imperialists make
investments in Europe, they only have to bring in ten
percent of the total amount invested, mobilizing the rest
of the resources within Europe itself.*

We know the degree of Yankee penetration in Europe. And we must say, seriously, that, perhaps to an extent unimagined by Europeans themselves, Yankee imperialism governs Europe.

Economic Sabotage

We know this; we have constant proof of it. Because, for example, the imperialists carry on incessant economic sabotage, economic blockage against us, doing everything possible to keep us from acquiring anything useful in any part of the world. The worst of this is that on many, many occasions the imperialists sabotage and frustrate our efforts in countries that consider themselves quite independent, quite sovereign, and quite developed.

The imperialists hold controlling interests in countless European enterprises; the imperialists control numerous patents used in Europe. And if we seek to purchase a machine that is manufactured under a patent held by a U.S. company, or if part of the machine has been manufactured under such a patent, we cannot buy the machine or the technological process involved. At times we may buy a part of a factory, but we cannot purchase the complete process because the patent is held by a U.S. company. In many other cases, in which neither patents nor the participation of U.S. capital in a factory is involved, we are also unable to purchase what we want because U.S. citizens are important clients of that industry and will be offended if the industry sells something to us. And in this way they sabotage and frustrate our efforts in the economic field. Thus they govern Europe, as owners of enterprises, as owners of patents, as important clients, and as allies of some European governments, using their influence to sabotage Cuba's economic activities.

And the lengths to which they go and their thoroughness in this activity seem incredible. Therefore, we without being Europeans, know to what extent the economy of Europe is ruled by the U.S. And the problem confronting Europe—including capitalist Europe—is to see if any way exists to control, to check that economic penetration, and if such a way exists within the capitalist conception,

*within a capitalist legal structure. No matter how much
they try to protect themselves with tariffs and import
duties, the financial and technological power of the U.S. is
so great that on many occasions it is able to sell cheaper
and even "dump" certain products, overcoming every kind
of trade barrier. And often the U.S. capitalists do not have
to overcome any barrier whatever because they simply buy
up the European enterprises.*

*We have even had the following type of experience:
after we have purchased trucks from a European firm and
received them, U.S. businessmen have bought the factory.
From that point on, we have been unable to purchase a
single part for those trucks. . . .*

*Therefore, there is an enemy that can indeed be
called a universal enemy. If, in the history of mankind,
there ever was a truly universal enemy, an enemy whose
attitude and deeds alarmed the whole world, threatened
the whole world, assaulted the whole world in one way or
another, that real enemy, that truly universal enemy, is
precisely Yankee imperialism. And, as mankind becomes
aware of this problem, mankind begins, in one way or
another to act.* [31]

In the early sixties, Castro sought to implement a Marxian
program of development in his country. His theory was taken
from the writings of Marx, whose influence can be noted in the
following passage touching on the meaning of work for the
Cuban laborer:

*In our country, work is no longer—nor will it ever be
again—a means of enriching a privileged minority; in our
country, work is no longer—nor will it ever be again—a
means of exploitation. The sweat of the men and women
of our country will never again serve the privileged or the
exploiters.*

*But it is not true that because of this, as a result of
the Revolution, we shall have fewer millionaires in this
country. Now, we have more millionaires! But they are not
millionaires in the old sense of those who amassed
hundreds of thousands of pesos and came to possess*

fortunes of millions of pesos, and even tens of millions of pesos, drawn from the blood and the sweat of the people. And there is no way to become a millionaire, nor has there ever been in any epoch of history, other than the exploitation of labor, because no one by his own work alone can produce sufficient wealth to accumulate millions of pesos.

Our millionaires of today are not those who exploit the work of others, but those who by their own work are capable of cutting a million arrobas of sugar cane—as is the case of the cane cutters present here, honored guests of this celebration. . . .

In the past the millionaires were different. There were only a few, and they did not cut cane or shed a drop of sweat. The millionaires were precisely those who did not work but made others work for them. Yes, there were a few millionaires, but the nation was poor, the people were poor. To justify their right to exploit the nation, they alleged that without their intelligence, their leadership, and their management, society couldn't function.

They alleged that they contributed their intelligence and their experience as businessmen to society. They also affirmed that man was a kind of animal motivated by selfish interests, that only unwholesome self-interest could make him put forth his best efforts, and that, in the fierce struggle of man against man, society would progress, a society guided by the most vulgar egoism. They believed that the people were devoid of any virtues; they believed that men were incapable of any disinterested and generous sentiments; they conceived human beings as wild beasts, beasts in both senses: capable of devouring each other and unable to function without the privileged minority of exploiters.[32]

Che Guevara, an Argentinean by birth, became acquainted with Marxian thought during his university years through Argentinean Marxist friends of his mother. He met Fidel Castro during the summer of 1955 in Mexico City and agreed to serve as a medical doctor in the Cuban Revolutionary invasion. After the Revolution Guevara was assigned to direct the national bank, but his overriding concern was the development of the "new Socialist man" in Cuba. He consistently translated Marx's economic thought into moral, personal terms. Capitalism is evil, according to Guevara, because it destroys human beings:

Under capitalism man is controlled by a pitiless code of laws which is usually beyond his comprehension. The alienated human individual is tied to society in its aggregate by an invisible umbilical cord—the law of value. It is operative in all aspects of his life, shaping its course and destiny.

The laws of capitalism, blind and invisible to the majority, act upon the individual without his thinking about it. He sees only the vastness of a seemingly infinite horizon before him. That is how it is painted by capitalist propagandists who purport to draw a lesson from the example of any successful capitalist about the possibilities of success.

The amount of poverty and suffering required for the emergence of a successful capitalist, and the amount of depravity that the accumulation of a fortune of such magnitude entails, are left out of the picture, and it is not always possible to make the people in general see this.

In any case the road to success is pictured as one beset with perils but which, it would seem, an individual with the proper qualities can overcome to attain the goal. The reward is seen in the distance; the way is lonely. Further on it is a route for wolves; one can succeed only at the cost of the failure of others. . . .

Capitalism lulls the masses since they see themselves as being oppressed by an evil against which it is impossible to struggle. Immediately following comes hope of improvement—and in this, capitalism differed from the preceding caste system which offered no possibilities for advancement.

For some people the ideology of the caste system will remain in effect: the reward for the obedient after death is to be transported to some fabulous other-world where, in accordance with the old belief, good people are rewarded. For other people there is this innovation: the division of

*society is predestined, but through work, initiative, etc.,
individuals can rise out of the class to which they belong.*

*These two ideologies and the myth of the self-made
man have to be profoundly hypocritical: they consist in
self-interested demonstrations that the lie of the permanence of class divisions is a truth. . . .For a long time
man has been trying to free himself from alienation
through culture and art. While he dies every day during the
eight or more hours that he sells his labor, he comes to life
afterwards in his spiritual activities.*

*But this remedy bears the germs of the same sickness;
it is as a solitary individual that he seeks communion with
his environment. He defends his oppressed individuality
through the artistic medium and reacts to esthetic ideas as
a unique being whose aspiration is to remain untarnished.*

*All that he is doing, however, is attempting to escape.
The law of value is not simply a naked reflection of
productive relations: the monopoly capitalists—even while
employing purely empirical methods—weave around art a
complicated web which converts it into a willing tool. The
superstructure of society ordains the type of art in which
the artist has to be educated. Rebels are subdued by its
machinery and only rare talents may create their own
work. The rest become shameless hacks or are crushed.*

*A school of artistic "freedom" is created, but its
values also have limits even if they are imperceptible until
we come into conflict with them—that is to say, until the
real problem of man and his alienation arises. Meaningless
anguish and vulgar amusement thus become convenient
safety valves for human anxiety. The idea of using art as a
weapon of protest is combated.*

*If one plays by the rules, he gets all the honors—such
honors as a monkey might get for performing pirouettes.
The condition that has been imposed is that one cannot
try to escape from the invisible cage.*[33]

CONTEMPORARY ANALYSIS

The validity of the selections quoted above rests not on their
immediate applicability to every situation in every country—

though their relevance is apparent—but on the questions they bring forward: What dehumanizes? What is a just society? How is work related to human fulfillment? How should nations relate to each other?, etc. The concern which the Marxists register comes from their understanding of the praxis of their societies; and their theory is derived from the praxis they are describing. The praxis upon which they based their judgments was not researched by means of the sophisticated methodologies of contemporary social science. Their theory was only "scientific" to the extent that it proceeded from the experience of their time within the economic, social, and political structures of their societies. The theory deals with global sources of alienation and therefore precludes the controlled methodologies of the behavioral sciences.

The reader of these selections from the Marxian corpus of literature can easily discern not only a distinctive onlook, a commitment perspective, but also basic units which serve as instruments for gauging the world. Before we attempt to show the similarity of Marxian and Christian onlooks of alienation, it is important to identify the basic Marxian units which will focus more specifically on possible sources of contemporary alienation.

The units, which can be framed within an infinite variety of problems, are here placed in the context of possible questions of analysis: What application does the notion of *alienated labor* have today? What effect do *technology* and cybernation have on *human labor*? Are people able to make basic decisions about (*take control over*) the quality of their lives? Are individuals forced into greater *isolation*, rather than initiated into deeper community? Do *authoritarian, hierarchical, elitist* institutions—political beauracracies, schools, military, churches—preclude the possibilities of egalitarian communities? Who creates *surplus labor*? Who reaps its reward? What are the effects of continually *expanding markets* in this country and abroad? Are human needs manipulated by the necessity to *expand markets*? Can *class conflict* be located in a contemporary *ruling class* and *proletariat*? Are the *state, churches, schools* or other established institutions allied with a *ruling class*? In what terms can the *proletariat* be defined today? Does *commodity production* cause *antagonism* and *competition* within classes and with other classes? What is the relationship of *war* to the economic system? Does *imperialism* explain the *ideological conflict* between the three great power blocks of the world—United States, Russia, China? If not, what are some possible explanations of the conflict? Is *ideological mystification* apparent in our society? Is the growing tendency toward *international monopolies* bringing the world under the sway of an *elite class*? Is the quality of our natural environment determined by the maintenance of *maximum surplus value* and *commodity consumption*? Is *alienation* the root cause of *social upheaval* and *conflict*?

A good example of contemporary social analysis that applies a Marxian theory of alienation to advanced corporate capitalist society appeared as an editorial statement in *Socialist Revolution*. The editors utilize Marxian units which spring from a Marxian onlook in their summary of American capitalism. The selection is taken from a discussion of what meaning can be given today to the notion of surplus value and an emerging new proletariat:

> *The realization of surplus value has required new, expanding markets, the substitution of values in exchange for values in use, and the creation of new needs, both domestically and internationally. Abroad, imperialism has transformed traditional, semi-feudal, and semi-capitalist modes of production. At home, commodity production has replaced pre-and-semi-capitalist production in small-scale industry, on the farm, and in the home. In most of the nineteenth century, factory production replaced basic commodities traditionally produced by artisans and craftsmen; the problem of finding new markets for the products of large-scale industry was minimal. In the twentieth century, the market for traditional "wage goods"—food, clothing, shelter, and the related demand for capital goods—has been too thin to absorb the product of large scale industry. To supplement the market for "wage goods," capital has been compelled to manipulate the production of the entire range of human needs.*
>
> *The realization of surplus value requires the ruling class to direct the proletariat's search for the satisfaction*

of its needs, its unconscious motivations and desires, to the marketplace. Modern advertising exploits people's need for accomplishment, status, prestige, even affection and love; it focuses their awareness of these needs upon commodities in the market rather than upon their relations with one another. The ruling class is also compelled to manufacture new needs by increasing the general level of expectations and hammering away at the theme that commodities are indispensable for the "good life," a "happy home", "good marriage," and, in general, "success" in all spheres of life. And this requires product differentiation, advertising, sales, public relations, entertainment, commercial sports—industries and activities that are need-producing. The realization of surplus value depends upon surveys of consumer behavior, motivational research, psychological depth studies, a greater emotional knowledge of the proletariat, the use of the mass media to educate the proletariat that commodities will satisfy their deepest emotional needs. Modern capitalism thus produces a kind of sensitivity of the salesman, the copywriter, the sports promoter, the television director.

Both of these tendencies—the expansion and upgrading of the proletariat and the search for new markets—have led to the interpenetration of the economic base and superstructures, not merely in the form of an expanded role of government in the economy, but also in the integration of all secondary institutions and activities into production itself. The state, especially the education system, petty commodity production, the farm, and the home are all sources of labor power and exploitable markets. Recreation, leisure-time, and cultural activity all constitute growing markets. And accompanying the spread of commodities and commodity culture into all spheres of life is the spread of instrumental social relations and new forms of social antagonisms from the sphere of direct production into the secondary institutions.

Advanced corporate capitalism also requires the development of a political system designed to maintain the social order by politically containing and integrating the proletariat into a corporate liberal consensus. Keynesian and neo-Keynesian planning is impossible without cost-of-living indexes, budgetary control, balance of payments analyses. Production and distribution planning is impossible without an extended government apparatus that serves to coordinate corporate policies. Social planning is impossible without city planning, welfare departments, "humanistic" approaches to child care, education, family counseling, schools of psychology. Military planning is impossible without an elaborate science apparatus. And all of these activities rest on the development of an information industry, an information explosion, which includes "presentation depots" and "interpretation networks." The development and consolidation of the corporate liberal social order also engenders a kind of rationality and a kind of sensitivity—the rationality of the economist, urban planner, "systems" expert, and cost accountant, and the sensitivity of the social worker, public health nurse, psychotherapist, and teacher. . . .

Capitalist Culture

Advanced capitalism has created a new proletariat and a new culture for that proletariat. It has spread into the home, leisure, recreation, culture, and education. The penetration of capital into spheres outside production and exchange has transformed the social relations, the needs, the expectations, and the values of the proletariat. In general, the proletariat experiences social relations as more impoverished, and alienated, in the sense that there exists a greater discrepancy between bourgeois thought and promise, and perceived reality. Capitalism has created a social and ecological environment in which people find themselves unable to establish trusting, loving, collective social relations.

The "traditional" proletarian cultures formed during earlier phases of capitalism in both urban and rural society have been replaced. The candy store gives way to the drive-in; the neighborhood block to the "strip"; the ethnic neighborhood to the homogeneous suburb; the rural

*sharecropping culture to the urban black ghetto; the village
and town to the megalopolis. Modern capitalism has
disintegrated earlier sub-cultures and reintegrated culture
around commodity production and consumption.*

*For these reasons, fewer traditional avenues of escape
from alienation in production are available.The milieus of
the family, neighborhood, village, and town have been all
but destroyed. The breakdown of neighborhood and
community social structures, and the growth of super-
organizations of capital and the state, and the social
relations they create combine to atomize large sectors of
the population—to transform associations, groups, and
families into masses. At a time when individuals feel the
heaviest pressures of alienation, escape from their situation
becomes impossible in bourgeois daily life.*

Produces Isolation

*A vast, variegated proletariat lives under conditions of
individual isolation, its life outside of work organized
around commodity consumption. As capital offers more
and more distractions in the form of new and different
commodities, these distractions become less and less
emotionally satisfying. As bourgeois ideology promises
personal liberation and fulfillment through commodities,
the proletariat becomes confused, irritated, and angry.
Students rise up against authoritarian institutions; Blacks
burn the cities; street people reject alienated labor and
attempt to establish their own turn in the streets;
drop-outs seek escape in drugs, in the intimacy of personal
encounters, mysticism, rural communes; the majority
search for meaning in fantasy, in new sexual relations,
escapist travel, televised heroism, controlled violence, and
the military precision of professional sports. Antagonistic
social relations, in the most chaotic, distorted, self-
deceptive, and violent forms, are displaced from the
factories and offices into the streets, the schools, and the
home.*

*Capital tries to contain the chaos in the only way it
knows how: by turning these forms of escape, these*

outbursts, these new experiments in living, into more capital. Eye drops are sold to counteract air pollution; depressants to relieve anxiety; speed to cure depression; "home-making" objects for families in crisis; mace and machine guns to solve the problem of the black ghetto; teaching machines to control the schools; "psychedelic items," pro football, and films that begin and end with the individual "doing his own thing" to camouflage a barren culture. And simultaneously corporate ideology "explains" these outbursts and this disintegration in terms of new, mystified theories of human behavior—or as "problems," soluble in time, with compromise.

When the distractions no longer distract and the explanations no longer explain, the use of force becomes necessary, which still further dehumanizes social relations. The attacks against the institutions are extended into the courts, the jails, the army stockades, "corrections" systems, into relations with school principals, probation officers, social workers. Anger and rage become social products, which are countered by producing more commodities, and by producing fear to divert and suppress this anger and rage. The effect, however, deepens the anger and rage. [34]

ALIENATION: A CHRISTIAN ONLOOK

Within the analytical level of a Marxian onlook lies a faith dimension that parallels a Christian understanding of alienation in the world. Comparable attitudes underlie both theories and make it possible for a Christian to utilize comfortably a Marxian methodology. At this point it is necessary to uncover a few of these points of contact.

The origins of a Christian religious onlook of alienation reach into the second millennium B.C. to the foundation of "Hebrew" tribes, culture, and tradition.[35] Because of the oppressive quality of many ancient Near Eastern societies, individuals often withdrew from their urban centers; by this action they forfeited their standing and status in the society. Their explicit or implicit posture gave others the description recorded in the Code of Hammurabi, "I hate my king and my city." The word "Hebrew," *Hab/piru, 'Apiru,* refers to those who withdraw in some way from the social order; in later Palestine "Hebrew" became almost identical with "Israelite." The major consequence of this act of alienation was the banding together of disaffected individuals, e.g., the "Hebrews" in David's gang of outlaws. Other "Hebrews" joined other political communities or entered the service of another king.

Mendenhall believes that the Hebrews who escaped from Egypt picked up support from other oppressed people throughout Palestine and thus were able to conquer a large territory in a short period of time: "Individuals who withdraw from an urbanized society rarely can cause a situation in which the society is threatened with extinction, but organized resistance within a political society is infinitely more dangerous than the plaintive voice of dissent of an individual, who can always be dismissed as a lunatic, or at least be decently put out of his misery by respectable, legal processes. There can be no doubt, however, that whole groups of persons possessed a solidarity of action in the ancient world which could be a great danger to constituted political organizations. This is the 'tribe.' The Hebrew conquest of Palestine took place because a religious movement and motivation created a solidarity among a large group of pre-existent social units, which was able to challenge and defeat the dysfunctional complex of cities which dominated the whole of Palestine and Syria at the end of the Bronze Age."[36]

It is not our purpose to examine the accuracy of Mendenhall's thesis in detail, but only to call attention to the certainty that underlies it: that early Israelite Yahwism was a religious movement which developed in the context of oppressive economic and political social structures. It was either the brutality of feudal lords and slave masters, or the persistance of tax collectors, or the confiscation of land, or dozens of other types of ancient exploitative activity that precipitated tribal resistance. In the days when the religious experience which was to become the Judaeo-Christian heritage was born, "Hebrews" felt no control over their own lives or destiny. This strain in the tradition never has disappeared.

Later the Yahwistic faith of the Hebrews would demand

protection for their nationalist political and economic interests. In the beginning, however, it was simple loyalty to a deity who was said to have identified himself with the oppressed in Egypt. The symbol for all who were allied with the Hebrews was a God whose content represented the inversion of the alienation and oppression they suffered. Hebrews from all parts of Palestine easily accepted the Exodus event as their own personal history. It was not difficult for a movement to grow and for inhabitants of an area to reject political, economic, and social institutions that caused so much grief. The tribes retained many of their own religious traditions, ritual, and customs but accepted an Overlord who represented freedom now.

After the kingship became institutionalized in Israel, the prophets were to point out that the existence of the Israelite kingdoms took the very form which early Hebrews had rejected, the monopoly of force and power. Once again the Hebrews in the northern kingdom rejected the oppressive powers of the south: "What portion have we in David?. . . . To your tents, O Israel!" (1 Kings 12:16). In every period of Israelite history institutions threatened the Jewish people with old and new forms of alienation. The problem became rooted in the onlook of their religion, its tradition, and literature. Different religious viewpoints responded to the problem in varying ways.

New oppression arose for the Palestinian community in the second century B.C. when the Hellenistic dynasty which succeeded Alexander the Great ruled the region. The structures of Hellenistic society that made its culture possible included slave labor, a heavy tax on the poor, and continual wars of territorial expansion. The constant struggle for power within the realm destroyed any sense of security among its inhabitants.

Part of the story of this period is told in the books of the Maccabees. The tale begins with Jason, a lover of Hellenistic culture, buying the high priesthood in order to introduce a fuller measure of Hellenism into Jerusalem. He built a gymnasium on the temple hill, "destroyed the lawful ways of living and introduced new customs contrary to the law" (2 Macc. 4:11). Although Jason did not attempt to outlaw the Jewish religion, this course of events brought down a crisis for orthodox Jews, who knew that pagan customs had not been tolerated in their city since the Jewish return from Babylon more than three centuries earlier. Menelaus soon outbid Jason for the high priesthood and paid for the position with gold vessels stolen from the temple, an outrageous act of sacrilege in the eyes of all Jews. Later King Antiochus Epiphanes further profaned the temple by stealing its funds to pay for military expenses. Consequent popular uprisings provoked the king into a mass slaughter of Jerusalem Jews, the selling of thousands into slavery, and eventually the proscription of Jewish customs and religion.

For people whose religious beliefs affirmed that God would keep their national heritage intact by delivering them from the evil in which they lived, these events appeared catastrophic. What happened to their God whom they believed to be the lord of history? The answer came in a type of religious literature at least partially influenced by Iranian religion called apocalyptic. The author of the Book of Daniel was probably the first of many Jewish writers to adopt this literary form. In former days Jews looked for historical deliverance in their own day; Daniel substituted an afterlife, but not the disembodied future life of Hellenistic belief. Daniel's future was the kingdom of God, where God's rule insured a new history, in peace, harmony, and communal happiness. Daniel injected new hope into Jewish faith by explaining that the successive worldly kingdoms that had enslaved Judaism heralded the coming of God's own kingdom.

Apocalyptic literature was the natural heir of prophecy, which used the Exodus experience as a model. Both outlooks, however, stemmed from man's existence in a hostile, oppressive, alienated world. Apocalyptic literature utilized highly allegorical images and mythical imagination to describe the evil forces, worldly power, and military might of their contemporary history coming in conflict with the powers of God in a supreme final battle. The faith of the community assured the Jewish people of final salvation after the struggle. The important point of apocalyptic writing lies in its starting point—oppressive economic and political forces which controlled the Jews.

It is not unusual that apocalyptic literature should flourish at the time of Jesus and that Jesus himself should speak in apocalyptic images. Josephus, a Jewish historian who wanted to explain the history and customs of his people to Roman society, fills in the sociopolitical background of Jesus' era, which is not unlike that of the previous two centuries.[37] Roman rulers, proconsuls, and legates milked the provinces of their revenue; religious customs were interfered with; political and economic structures strangled the lifelines of the people. Archelaus succeeded his father Herod in Judea in 4 B.C. and because of a riot soon afterward, sent his troops to slaughter hundreds of Jews as they offered their sacrifices at the temple. Other insurrections led to the intervention of Roman troops under Varus, who crucified perhaps as many as two thousand Jews.

Judea was then placed under a procurator, or financial officer, named Coponius. The legate of Syria, Quirinius, came to Judea to conduct a census, probably to determine the financial situation of the area. A Zealot revolutionary, Judas the Galilean, led a revolt because of the census, the first of a long series of terrorist tactics by him and his followers to precipitate the coming of the kingdom, or at least to force national independence.

Pontius Pilate entered the scene in 26 A.D. and ruled for ten years. Among other administrative provocations of the Jews, Pilate seized the sacred treasure of the temple, provoking a demonstration and consequent murder of many of the demonstrators by his plainclothes security guard. He continued an adamant policy toward dissenters throughout his tenure. Although only a small group of Zealots actively sought to bring down the Roman Empire, they undoubtedly enjoyed much support in an era that was prolific in apocalyptic writing. S. G. F. Brandon claims that Jesus himself was sympathetic to the Zealot revolutionaries and possibly even their ally, that the early Jewish Christians lived in apocalyptic expectation in their political and religious rejection of Rome, and that they considered themselves commissioned to prepare Israel for the imminent coming of the kingdom in the person of the Risen Jesus.[38] The testimony of the Gospels admits a variety of interpretations about the revolutionary quality of Jesus' life, but the times were ripe for a religious community to frame its belief within the framework of an alienation-liberation dynamic.

This background leads to the subject matter of the New

Testament, which relies heavily on apocalyptic literature and which is the foundation of a Christian onlook. The central symbol of the New Testament counterpart of Marxian alienation is the figure of Satan, which stands for much more than a personal being who harasses unfortunate earthlings. The Gospel of Mark points up the many conditions of man's life over which he has no control; disease, ritual defilement, and suffering are manifestations of Satan's control over the common life of man. Matthew extends the concept to include Satan's power in society, a "brood of vipers" (12:34), "an evil and adulterous generation" (12:39), and "this evil generation" (12:45). Jesus places himself in opposition to the evil of his society represented by Satan. Matthew further describes Jesus lamenting over the evil that has come upon his people, evil so thoroughly ingrained in the structures of social life that a single exorcism of his disciples proved unavailing. An entire new society with a new Spirit is needed to correct the problem of his "generation," that is, the religio-cultural and political life of Palestine.

In this context it is unimportant whether or not Satan is a personal creature bent upon the moral destruction of the world; it is important, however, to know that the people of New Testament times were oppressed on many fronts and that religious literature was written to express and cope with this suffering. Trevor Ling maintains "that when a careful consideration of the whole range of New Testament references to Satan has been made, the outline which emerges is that of the spirit of a society . . . the spirit of unredeemed man's collective life, that which dominates the individual and stifles his growth in truly personal life."[39] This onlook has penetrated the core of the Christian message.

In Johannine writings of the New Testament a connection is not difficult to establish between the hostile structures of society and the symbol of Satan. For John the "world" stands for the old order of life, that which "passes away" (1 John 2:17). It contrasts with the new order inaugurated by Christ. C. H. Dodd says that John uses the term to signify "the life of human society as organized under the power of evil."[40] Raymond Brown gives the term four different usages in John, including one that expresses hostile social structure,[41] and Ling says simply that in John "world" means "the complex of inter-related human individuals and institutions, which nowadays would be described as 'human society.' "[42]

In Johannine writings the "world" is also given a personal quality in its manifestation of hostility, in its control over people's lives, and its hatred for the disciples of Jesus (John 7:7; 15:18; 17:14; 1 John 3:13). Parallelisms in John's First Epistle indicate that "world" and "evil one" have very close relationships. It is the hostile quality of the world's oppression that Christians are to overcome.

Herbert McCabe uses the passage in John 17—"the world has hated them because they are not of the world"—in a political sense. He claims that John saw the world as the Roman colonial empire, "a kind of human organization and unity based on the domination of man by man."[43] The reason the world hates the followers of Jesus lies in their opposition to its destructive, alienating power and their intent to subvert those structures. His followers find a precedent in Jesus' opposition to Satan and what Satan represents.

Of course the symbol of Satan includes many more individualistic interpretations. But if the notion primarily represents the corporate alienating aspects of man's life in keeping with the apocalyptic writings of the time, a Christian understanding of the world is profoundly influenced by the idea. In the words of Trevor Ling, "Satanic temptation occurs when society exerts pressure upon the individual to do that which is contrary to the development of free personality in himself or in others. . . . In order to aggrandize its power at the expense of the individual, the collective offers him an apparent good." (By Satanic temptation Ling means social structures that control the individual and stop development. Satan signifies false needs and mystification arising from social domination.) Ling further aligns the problem of depersonalization and the reification of human relationships through which "pecuniary values pervade the whole hierarchy of human values" with the New Testament idea of Satan.[44] This interpretation bears a close relationship to the Marxian idea of alienation. The traditions of both Marxism and Christianity begin with an acute vision of man's social predicament.

This chapter proposed to indicate the similarity of onlooks

between Marxism and Christianity regarding alienation and to offer a Marxian instrument to gauge alienating aspects of contemporary society. The effort is clearly not exhaustive, nor is it the only mode of analysis by which political theology could look at social institutions. Nevertheless it brings important light to bear on dehumanized social relationships.

The Marxian outlook and analysis was presented first and later it became clear that the Christian onlook toward alienation runs᷄ in a parallel direction. Both Christian and Marxian traditions were born in historical settings that strongly reacted to man's oppression, his isolation and deprivation of community and a fully human life. The same kind of social relationships which Old and New Testament tradition deplored or viewed as satanic, Marx later analyzed more impersonally. For early Christian as well as Marxist writers, oppressive or exploitative social, economic, and political structures represent the "old order of life." Alienation stems from expropriated labor power, the loss of a person's control over his existence, and class domination, whether the historical category is slave trade or capitalism, monarchy or bourgeois democracy, a priestly caste or a ruling class, the Pax Romana or imperialist adventures, foreign interference with local customs or local ideological domination. Both traditions have left deep marks on Western civilization. Because of the similarity of onlooks toward alienation, political theology could fruitfully test the Marxian analysis in the application of its own task.

The more fundamental question deals with the political theologian's involvement in social change. A mere theoretical understanding of alienated human existence does not activate a community to overturn oppressive social structures. Analysis must be translated into collective understanding, understanding into strategy, and strategy into intentional activity. First, however, we should examine the content of Marxian and Christian notions of liberation.

Notes

1. The bulk of the material presented in these chapters is derived from Marx rather than Engels, but the two

collaborated on a few significant works in a way that makes separating them difficult. Recent Marxian scholarship has identified significant differences in their philosophical positions, but this is not the place to discuss them.

2. Karl Marx, *Pre-Capitalist Economic Formations* (New York: International, 1966), pp. 84-85.
3. *Ibid.*, p. 83.
4. *Wage-Labour and Capital* (New York: International, 1933), p. 19.
5. *Cf. Capital*, Vol. 1, "The Two-Fold Character of the Labour Embodied in Commodities" (New York: International, 1967), pp. 41 ff.
6. *The Poverty of Philosophy* (New York: International, 1963), p. 34.
7. *Early Writings* (New York: McGraw Hill, 1964), pp. 168-169.
8. *Wage-Labour and Capital*, p. 33.
9. *Early Writings*, pp. 124-125.
10. *Ibid.*, p. 138.
11. *Wage-Labour and Capital*, pp. 20, 27.
12. Marx's elaborate development of this idea is found in the first volume of *Capital*. See also "The Eighteenth Brumaire of Louis Bonaparte" in *Selected Works*, Vol. I, (Moscow: Foreign Languages, 1962), p. 273.
13. *Early Writings*, pp. 177-178.
14. *The Poverty of Philosophy*, pp. 122-123.
15. "Manifesto of the Communist Party" in *Selected Works*, Vol. I, pp. 34-35, 37-38.
16. *Cf. The German Ideology* (New York: International, 1966), pp. 3 ff.
17. *Ibid.*, pp. 13-15, 19-21, 26.
18. *Ibid.*, pp. 39-40.
19. *Capital*, Vol. I, p. 645.
20. "Speech at the Anniversary of the *People's Paper*," *Selected Works*, Vol. I, pp. 359-360.
21. *Wage-Labour and Capital*, pp. 43-44.
22. *The Poverty of Philosophy*, p. 152.
23. *Ibid.*, pp. 218-219.
24. *Selected Correspondence* (New York: International, 1942), p. 117.

25. *Socialism: Utopian and Scientific* (New York: International, 1935), pp. 60-61, 63.

26. Lenin's economic theory of imperialism has been hotly debated for the past fifty years: e.g., whether or not monopoly imperialism is characterized by export of surplus capital to offset a crisis of an increasing disparity between expanding forces of production and restricted consumption, whether or not imperialism results from the growth of monopoly capitalism and its drive for hegemony, whether or not imperialists are simply attracted by a higher rate of profit that is derived from colonial exploitation, whether or not foreign capital is invested in underdeveloped regions primarily to exploit the cheap labor market, etc. These considerations of economic questions are beyond the scope of our analysis.

27. *Imperialism: The Highest Stage of Capitalism* (New York: International, 1939), pp. 62-63, 65-67, 75, 81, 83, 88, 107.

28. *War and the Workers* (New York: International, 1940), pp. 13-15.

29. "On the National Pride of the Great Russians," in *Collected Works*, Vol. 21 (Moscow: Progress Publishers, 1964), p. 104.

30. "Speech at the United Nations," September 26, 1960, distributed by Fair Play for Cuba Committee, New York.

31. "Speech at the Cultural Conference," January 12, 1968, printed by the Stenographic Department of the Cuban Revolutionary Government, Havana.

32. "May Day Speech," May 1, 1966, Havana.

33. *Socialism and Man* (New York: Merit, 1968), pp. 6-7, 10, 14-15.

34. *Socialist Revolution*, I No. 2 (March-April, 1970), 11-13, 15-17. Agenda Publishing Company, 1445 Stockton St., San Francisco, California, 94133.

35. This account of the Habiru groups is taken from George E. Mendenhall, "The Hebrew Conquest of Palestine" in *The Biblical Archaeologist*, 25, (September, 1962), 66-87.

36. *Ibid.*, p. 73.

37. *Cf.* Josephus, *Jewish Antiquities*, Loeb Classical Library (Cambridge, Massachusetts: Harvard University Press, 1965), Book XVIII.

38. Brandon has compiled an impressive survey of evidence to support his thesis in *Jesus and the Zealots* (Manchester: Manchester University Press, 1967); Oscar Cullmann presents his arguments against the position in *The State in the New Testament* (New York: Scribners, 1956), pp. 20 ff.

39. Trevor Ling, *The Significance of Satan* (London: S.P.C.K., 1961), pp. 83-84.

40. *The Johannine Epistles,* (New York: Harper, 1946), p. 39.

41. *The Anchor Bible: John,* Vol. 1, (Garden City: Doubleday, 1966), pp. 508-510.

42. *The Significance of Satan,* p. 32.

43. "Priesthood and Revolution" in *Commonweal,* 88, (March 1, 1968), 621-622.

44. *The Significance of Satan,* pp. 90-91.

CHAPTER THREE

Theory: Liberation

MARX AND ENGELS

Perhaps the most valuable portion of the Marxian inheritance lies in its vision of future society. What makes Marx's contribution different from dozens of other utopian visions, however, is his insistence that the new world is being born now within the old order. This distinguishes his "scientific" method from a uotopian view. He puts the question in economic terms: "No social order ever perishes before all the productive forces for which there is room in it have developed; and new, higher relations never appear before the material conditions of their existence have matured in the womb of the old society itself."[1] For Marx the relations of production in capitalist society necessitate a conflict of classes; these relations are running their course and the new relations which will bloom into a socialist society are unfolding in the old order.

The Resolution of Class Conflict

Marx usually identified affiliation to a class with the class's relationship to the means of production and its consequent struggle over newly created surplus value. The distinction between those who sell their labor and those who buy it furnished the foundation of Marx's theory of class conflict.

Marx never claimed credit for "discovering the existence of classes in modern society, nor yet the struggle between them."[2] He did say that he was the first to understand the historical development of class conflict that will ultimately lead to the resolution of this struggle in a classless, socialist society. Marx pointed to history to indicate that changes from one society to another—from ancient to feudal to capitalist—always climaxed in class struggle. The basis of the conflict in the Marxian paradigm lies in the social relations of production between the proletariat (working class) and the ruling class (capitalist class). Out of the social relations of production grows the awareness of class interests and class solidarity.

Marx saw the working class in terms of a group with a newly developing consciousness dependent on its class condition, not an awareness created by moral appeals. He asserted that a social revolution will come only when the proletariat becomes aware of its own interests:

Material force can only be overthrown by material force; but theory itself becomes a material force when it has seized the masses. Theory is capable of seizing the masses when it demonstrates ad hominem, and it demonstrates ad hominem as soon as it becomes radical. To be radical is to grasp things by the root. But for man the root is man himself. What proves beyond doubt the radicalism of German theory, and thus its practical energy, is that it begins . . . with the categorical imperative to overthrow all those conditions in which man is an abased, enslaved, abandoned, contemptible being—conditions which can hardly be better described than in the exclamation of a Frenchman on the occasion of a proposed tax upon dogs: "Wretched dogs! They want to treat you like man!"[3]

The unique feature of the evolving class awareness of the proletariat, however, is found in its universality. For the first time in history, according to Marx, the interests of a particular class coincide with the interests of mankind as a whole. The proletariat is fast becoming the historically privileged class to emancipate all of society because its consciousness includes the vision of a classless society, finally purged of divisions, inequalities, and antagonisms. This awareness is not given as ideology from above but comes from experience and understanding.

What Marx is rejecting here is Hegel's notion that the bureaucracy of the state serves as a "universal class," representing the needs of every segment of society. The state bureaucracy pretends to embody universality but represents only the particular interests of the ruling class. Marx substitutes the historical emergence of the proletariat for the state bureaucrats and predicts that this new class will abolish itself as a class when it liberates all of humanity:

> It is not radical revolution, universal human emancipation, which is a Utopian dream for Germany, but rather a partial, merely political revolution which leaves the pillars of the building standing. What is the basis of a partial, merely political revolution? Simply this: a section of civil society emancipates itself and attains universal domination; a determinate class undertakes, from its particular situation, a general emancipation of society. This class emancipates society as a whole, but only on condition that the whole of society is in the same situation as this class; for example, that it possesses or can easily acquire money or culture.
>
> No class in civil society can play this part unless it can arouse, in itself and in the masses, a moment of enthusiasm in which it associates and mingles with society at large, identifies itself with it, and is felt and recognized as the general representative of this society. Its aims and interests must genuinely be the aims and interests of society itself, of which it becomes in reality the social head and heart. It is only in the name of general interests that a particular class can claim general supremacy.
>
> A class must be formed which has radical chains, a class in civil society which is not a class of civil society, a class which is the dissolution of all classes, a sphere of society which has a universal character because its sufferings are universal, and which does not claim a particular redress because the wrong which is done to it is not a particular wrong but wrong in general. There must be

*formed a sphere of society which claims no traditional
status but only a human status, a sphere which is not
opposed to particular consequences but is totally opposed
to the assumptions of the . . . political system; a sphere,
finally, which cannot emancipate itself without emancipating itself from all the other spheres of society, without,
therefore, emancipating all these other spheres, which is, in
short, a total loss of humanity and which can only redeem
itself by a total redemption of humanity.*[4]

When the alienation and oppression of the proletariat reaches its
final stage, the awareness of the class reaches its peak. Their
consciousness produces the understanding that no human
fulfillment is possible outside the fulfillment of the entire
human community. Class conflict is understood by the proletariat as a means to the mutuality of human community. But
Marx was clear in his insistence that the first step in the
direction of the abolition of class domination is the polarization
of antagonistic social relations. The phenomenon occurs for two
reasons: (1) Because the proletariat gains more perfect universal
human awareness as they are forced into further alienation, and
(2) because the ruling class will give way only when it is
overcome and compelled to resign its privileged status:

*An oppressed class is the vital condition of every society
based upon the antagonism of classes. The emancipation of
the oppressed class therefore necessarily implies the
creation of a new society. In order for the oppressed class
to be emancipated it is necessary that the productive
powers already acquired and the existing social relations
should no longer be able to exist side by side. Of all the
instruments of production the greatest productive power is
the revolutionary class itself. The organisation of the
revolutionary elements as a class supposes the existence of
all the productive forces which can be engendered in the
bosom of the old society.*
*Is that to say that after the fall of the old society
there will be a new class domination, comprised in a new
political power? No.*
The essential condition of the emancipation of the

*working class is the abolition of all classes, as the condition
of the emancipation of the third estate of the bourgeois
order, was the abolition of all estates, all orders.*

*The working class will substitute, in the course of its
development, for the old order of civil society an
association which will exclude classes and their antagonism, and there will no longer be political power, properly
speaking, since political power is simply the official form
of the antagonism in civil society.*

*In the meantime, the antagonism between the pro-
letariat and the bourgeoisie is a struggle between class and
class, a struggle which, carried to its highest expression, is
a complete revolution. Would it, moreover, be matter for
astonishment if a society, based upon the antagonism of
classes, should lead ultimately to a brutal conflict, to a
hand-to-hand struggle as its final denouement?*

*Do not say that the social movement excludes the
political movement. There has never been a political
movement which was not at the same time social.*

*It is only in an order of things in which there will be
no longer classes or class antagonism that social evolutions
will cease to be political revolutions.*[5]

Class polarization is the shock that precedes revolutionary
change. Engels softens the Marxian theory of revolution with
his explanation that the certain evolution of the forces of
production necessarily will bring with them new harmonious
relationships. New technological advances integrate every sector
of society into a high degree of interdependency. Antagonisms
among the segments of society will no longer provide viable
relationships for any sector, including the ruling class. Therefore, new cooperative relationships must in the course of
history replace old oppressive ones. Engels sees the signs of a
new society coming out of old relations of production:

*Since the historical appearance of the capitalist mode of
production, the appropriation by society of all the means
of production has often been dreamed of, more or less
vaguely, by individuals, as well as by sects, as the ideal of
the future. But it could become possible, could become a*

historical necessity, only when the actual conditions for its realisation were there. Like every other social advance, it becomes practicable, not by men understanding that the existence of classes is in contradiction to justice, equality, etc., not by the mere willingness to abolish these classes, but by virtue of certain new economic conditions. The separation of society into an exploiting and an exploited class, a ruling and an oppressed class, was the necessary consequence of the deficient and restricted development of production in former times. So long as the total social labour only yields a produce which but slightly exceeds that barely necessary for the existence of all; so long, therefore, as labour engages all or almost all the time of the great majority of the members of society—so long, of necessity, this society is divided into classes. Side by side with the great majority, exclusively bond slaves to labour, arises a class freed from directly productive labour, which looks after the general affairs of society, the direction of labour, state business, law, science, art, etc. It is, therefore, the law of division of labour that lies at the basis of the division into classes. But this does not prevent this division into classes from being carried out by means of violence and robbery, trickery and fraud. It does not prevent the ruling class, once having the upper hand, from consolidating its power at the expense of the working class, from turning their social leadership into an intensified exploitation of the masses.

But if, upon this showing, division into classes has a certain historical justification, it has this only for a given period, only under given social conditions. It was based upon the insufficiency of production. It will be swept away by the complete development of modern productive forces. And, in fact, the abolition of classes in society presupposes a degree of historical evolution, at which the existence, not simply of this or that particular ruling class, but of any ruling class at all, and, therefore, the existence of class distinction itself has become an obsolete anachronism. It presupposes, therefore, the development of production carried out to a degree at which appropriation of the means of production and of the products, and, with

*this, of political domination, of the monopoly of culture,
and of intellectual leadership by a particular class of
culture, has become not only superfluous, but economically, politically, intellectually a hindrance to development.*[6]

The Conquest of Alienation

Essentially the "new society" implies the inversion of all
the oppressive, alienating, dehumanizing forces of the old
society. The world that man creates is no longer separated from
him or hostile to him. Men are free to tap their own potential
because they are no longer forced to create only to sustain
themselves and because they are aware that they are making a
new world in concert with other men. Competitive privatization
of individual lives terminates. Men are liberated from the
necessity of satisfying their own needs at the expense of other
men.

When Marx speaks of communism as the "positive abolition of private property," he is talking about overcoming
"human self-alienation," and about the "real appropriation of
human nature through and for man." He never placed any
primacy on the abolition of private property as such since
alienation maintains a powerful hold over a society which only
attempts to equalize property relations without reconstitution
of human relations. Communism that simply divided up the
property is what Marx terms "crude communism".[7]

The problem of property must be transcended in true
communism. Marx shows in the following passage that man has
to be reoriented towards a unity with the world he creates with
other men. He unveils an anthropology which establishes that
man is incomplete in himself; he needs to create a harmonious
life with other men:

*Communism is the positive abolition of private property,
of human self-alienation, and thus the real appropriation
of human nature through and for men. It is therefore, the
return of man himself as a social, i.e. really human, being,
a complete and conscious return which assimilates all the
wealth of previous development. Communism as a fully*

*developed naturalism is humanism and as a fully developed
humanism is naturalism. It is the definitive resolution of
the antagonism between man and nature, and between
man and man. It is the true solution of the conflict
between existence and essence, between objectification
and self-affirmation, between freedom and necessity,
between individual and species. It is the solution of the
riddle of history and knows itself to be this solution. . . .*

*The human significance of nature only exists for
social man, because only in this case is nature a bond with
other men, the basis of his existence for others and of their
existence for him. Only then is nature the basis of his own
human experience and a vital element of human reality.
The natural existence of man has here become his human
existence and nature itself has become human for him.
Thus society is the accomplished union of man with
nature, the veritable resurrection of nature, the realized
naturalism of man, and the realized humanism of nature.*

*Social activity and social mind by no means exist
only in the form of activity of mind which is directly
communal. Nevertheless, communal activity and mind, i.e.
activity and mind which express and confirm themselves
directly in a real association with other men, occur
everywhere where this direct expression of sociability
arises from the content of the activity or corresponds to
the nature of mind.*

*Even when I carry out scientific work, etc., an
activity which I can seldom conduct in direct association
with other men, I perform a social, because human, act. It
is not only the material of my activity—such as the
language itself which the thinker uses—which is given to
me as a social product. My own existence is a social
activity. For this reason, what I myself produce I produce
for society, and with the consciousness of acting as a social
being. . . .*

*It is above all necessary to avoid postulating
"society" once again as an abstraction confronting the
individual. The individual is the social being. The manifestation of his life—even when it does not appear directly in
the form of a communal manifestation, accomplished in*

association with other men—is, therefore, a manifestation and affirmation of social life. Individual human life and species-life are not different things, even though the mode of existence of individual life is necessarily either a more specific or a more general mode of species-life, or that of species-life a specific or more general mode of individual life.

   In his species-consciousness man confirms his real social life, and reproduces his real existence in thought; while conversely, species-life confirms itself in species-consciousness and exists for itself in its universality as a thinking being. Though man is a unique individual—and it is just his particularity which makes him an individual, a really individual communal being—he is equally the whole, the ideal whole, the subjective existence of society as thought and experienced. He exists in reality as the representation and the real mind of social existence, and as the sum of human manifestations of life.[8]

The content of the revolution for Marx has less to do with property (much less violence) than with men's new relationships with each other and the world. No longer will men look upon the goods in the world around them as objects to be possessed, manipulated, or consumed. Nature is tied in with the mutuality of human relationships, not in the capitalist system of profit and accumulation through which men exploit each other. Man's free, creative praxis becomes like artistic activity. Just as many men can share an artist's satisfaction with his work without diminishing or depriving each other of enjoyment, so the normal way of relating in the new society will be nonpossessive and nonexploitive. Each person's work is available to all in a way that the entire society may benefit from it:

   Just as private property is only the sensuous expression of the fact that man is at the same time an objective fact for himself and becomes an alien and non-human object for himself; just as his manifestation of life is also his alienation of life and his self-realization a loss of reality, the emergence of an alien reality; so the positive supersession of private property, i.e. the sensuous appropriation of

*the human essence and of human life, of objective man
and of human creations, by and for man, should not be
taken only in the sense of immediate, exclusive enjoyment,
or only in the sense of possession or having. Man
appropriates his manifold being in an all-inclusive way, and
thus as a whole man. All his human relations to the
world—seeing, hearing, smelling, tasting, touching, thinking, observing, feeling, desiring, acting, loving—in short, all
the organs of his individuality, like the organs which are
directly communal in form, are in their objective action
(their action in relation to the object) the appropriation of
this object, the appropriation of human reality. The way in
which they react to the object is the confirmation of
human reality. It is human effectiveness and human
suffering, for suffering humanly considered is an enjoyment of the self for man.*

*Private property has made us so stupid and partial
that an object is only ours when we have it, when it exists
for us as capital or when it is directly eaten, drunk, worn,
inhabited, etc., in short, utilized in some way. But private
property itself only conceives these various forms of
possession as means of life, and the life for which they
serve as means is the life of private property—labour and
creation of capital.* [9]

Man's glory in a socialist society lies in his ability to open
his entire being in a way that continually furthers his creative
development. It is the person who matters, not what he
possesses or what rank he enjoys. Marx insists that no
intermediary—money, property, job, status, class—will interrupt
relationships among man in the new society:

*Let us assume man to be man, and his relation to the
world to be a human one. Then love can only be
exchanged for love, trust for trust, etc. If you wish to
enjoy art you must be an artistically cultivated person; if
you wish to influence other people you must be a person
who really has a stimulating and encouraging effect upon
others. Every one of your relations to man and to nature*

must be a specific expression, corresponding to the object
of your will, of your real individual life. If you love
without evoking love in return, i.e., if you are not able, by
the manifestations of yourself as a loving person, to make
yourself a beloved person, then your love is impotent and
a misfortune. [10]

To the objection that relationships of this kind are possible
in any society Marx would reply that a complete inversion of
the capitalist economic system is necessary before men can
cooperatively control the external conditions of life that
manipulate them. He was acutely aware of the influence of
societal economic structures on man's consciousness, i.e., how it
causes privatization, competitive struggle, the search for economic security, etc. In the final stage of socialism, communism,
men realize that dehumanizing economic structures must be
transformed. No longer will economic institutions or men's own
created objects shape or control their makers. Men will
reorganize their own future and collectively control it. The
action cannot be undertaken or completed by isolated individuals; it is a social task:

Communism differs from all previous movements in that it
overturns the basis of all earlier relations of production
and intercourse, and for the first time consciously treats all
natural premises as the creatures of men, strips them of
their natural character and subjugates them to the power
of individuals united. Its organization is, therefore, essen-
tially economic, the material production of the conditions
of this unity; it turns existing conditions into conditions of
unity. The reality, which communism is creating, is pre-
cisely the real basis for rendering it impossible that
anything should exist independently of individuals, in so
far as things are only a product of the preceding
intercourse of individuals themselves. Thus the com-
munists in practice treat the conditions created by
production and intercourse as inorganic conditions, with-
out, however, imagining that it was the plan or the
destiny of previous generations to give them material, and
without believing that these conditions were inorganic for
the individuals creating them . . .

The transformation, through the division of labour, of personal powers (relationships) into material powers, cannot be dispelled by dismissing the general idea of it from one's mind, but only by the action of individuals in again subjecting these material powers to themselves and abolishing the division of labour. This is not possible without the community. Only in community with others has each individual the means of cultivating his gifts in all directions; only in the community, therefore, is personal freedom possible. In the previous substitutes for the community, in the State, etc., personal freedom has existed only for the individuals who developed within the relationships of the ruling class, and only in so far as they were individuals of this class. The illusory community, in which individuals have up till now combined, always took on an independent existence in relation to them, and was at the same time, since it was the combination of one class over against another, not only a completely illusory community, but a new fetter as well. In the real community the individuals obtain their freedom in and through their association.

It follows from all we have been saying up till now that the communal relationship into which the individuals of a class entered, and which was determined by their common interests over against a third part, was always a community to which these individuals belonged only as average individuals, only in so far as they lived within the conditions of existence of their class—a relationship in which they participated not as individuals but as members of a class. With the community of revolutionary proletarians, on the other hand, who take their conditions of existence and those of all members of society under their control, it is just the reverse; it is as individuals that the individuals participate in it. It is just this combination of individuals (assuming the advanced stage of modern productive forces, of course) which puts the conditions of the free development and movement of individuals under their control—conditions which were previously abandoned to chance and had won an independent existence over against the separate individuals just because of their separation as individuals, and because their combination had been determined by the division of labour, and through their separation had become a bond alien to them. Combination up till now (by no means an arbitrary one, such as is expounded for example in the Contrat Social, *but a necessary one) was permitted only upon these conditions, within which the individuals were at the mercy of chance (compare, e.g., the formation of the North American State and the South American republics). This right to the undisturbed enjoyment, upon certain conditions, of fortuity and chance has up till now been called personal freedom: but these conditions are, of course, only the productive forces and forms of intercourse at any particular time.* [11]

In the present society the seeds of a new order are germinating, not only in the economic realm but also in a new social awareness. Men are made for the mutuality of community and will seek it even when the economic side of society seems to conspire against its realization. Marx saw trade associations and other social groupings as the prelude to a socialist society:

When communist artisans form associations, teaching and propaganda are their first aims. But their association itself creates a new need—the need for society—and what appeared to be a means has become an end. The most striking results of this practical development are to be seen when French socialist workers meet together. Smoking, eating, and drinking are no longer simply means of bringing people together. Society, association, entertainment which also has society as its aim, is sufficient for them; the brotherhood of man is no empty phase but a reality, and the nobility of man shines forth upon us from their toil-worn bodies. [12]

Although Marx did not think that the cooperative movement embodied every ideal of the revolution he awaited, he knew that its presence augured well for the future. In cooperatives men find community and begin to take control over their destinies:

*But there was in store a still greater victory of the political
economy of labour over the political economy of property.
We speak of the co-operative movement, especially the
co-operative factories raised by the unassisted efforts of a
few bold "hands." The value of these great social
experiments cannot be over-rated. By deed, instead of by
argument, they have shown that production on a large
scale, and in accord with the behests of modern science,
may be carried on without the existence of a class of
masters employing a class of hands; that to bear fruit, the
means of labour need not be monopolised as a means of
dominion over, and of extortion against, the labouring man
himself; and that, like slave labour, like serf labour, hired
labour is but a transitory and inferior form, destined to
disappear before associated labour plying its toil with a
willing hand, a ready mind, and a joyous heart.*[13]

Alienation begins with labor and is compounded in the social
division of labor. In his early writings Marx attacked Adam
Smith's contention that the division of labor corresponded to
different personalities of different people. He reversed Smith's
argument and said that the division of labor is responsible for
the formation of different capacities in people who are forced
into narrowly specialized detail work. Although Marx never
discussed the problem of how modern industrial society could
ever completely eliminate the divisions of labor, he did
underline the prior necessity of communal labor and collective
effort by which men could share in each other's labor and
contribute to the well-being of the total society. Along with the
importance of collective decision-making, Marx stressed the
value of combining intellectual activity with physical labor for
complete human growth:

*In a higher phase of communist society, after the enslaving
subordination of individuals under division of labour, and
therewith also the antithesis between mental and physical
labour, has vanished, after labour has become not merely a
means to live but has become itself the primary necessity
of life, after the productive forces have also increased with*

*the all-round development of the individual, and all the
springs of co-operative wealth flow more abundantly—only
then can the narrow horizon of bourgeois right be fully
left behind and society inscribe on its banners: "from each
according to his ability, to each according to his needs."*[15]

The final phrase comes from the socialist Saint-Simon, though
communists have relished its use for their own propagandistic
purposes. In the context of the Marxian selections already cited,
however, a new meaning can be given to the slogan. Man's needs
can never be assessed and satisfied by any paternalist authority
which hands out social welfare to law-abiding citizens. An
individual develops his abilities through the labor that is its own
reward. He freely contributes to society and personally grows
because of his contribution; in this sense he is receiving
"according to his needs." No two men ever have exactly the
same needs. Neither do two societies. Marx is claiming that the
communist society will be the first in history to satisfy its exact
needs according to its production, because men will have
conscious awareness of their own needs and conscious control
of their own history.

The usual complaint about Marx deals with his supposed
neglect of the individual in his relationship with the community. This objection can find no basis in Marx's analysis. He
was clear that liberation signifies the individual's ability to
develop through the community: "Society cannot free itself
unless every individual is freed." Engels picks up this idea and
gives it the support of economic necessity. He quotes from
Marx to show that productive forces are coming to the point
where men can share decision-making in industry as well as the
use of technology. In this way Engels makes his peace with the
problem of the division of labor:

*In making itself the master of all the means of production
to use them in accordance with a social plan, society puts
an end to the former subjection of men to their own means
of production. It goes without saying that society cannot
free itself unless every individual is freed. The old mode of
production must therefore be revolutionized from top to
bottom, and in particular the former division of labour*

*must disappear. Its place must be taken by an organization
of production in which, on the one hand, no individual can
throw on the shoulders of others his share in productive
labour, this natural condition of human existence; and in
which, on the other hand, productive labour, instead of
being a means of subjugating men, will become a means of
their emancipation, by offering each individual the opportunity to develop all his faculties, physical and mental, in
all directions and exercise them to the full—in which,
therefore, productive labour will become a pleasure instead
of being a burden.*

*Today this is no longer a fantasy, no longer a pious
wish. With the present development of the productive
forces, the increase in production that will follow from the
very fact of the socialization of the productive forces,
coupled with the abolition of the barriers and dis-
turbances, and of the waste of products and means of
production resulting from the capitalist mode of production, will suffice, with everybody doing his share of work,
to reduce the time required for labour to a point which,
measured by our present conceptions, will be small indeed.*

*Nor is the abolition of the old division of labour a
demand which could only be carried through to the
detriment of the productivity of labour. On the contrary.
Thanks to modern industry it has become a condition of
production itself. "The employment of machinery does
away with the necessity of crystallizing this distribution
after the manner of Manufacture, by the constant annexa-
tion of a particular man to a particular function. Since the
motion of the whole system does not proceed from the
workman, but from the machinery, a change of persons
can take place at any time without an interruption of the
work . . . Lastly, the quickness with which machine-work
is learnt by young people, does away with the necessity of
bringing up for exclusive employment by machinery, a
special class of operatives." (Capital, Vol. I, Moscow 1954,
p. 421) But while the capitalist mode of employment of
machinery necessarily perpetuates the old division of
labour with its fossilized specialization, although it has
become superfluous from a technical standpoint, the*

machinery itself rebels against this anachronism. The technical basis of modern industry is revolutionary. "By means of machinery, chemical processes, and other methods, it is continually causing changes not only in the technical basis of production, but also in the functions of the labourer, and in the social combinations of the labour process. At the same time, it thereby also revolutionizes the division of labour within the society, and incessantly launches masses of capital and of workpeople from one branch of production to another. Modern industry, by its very nature, therefore necessitates variation of labour, fluency of function, universal mobility of the labourer . . . " (Capital, Vol. I, Moscow 1954, pp. 487-488).

Once more, only the abolition of the capitalist character of modern industry can bring us out of this new vicious circle, can resolve this contradiction in modern industry, which is constantly reproducing itself. Only a society which makes it possible for its productive forces to dovetail harmoniously into each other on the basis of one single vast plan can allow industry to be distributed over the whole country in the way best adapted to its own development, and to the maintenance and development of the other elements of production.

Accordingly, abolition of the antithesis between town and country is not merely possible. It has become a direct necessity of industrial production and, besides, of public health. The present poisoning of the air, water, and land can be put an end to only by the fusion of town and country; and only such fusion will change the situation of the masses now languishing in the towns, and enable their excrement to be used for the production of plants instead of for the production of disease.

The abolition of the separation of town and country is therefore not utopian, also, in so far as it is conditioned on the most equal distribution possible of modern industry over the whole country. It is true that in the huge towns civilization has bequeathed us a heritage which it will take much time and trouble to get rid of. But it must and will be got rid of, however protracted a process it may be.[16]

Resolution of the conflict between man and nature includes the problem of ecological balance and man's contact with the world he creates. In a socialist society the balance is possible and necessary because men have become aware of their collective responsibility towards nature and have the power to regulate their relationships with it. Capitalism tends to breed exploitation, both of people and of natural surroundings.

In the Marxian schema the problems of production, distribution, and consumption, the relationships between city and country, the harmony of man with nature, all are resolved by a new economic organization. Capitalists turn into administrators of the people's capital, stock companies become social property, and all engaged in any kind of industry make decisions about their products, their production, and the distribution of their products. Only if the economic base of society is transformed can global alienation be overcome. Marx indicated that already in capitalist society stock companies are converting the means of production from private hands into social hands. It is only one small step to the social corporate ownership of these companies by the workers:

[What we see today is] transformation of the actual functioning capitalist into a mere manager, administrator of other people's capital, and of the owner of capital into a mere owner, a mere money-capitalist. Even if the dividends which they receive include the interest and the profit of enterprise, i.e., the total profit (for the salary of the manager is, or should be, simply the wage of a specific type of skilled labour, whose price is regulated in the labour-market like that of any other labour), this total profit is henceforth received only in the form of interest, i.e., as mere compensation for owning capital that now is entirely divorced from the function in the actual process of reproduction, just as this function in the person of the manager is divorced from ownership of capital. Profit thus appears . . . as a mere appropriation of the surplus-labour of others, arising from the conversion of means of production into capital, i.e., from their alienation vis-a-vis the actual producer, from their antithesis as another's property to every individual actually at work in produc-

tion, from manager down to the last day-labourer. In stock companies the function is divorced from capital owner-ship, hence also labour is entirely divorced from ownership of means of production and surplus-labour. This result of the ultimate development of capitalist production is a necessary transitional phase towards the reconversion of capital into the property of producers, although no longer as the private property of the individual producers, but rather as the property of associated producers, as outright social property. On the other hand, the stock company is a transition toward the conversion of all functions in the reproduction process which still remain linked with capi-talist property, into mere functions of associated pro-ducers, into social functions. [17]

If men take control of the totality of the production process, their labor—even specialized labor—can really take on deeper personal significance. Their growth is enriched by the sharing of different responsibilities, and their freedom is enhanced by technological advances that shorten the working day. All sides of the human personality can be cultivated in a society which provides educational, cultural, recreational, physical, and social opportunities to all of its members. Marx did not hold that man's life was to consist of nothing but manual or intellectual labor:

In fact, the realm of freedom actually begins only where labour which is determined by necessity and mundane considerations ceases; thus in the very nature of things it lies beyond the sphere of actual material production. Just as the savage must wrestle with Nature to satisfy his wants, to maintain and reproduce life, so must civilised man, and he must do so in all social formations and under all possible modes of production. With his development this realm of physical necessity expands as a result of his wants; but, at the same time, the forces of production which satisfy these wants also increase. Freedom in this field can consist in socialised man, the associated pro-ducers, rationally regulating their interchange with Nature, bringing it under their common control, instead of being ruled by it as by the blind forces of Nature; and achieving this with the least expenditure of energy and under conditions most favourable to, and worthy of, their human nature. But it nonetheless still remains a realm of necessity. Beyond it begins that development of human energy which is an end in itself, the true realm of freedom, which, however, can blossom forth only with this realm of necessity as its basis. The shortening of the working-day is its basic prerequisite. [18]

Marx thus attempts to resolve the conflict between freedom and necessity. The human condition presupposes the realm of necessity, which first must be dealt with by an equitable distribution of the work load:

The intensity and productiveness of labour being given, the time which society is bound to devote to material production is shorter, and as a consequence, the time at its disposal for the free development, intellectual and social, of the individual is greater, in proportion as the work is more and more evenly divided among all the able-bodied members of society, and as a particular class is more and more deprived of the power to shift the natural burden of labour from its own shoulders to those of another layer of society. [19]

In his early writings Marx conditioned his notion of freedom with a theory of man's social nature. For Marx freedom is possible only when man works conjointly with other men. He attacks every definition of freedom that excludes the idea of community.

Marx accepted Hegel's distinction between civil society, in which egoistic men fight for their own interests in everyday life, and the state, in which these conflicts were supposed to be resolved. Marx denied that the state could offer complete emancipation to men who have isolated themselves from each other through more fundamental economic institutions which the state defends. True emancipation "is a restoration of the human world and of human relationships to man himself," as Marx indicates in the following selection. The state's freedom is privatized, abstract; it does not affirm the citizens' species-life, Marx's term for man's essence, his social life. Political and religious liberties are simply abstract, individualistic qualities that do not abolish the egoism of civil society. They do not permit freedom in the community of man's species-life because their foundation rests on alienated economic, political, and social institutions. Freedom can be enjoyed only in communality. The dichotomy between civil society and the state can be resolved by complete human liberation, not simply by adding individualistic liberties:

Let us notice first of all that the so-called rights of man, as distinct from the rights of the citizen, are simply the rights of a member of civil society, that is, of egoistic man, of men separated from other men and from the community. The most radical constitution, that of 1793, says: Declaration of the Rights of Man and of the Citizen: Article 2. "These rights, etc. (the natural and imprescriptible rights) are: equality, liberty, security, property.

What constitutes liberty?

Article 6. "Liberty is the power which man has to do everything which does not harm the rights of others."

Liberty is, therefore, the right to do everything which does not harm others. The limits within which each individual can act without harming others are determined by law, just as the boundary between two fields is marked by a stake. It is a question of the liberty of man regarded as an isolated monad, withdrawn into himself . . .

But liberty as a right of man is not founded upon the relation between man and man, but rather upon the separation of man from man. It is the right of such separation. The right of the circumscribed individual, withdrawn into himself.

The practical application of the right of liberty is the right of private property. What constitutes the right of private property?

Article 16 (Constitution of 1793). "The right of property is that which belongs to every citizen of enjoying and disposing as he will of his goods and revenues, of the fruits of his work and industry."

The right of property is, therefore, the right to enjoy one's fortune and to dispose of it as one will; without regard for other men and independently of society. It is the right of self-interest. This individual liberty, and its application, form the basis of civil society. It leads every man to see in other men, not the realization, but rather the limitation of his own liberty. It declares above all the right "to enjoy and to dispose of as one will, one's goods and revenues, the fruits of one's work and industry."

There remain the other rights of man, equality and security.

The term "equality" has here no political significance. It is only the equal right to liberty as defined above; namely that every man is equally regarded as a self-sufficient monad. The Constitution of 1795 defines the concept of liberty in this sense.

Article 5 (Constitution of 1795). "Equality consists in the fact that the law is the same for all, whether it protects or punishes."

And security?

Article 8 (Constitution of 1793). "Security consists in the protection afforded by society to each of its members for the preservation of his person, his rights, and his property."

Security is the supreme social concept of civil society, the concept of the police. The whole society exists only in order to guarantee for each of its members the preservation of his person, his rights and his property. It is in this sense that Hegel calls civil society "the state of need and of reason."

The concept of security is not enough to raise civil society above its egoism. Security is, rather, the assurance of its egoism.

None of the supposed rights of man, therefore, go beyond the egoistic man, man as he is, as a member of civil society; that is, an individual separated from the community, withdrawn into himself, wholly preoccupied with his private interest and acting in accordance with his private caprice. Man is far from being considered, in the rights of man, as a species-being; on the contrary,

*species-life itself—society—appears as a system which is
external to the individual and as a limitation of his original
independence. The only bond between men is natural
necessity, need and private interest, the preservation of
their property and their egoistic persons.*

The Paradox

*It is difficult enough to understand that a nation
which has just begun to liberate itself, to tear down all the
barriers between different sections of the people and to
establish a political community, should solemnly proclaim
(Declaration of 1791) the rights of the egoistic man,
separated from his fellow men and from the community,
and should renew this proclamation at a moment when
only the most heroic devotion can save the nation (and is,
therefore, urgently called for), and when the sacrifice of all
the interests of civil society is in question and egoism
should be punished as a crime. (Declaration of the Rights
of Man, etc. 1793). The matter becomes still more
incomprehensible when we observe that the political
liberators reduce citizenship, the political community, to a
mere means for preserving these so-called rights of man;
and consequently, that the citizen is declared to be the
servant of egoistic "man," that the sphere in which man
functions as a species-being is degraded to a level below the
sphere where he functions as a partial being, and finally
that it is man as a bourgeois and not man as a citizen who
is considered the true and authentic man . . . Man in this
aspect, the member of civil society, is now the foundation
and presupposition of the political state. He is recognized
as such in the rights of man.*

*But the liberty of the egoistic man, and the recogni-
tion of this liberty, is rather the recognition of the frenzied
movement of the cultural and material elements which
form the content of his life.*

*Thus man was not liberated from religion; he received
religious liberty. He was not liberated from property; he
received the liberty to own property. He was not liberated
from the egoism of business; he received the liberty to
engage in business.*

The Result

The formation of the political state, and the dissolution of civil society into independent individuals whose relations are regulated by law, as the relations between men in the corporations and guilds were regulated by privilege, are accomplished by one and the same act. Man as a member of civil society—nonpolitical man—necessarily appears as the natural man. The rights of man appear as natural rights because conscious activity is concentrated upon political action. Egoistic man is the passive, given result of the dissolution of society, an object of direct apprehension and consequently a natural object. The political revolution dissolves civil society into its elements without revolutionizing these elements themselves or subjecting them to criticism. This revolution regards civil society, the sphere of human needs, labour, private interests and civil law, as the basis of its own existence, as a self-subsistent pre-condition, and thus as its natural basis, Finally, man as a member of civil society is identified with authentic man, man as distinct from citizen, because he is man in his sensuous, individual, and immediate existence, whereas political man is only abstract, artificial man, man as an allegorical, moral person. Thus man as he really is, is seen only in the form of egoistic man, and man in his true nature only in the form of the abstract citizen.

The abstract notion of political man is well formulated by Rousseau: "Whoever dares undertake to establish a people's institutions must feel himself capable of changing, as it were, human nature itself, of transforming each individual who, in isolation, is a complete but solitary whole, into a part of something greater than himself, from which in a sense, he derives his life and his being; (of changing man's nature in order to strengthen it;) of substituting a limited and moral existence for the physical and independent life (with which all of us are endowed by nature). His task, in short, is to take from a man his own powers, and to give him in exchange alien powers which he can only employ with the help of other men."

Every emancipation is a restoration of the human world and of human relationships to man himself.

Political emancipation is a reduction of man, on the one hand to a member of civil society, an independent and egoistic individual, and on the other hand, to a citizen, to a moral person.

*Human emancipation will only be complete when the real, individual man has absorbed into himself the abstract citizen; when as an individual man, in his everyday life, in his work, and in his relationships, he has become a species-being; and when he has recognized and organized his own powers (*forces propres*) as social powers so that he no longer separates this social power from himself as political power.* [20]

LENIN

More than twenty years before the 1917 Russian Revolution Lenin organized the Social-Democratic Party to attempt to develop the social consciousness of the Russian working class. Lenin's new organization took the name "The League of Struggle for the Emancipation of the Working Class." The group organized worker study circles, published tracts, and promoted strikes. Lenin was primarily interested in giving Marxian economic theory a wide audience. His themes were similar to those of his mentor:

The increase of wealth that comes from combining the labour of large masses of workers, or from improvements in the methods of production, goes to the capitalists, and the workers, who toil from generation to generation, remain propertyless proletarians as before. Hence, there is only one way of putting an end to the exploitation of labour by capital, and that is to abolish private ownership in the means of production and to transfer all the factories, workshops, mines, and all the large landed estates to society as a whole and to carry on industry on socialist lines under the management of the workers themselves. The goods produced by common labour will then be used for the benefit of the workers, and all wealth produced over and above that which is required for their

*mantenance will be used to satisfy the requirements of the
workers themselves for the fullest development of all their
capabilities and the equal enjoyment of all the benefits of
science and art.* [21]

At the time of the Russian Revolution Lenin was genuinely
interested in social equality, the abolition of classes and
workers' control of factories. The Revolution confiscated the
large landed estates for distribution among the peasants and
nationalized the banks but did not nationalize industry. Lenin
hoped that the workers would soon learn to take charge of their
own factories. A few months after the Revolution he spoke
about this matter in a speech at Petrograd: "Very often
delegations of workers and peasants come to the Soviet
Government and ask what to do with such and such a piece of
land, for example. And very frequently I myself have felt
embarrassment when I saw that they had no very definite views.
And I said to them: do as you please, you are the government,
take all you want, we will support you, but take care of
production, see that production is useful." [22] The Revolutionary
government had to nationalize its industry more quickly than it
had planned to; capitalists left their factories and fled the
country.

Lenin wanted experimentation in the new Soviet society;
he saw that the Revolution had to institute new structures to
facilitate cooperative sharing, that only a "permanent revolution" would liberate the lives of the Soviet people, that seizure
of power was not the final act of his Party. In 1917 Lenin knew
that his seizure of power had over-run the consciousness of the
Russian people, that objective conditions were not ripe for
socialism. The Party's acts of repression against individual
groups were carried out with the hope that in a short time all
factions would work in harmony with the Revolution. This
optimism, as subsequent events especially during the Stalin
purges bore out, was naively sanguine. But Lenin himself never
lost hope that a broader, deeper freedom could be attained in
his country in his lifetime:

*Democracy means equality. The great significance of the
struggle of the proletariat for equality, and the significance*

of equality as a slogan, are apparent, if we correctly interpret it as meaning the abolition of classes. But democracy. means only formal equality. Immediately after the attainment of equality for all members of society in respect of the ownership of the means of production, that is, of equality of labour and equality of wages, there will inevitably arise before humanity the question of going further from formal equality to real equality, i.e., to realising the rule, "From each according to his ability; to each according to his needs." By what stages, by means of what practical measures humanity will proceed to this higher aim—this we do not and cannot know. But it is important to realise how infinitely mendacious is the usual bourgeois presentation of Socialism as something lifeless, petrified, fixed once for all, whereas in reality, it is only with Socialism that there will commence a rapid, genuine, real mass advance, in which first the majority and then the whole population will take part—an advance in all domains of social and individual life. [23]

Lenin came to be disappointed in the workers and peasants because they did not assume responsibility for the ideals of the Revolution. He was even more disgusted, though, in his Party's growing state bureaucracy that tied up the entire country in red tape. He focused his attack on two groups which he believed were impeding the progress of the Revolution—his own Party and the greedy petit bourgeois capitalists, whom he tried to persuade to work for the benefit of all of society. While Lenin retained power he never ceased to try new methods of solving the difficult problems of his country. At one stage of his career he spent most of his time pleading with the people:

What are classes in general? Classes are that which permits one section of society to appropriate the labour of another section. If one section of society appropriates all the land, we have a landowner class and a peasant class. If one section of society owns the factories, shares, and capital, while another section works in these factories, we have a capitalist class and a proletarian class.

It was not difficult to drive out the tsar—that

*required only a few days. It was not very difficult to drive
out the landowners—that was done in a few months. Nor
was it very difficult to drive out the capitalists. But it is
incomparably more difficult to abolish classes; we still
have the division into workers and peasants. If the peasant
is installed on his plot of land and appropriates his surplus
grain, that is, grain that he does not need for himself or for
his cattle, while the rest of the people have to go without
bread, then the peasant becomes an exploiter. The more
grain he clings to, the more profitable he finds it; as for the
rest, let them starve: "The more they starve, the dearer I
can sell this grain." All should work according to a single
common plan, on common land, in common factories and
in accordance with a common system . . .*

    *The class struggle is continuing; it has merely changed
its forms. It is the class struggle of the proletariat to
prevent the return of the old exploiters, to unite in a single
union the scattered masses of unenlightened peasants. The
class struggle is continuing and it is our task to subordinate
all interests to that struggle. Our communist morality is
also subordinated to that task. We say: Morality is what
serves to destroy the old exploiting society and to unite all
the working people around the proletariat, which is
building up a new, a communist society.*

    *Communist morality is that which serves this struggle
and unites the working people against all exploitation,
against all petty private property; for petty property puts
into the hands of one person that which has been created
by the labour of the whole of society. In our country the
land is common property.*

    *But suppose I take a piece of this common property
and grow on it twice as much grain as I need, and profiteer
on the surplus? Suppose I argue that the more starving
people there are, the more they will pay? Would I then be
behaving like a Communist? No, I would be behaving like
an exploiter, like a proprietor. That must be combated. If
that is allowed to go on, things will revert to the rule of
the capitalists, to the rule of the bourgeoisie, as has more
than once happened in previous revolutions. To prevent
the restoration of the rule of the capitalists and the*

bourgeoisie, we must not allow profiteering; we must not allow individuals to enrich themselves at the expense of the rest; the working people must unite with the proletariat and form a communist society. This is the principal feature of the fundamental task of the League and the organisation of the communist you⁚h.

The old society was based on the principle: rob or be robbed; work for others or make others work for you; be a slave-owner or a slave. Naturally, people brought up in such a society assimilate with their mother's milk, one might say, the psychology, the habit, the concept which says: you are either a slave-owner or a slave, or else, a small owner, a petty employee, a petty official, or an intellectual—in short, a man who is concerned only with himself, and does not care a rap for anybody else.

If I work this plot of land, I do not care a rap for anybody else; if others starve, all the better; I shall get more for my grain. If I have a job as a doctor, engineer, teacher, or clerk, I do not care a rap for anybody else. If I toady to and please the powers that be, I may be able to keep my job, and even get on in life and become a bourgeois. A Communist cannot harbour such a psychology and such sentiments. When the workers and peasants proved that they were able, by their own efforts, to defend themselves and create a new society—that was the beginning of the new and communist education, education in the struggle against the exploiters, education in alliance with the proletariat against the self-seekers and petty proprietors, against the psychology and habits which say: I seek my own profit and don't care a rap for anything else . . .

To make this clearer to you, I shall quote an example. We call ourselves Communists. What is a Communist? Communist is a Latin word. Communis is the Latin for "common." Communist society is a society in which all things—the land, the factories—are owned in common and the people work in common. That is communism.[24]

MAO TSE-TUNG

Because of incomplete information dispensed by the popular media and "revolutionary" Maoist student groups in the West, Chairman Mao is usually thought of in terms of violence and guerrilla warfare. His role in the transformation of the social structures of the world's largest nation and his unique contribution to the body of Marxian literature are far more significant, however, than his military writings.

Mao identified himself as a Marxist-Leninist over fifty years ago and at the same time worked on a theory of revolutionary war for which he has since become famous. For thirty years he combined guerrilla warfare with organizing of the peasants, "the masses of the Chinese people." After the defeat of Japan in 1945 he consolidated his support and moved toward a final military victory against Chiang Kai-Shek's forces in 1949. He never lost sight of his original Marxian goals, the problems that blocked their attainment, or the role of the Chinese people in bringing about the revolution. Shortly before the final defeat of Japan in 1945, Mao delivered an address at a Communist Party congress, from which this well-known selection is taken:

There is an ancient Chinese fable called "The Foolish Old Man Who Removed the Mountains." It tells of an old man who lived in northern China long, long ago and was known as the Foolish Old Man of North Mountain. His house faced south and beyond his doorway stood the two great peaks, Taihang and Wangwu, obstructing the way. With great determination, he led his sons in digging up these mountains hoe in hand. Another grey-beard, known as the Wise Old Man, saw them and said derisively, "How silly of you to do this! It is quite impossible for you few to dig up these two huge mountains." The Foolish Old Man replied, "When I die, my sons will carry on; when they die, there will be my grandsons, and then their sons and grandsons, and so on to infinity. High as they are, the mountains cannot grow any higher and with every bit we dig, they will be that much lower. Why can't we clear them away?" Having refuted the Wise Old Man's wrong view, he went on

*digging every day, unshaken in his conviction. God was
moved by this, and he sent down two angels, who carried
the mountains away on their backs. Today, two big
mountains lie like a dead weight on the Chinese people.
One is imperialism, the other is feudalism. The Chinese
Communist Party has long made up its mind to dig them
up. We must persevere and work unceasingly, and we, too,
will touch God's heart. Our God is none other than the
masses of the Chinese people. If they stand up and dig
together with us, why can't these two mountains be
cleared away?*[25]

Mao's concept of the revolutionary power of the masses was
always conditioned by his theory of the advanced class, not
limited in membership to the working class. In the following
selection Mao summarizes his theory of praxis. The experience
of the advanced class provides a theory of society that the
masses embrace and live, and their "permanent revolution"
signifies permanent social change; "the one and only purpose of
the proletariat in knowing the world is to change it," an obvious
reference to Marx:

*It is man's social being that determines his thinking. Once
the correct ideas characteristic of the advanced class are
grasped by the masses, these ideas turn into a material
force which changes society and changes the world. In
their social practice, men engage in various kinds of
struggle and gain rich experience, both from their successes
and from their failures . . . .*

*In social struggle, the forces representing the
advanced class sometimes suffer defeat not because their
ideas are incorrect but because, in the balance of forces
engaged in struggle, they are not as powerful for the time
being as the forces of reaction; they are therefore
temporarily defeated, but they are bound to triumph
sooner or later. Man's knowledge makes another leap
through the test of practice. This leap is more important
than the previous one. For it is this leap alone that can
prove the correctness or incorrectness of the first leap in
cognition, i.e., of the ideas, theories, policies, plans or*

measures formulated in the course of reflecting the objective external world. There is no other way of testing truth. Furthermore, the one and only purpose of the proletariat in knowing the world is to change it. [26]

The process of social change, Mao often repeated, necessitates economic change. Mao utilized the theory of "buying out" the capitalists in a gradual, "peaceful transformation." He reconstituted capitalist enterprises in the following way: after 1949 industrialists simply sold their products to the state on government contracts; by 1952 government assumed a half-share in industrial production and distribution; from 1952-1956 the capitalists were bought out and given a share of the profits.

Mao introduced a far more important venture in 1953 with his agricultural collectivization of hundreds of millions of Chinese. At first the collectivization moved slowly, but Mao appealed to his constituency for a more rapid change-over. Mao was convinced that only this procedure could increase agricultural production and inspire socialist cooperation, that it represented the thinking of the "advanced class" and that it "was bound to triumph sooner or later." The following excerpt from a July 31, 1955 speech represents the impetus for the largest economic collectivization in history:

On the question of developing the co-operatives, the problem now is not one of having to criticize rashness. It is wrong to say that the present development of the co-operatives has "gone beyond the real possibilities" or "gone beyond the level of political consciousness of the masses". This is how things stand: China has an enormous population with insufficient cultivated land (only three mou of land per head taking the country as a whole, and only one mou or even less on the average in many parts of the southern provinces), natural calamities are frequent (every year large areas of farmland suffer from flood, drought, gales, frost, hail or insect pests in varying degrees), and farming methods are backward. Consequently, although the standard of living of the peasant masses since the land reform has improved or has even improved a good deal, many are still in difficulty or are still not well off, there being relatively few who are well off, and hence most of the peasants show enthusiasm for taking the socialist road. Their enthusiasm is being constantly heightened by China's socialist industrialization and its achievements. For them, socialism is the only way out. These peasants make up 60 to 70 per cent of the entire rural population. In other words, the only way for the majority of the peasants to shake off poverty, improve their livelihood and fight natural calamities is to unite and go forward along the high road of socialism . . .

Some comrades have a wrong approach to the vital question of the worker-peasant alliance, proceeding as they do from the stand of the bourgeoisie, of the rich peasants, or of the well-to-do middle peasants with their spontaneous tendency towards capitalism. They think that the present situation in the co-operative movement is very dangerous, and they advise us to "get off the horse quickly" in our present advance along the road of co-operation. "If you do not," they warn us, "you are in danger of breaking up the worker-peasant alliance." We think exactly the opposite. If we do not get on the horse quickly, there will be danger of breaking up the worker-peasant alliance. There is a difference of only a single word here—one says "off" while the other says "on"—yet it demonstrates the difference between two opposing lines. As everybody knows, we already have a worker-peasant alliance built on the basis of the bourgeois-democratic revolution against imperialism and feudalism, a revolution which took the land from the landlords and distributed it to the peasants in order to free them from the bondage of the feudal system of ownership. But this revolution is past and feudal ownership has been abolished. What exists in the countryside today is capitalist ownership by the rich peasants and a vast sea of private ownership by the individual peasants. As is clear to everyone, the spontaneous forces of capitalism have been steadily growing in the countryside in recent years, with new rich peasants springing up everywhere and many well-to-do middle peasants striving to become rich peasants. On the other hand, many poor peasants are still living in poverty for lack of sufficient means of production, with some in debt and others selling or renting out their land. If this tendency goes unchecked, the polarization in the countryside will inevitably be aggravated day by day. Those peasants who lose their land and those who remain in poverty will complain that we are doing nothing to save them from ruin or to help them overcome their difficulties. Nor will the well-to-do, middle peasants who are heading in the capitalist direction be pleased with us, for we shall never be able to satisfy their demands unless we intend to take the capitalist road. Can the worker-peasant alliance continue to stand firm in these circumstances? Obviously not. There is no solution to this problem except on a new basis. And that means to bring about, step by step, the socialist transformation of the whole of agriculture simultaneously with the gradual realization of socialist industrialization and the socialist transformation of handicrafts and capitalist industry and commerce; in other words, it means to carry out co-operation and eliminate the rich-peasant economy and the individual economy in the countryside so that all the rural people will become increasingly well off together. We maintain that this is the only way to consolidate the worker-peasant alliance. Otherwise, this alliance will be in real danger of breaking up. The comrades who advise us to "get off the horse" are completely wrong in their thinking on this question.[27]

Mao was eminently concerned that the masses of peasants join in the cooperative movement. The people responded with great enthusiasm, but not without the help of a well-organized Party campaign. Mao knew that in order to equalize relationships in the countryside, a strong ideological message had to convince the people to back economic changes:

Political work is the life-blood of all economic work. This is particularly true at a time when the social and economic system is undergoing fundamental change. The agricultural cooperative movement has been a severe ideological and political struggle from the very beginning. No cooperative can be established without going through such a struggle.

*Before a brand-new social system can be built on the site
of the old, the site must be swept clean. Invariably, the
remnants of old ideas reflecting the old system remain in
people's minds for a long time.* [28]

Although the collectivization program generally proved successful, in other sections of the above-quoted document on
agricultural cooperation Mao denounced "counter-revolution-
aries" who opposed collectivization in order to keep their own
economic and social advantage. Mao insisted that the share of
each member of a collective be calculated according to his
labor. Other factors of the time, including a poor harvest and
industrial disorganization, caused Mao to intensify his political
and ideological education program. In 1957 once again he urged
all the Chinese people to "struggle" in behalf of the socialist
state, reaffirming his faith in the power of collectivized
ownership of industry and agriculture to develop the people's
consciousness:

*We are living in a period of great social change. Chinese
society has been going through great changes for a long
time. The War of Resistance Against Japan was one period
of great change and the War of Liberation another. But the
present change is much more profound in character than
the earlier ones. We are now building socialism. Hundreds
of millions of people are taking part in the movement for
socialist transformation. Class relations are changing
throughout the country. The petty bourgeoisie in agriculture and handicrafts and the bourgeoisie in industry and
commerce have both undergone a change. The social
economic system has been changed; individual economy
has been transformed into collective economy, and capitalist private ownership is being transformed into socialist
public ownership. Changes of such magnitude are of course
reflected in people's minds. Man's social being determines
his consciousness. People of different classes, strata and
social groups react differently to the great changes in our
social system. The masses eagerly support them for life
itself has confirmed that socialism is the only way out for
China. Overthrowing the old social system and establishing*

a new one, the system of socialism, is a great struggle, a
great change in the social system and in men's relations
with each other. It should be said that the situation is
basically sound. But the new social system has only just
been established and requires time for its consolidation. It
must not be assumed that the new system can be
completely consolidated the moment it is established, for
that is impossible. It has to be consolidated step by step.
To achieve its ultimate consolidation, it is necessary not
only to bring about the socialist revolution on the
economic front, but to carry on constant and arduous
socialist revolutionary struggles and socialist education on
the political and ideological fronts. Moreover, various
contributory international factors are required. In China
the struggle to consolidate the socialist system, the struggle
to decide whether socialism or capitalism will prevail, will
still take a long historical period. But we should all realize
that the new system of socialism will unquestionably be
consolidated. We can assuredly build a socialist state with
modern industry, modern agriculture, and modern science
and culture. [29]

In one of the most important of his writings, Mao defined the
limits of freedom in Chinese socialist society shortly before the
final victory of his armies. Mao desired the participation of all
the people in the political and economic life of the country, but
was careful to announce that he would curb the rights of all
who would undermine the new society. Even the petty local
bourgeois merchants and the national bourgeoisie were included
among the "people," but the landlords and political bureaucrats
of the old regime were considered reactionary. Mao's goal lay in
bringing all sectors of the population into the task of building a
new China, but he was wary of possible counter-revolutionary
activity. His model for "socialist" freedom was both flexible
and rigid, a step still far short of Marx's ideal state of complete
human emancipation:

"You are dictatorial." My dear sirs, you are right, that is
just what we are. All the experience the Chinese people
have accumulated through several decades teaches us to

enforce the people's democratic dictatorship, that is, to deprive the reactionaries of the right to speak and let the people alone have that right.

Who are the people? At the present stage in China, they are the working class, the peasantry, the urban petty bourgeoisie and the national bourgeoisie. These classes, led by the working class and the Communist Party, unite to form their own state and elect their own government; they enforce their dictatorship over the running dogs of imperialism—the landlord class and bureaucrat-bourgeoisie, as well as the representatives of those classes, the Kuomintang reactionaries and their accomplices—suppress them, allow them only to behave themselves and not to be unruly in word or deed. If they speak or act in an unruly way, they will be promptly stopped and punished. Democracy is practised within the ranks of the people, who enjoy the rights of freedom of speech, assembly, association and so on. The right to vote belongs only to the people, not to the reactionaries. The combination of these two aspects, democracy for the people and dictatorship over the reactionaries, is the people's democratic dictatorship.

Why must things be done this way? The reason is quite clear to everybody. If things were not done this way, the revolution would fail, the people would suffer, the country would be conquered.

"Don't you want to abolish state power?" Yes, we do, but not right now; we cannot do it yet. Why? Because imperialism still exists; because domestic reaction still exists; because classes still exist in our country. Our present task is to strengthen the people's state apparatus— mainly the people's army, the people's police, and the people's courts—in order to consolidate national defence and protect the people's interests. Given this condition, China can develop steadily, under the leadership of the working class and the Communist Party, from an agricultural into an industrial country and from a new-democratic into a socialist and communist society, can abolish classes and realize the Great Harmony. The state apparatus, including the army, the police, and the courts, is the

instrument by which one class oppresses another. It is an instrument for the oppression of antagonistic classes; it is violence and not "benevolence." "You are not benevolent!" Quite so. We definitely do not apply a policy of benevolence to the reactionaries and towards the reactionary activities of the reactionary classes. Our policy of benevolence is applied only within the ranks of the people, not beyond them to the reactionaries or to the reactionary activities of reactionary classes.

The people's state protects the people. Only when the people have such a state can they educate and remould themselves by democratic methods on a country-wide scale, with everyone taking part, and shake off the influence of domestic and foreign reactionaries (which is still very strong, will survive for a long time and cannot be quickly destroyed), rid themselves of the bad habits and ideas acquired in the old society, not allow themselves to be led astray by the reactionaries, and continue to advance—to advance towards a socialist and communist society.

Here, the method we employ is democratic, the method of persuasion, not of compulsion. When anyone among the people breaks the law, he too should be punished, imprisoned or even sentenced to death; but this is a matter of a few individual cases, and it differs in principle from the dictatorship exercised over the reactionaries as a class.

As for the members of the reactionary classes and individual reactionaries, so long as they do not rebel, sabotage or create trouble after their political power has been overthrown, land and work will be given to them as well in order to allow them to live and remould themselves though labour into new people. If they are not willing to work, the people's state will compel them to work. Propaganda and educational work will be done among them too and will be done, moreover, with as much care and thoroughness as among the captured army officers in the past. This, too, may be called a "policy of benevolence" if you like, but it is imposed by us on the members of the enemy classes and cannot be mentioned in the same breath with the work of self-education which we carry on within the ranks of the revolutionary people.[30]

CASTRO AND GUEVARA

Fidel Castro outlined his vision of liberation and freedom for the Cuban people in his speech at the United Nations not long after his Revolutionary government took power:

Therefore, the National General Assembly of the People of Cuba proclaims before America:
The right of the peasants to the land; the right of the workers to the fruit of their labor, the right of children to education; the right of the ill to medical and hospital attention; the right of youth to work; the right of students to free, experimental, and scientific education; the right of Negroes and Indians to "the full dignity of man," the right of women to civil, social and political equality; the right of the aged to secure old age; the right of intellectuals, artists, and scientists to fight, with their works, for a better world; the right of nations to their full sovereignty; the right of nations to turn fortresses into schools, and to arm their workers, their peasants, their students, their intellectuals, the Negro, the Indian, the women, the young and the old, the oppressed and exploited people, so that they may themselves defend their rights and their destinies.[31]

At this early period of the Revolutionary Cuban government, Castro did not identify himself as a communist. Neither did he nationalize industry or agriculture, though he set upon the task of equalizing land, goods, and services. He confiscated land-holdings in excess of about a thousand acres and distributed it to renters, sharecroppers, and landless peasants. This land now remains in the private sector and may be sold only to the state. Presently the private sector in agriculture represents about 43 percent of arable land on the island. By the middle of 1968, however, all private industries and businesses were nationalized, including shops and services.

Although Castro sometimes talks in romantic terms about his "revolutionary days" in the hills, his revolution is most concerned in practice with technological development, economic diversification, food, education, hospitals, houses, roads, and the spirit of cooperation. He seems to approach every problem with an eye for enriching the lives of the Cuban people. The quality of the Cuban Revolution, according to Castro, is found in the quality of life in Cuba today:

> *Because, while repeating once more that I consider myself no more than an apprentice in revolution, I believe that socialism can be built in a single country and that communism can be built to a certain degree. But communism, as a formula of absolute abundance in the midst of an underdeveloped world, cannot be built in a single country, without running the risk, involuntarily and unintentionally in future years, of immensely rich countries finding themselves trading and dealing with immensely poor countries. Some peoples in communism and other peoples in loincloths! And we ask ourselves—we who wish the best for our people, who wish that not a single child in this country grows up without all the proteins and vitamins and mineral salts and generally indispensable foodstuffs, we who wish them all to receive a complete education—we ask ourselves whether, in the midst of a world full of misery, we will be able to think tomorrow only of ourselves, to live in super-abundance with our tens of thousands of agricultural engineers, teachers, with our superdeveloped technology. How will we be able to live in that super-abundance—resulting from communism based on abundance, or super-abundance— while we see around us other peoples who, by not having had the opportunity or the good fortune to make a revolution in the epoch in which we are making ours, will, within ten years, be living even more miserably than they are living today.*
>
> *And I believe we should aspire to higher levels of food supply for our people, as well as education for our people, so that our citizens may develop both physically and mentally, and we should satisfy our needs for medical care and housing.*

We do not need very much in order to achieve this. I am sure that with our country's natural resources, plus work and the use of technology, it will not be long before we reach those levels. But from there on, we must not think that our duty is to strive so that each one of us may have his own automobile, before first concerning ourselves about whether or not each family in those countries which are behind us owns at least a plow.

Our present duty as a poor, underdeveloped country, is to make the maximum effort to rid ourselves of poverty, misery and underdevelopment. But in the future we must not think of great affluence while other peoples still need our help. We must begin now to educate our children in the idea that tomorrow, when all our pressing needs are supplied, our goal will be more than simple affluence. Our ideal is not wealth. Our principal ideal and our duty must be to help those peoples who are left behind. Let us educate our people in this concept of our international duty, so that within ten years not one person in this country will say that he does not have more because we are helping someone else, but instead, so that we will have a type of man capable of thinking of other human beings, men who are willing to deprive themselves in order to give, instead of giving to themselves by depriving others.

And if in future years, some of our people should still think this way, it would be without a doubt, because we, leaders of this people, have not been able to educate our people politically. It would be because our Party had been unable to teach the deep sense of internationalism, without which no one may be called a Marxist-Leninist, and without which even this May Day, International Workers' Day, would have no meaning; it would be meaningless without that profound and permanent sense of international duty.[32]

Castro blames the capitalist heritage for the moral under-development of the Cuban people as well as for the economic underdevelopment of the country. A 1968 monograph of the Cuban Communist Party states, "It is well-known that to build communism we must confront, in the economic sphere, the underdevelopment imposed on us by imperialism and, in the ideological sphere, the extraordinary weight of the ideas, habits, and concepts that society has accumulated for centuries." Capitalist "ideas, habits, and concepts" refer to individualism, selfish attitudes, and competition.

The Communist leadership has established institutions to facilitate the development of the opposite virtues, and Fidel ceaselessly exhorts his people to participate in the new institutions: to be willing to do volunteer weekend labor, to contribute leisure time to organizational service work during the week, to fight absenteeism on the job, to sacrifice all luxury items and submit to rationing in the interests of economic growth, to sign up for adult education courses, etc. His slogans abound and penetrate every corner of the media: "To cease working for profit—to work to satisfy needs"; "Not to create awareness with wealth but to create wealth through awareness"; "Social equality is not possible without cultural equality"; "To feel like human beings, to cease being nothing—to become someone"; "Rather cease to be than cease to be revolutionary."

The Marxian inspiration of these aphorisms points to the origin of Castro's ideology. He hopes to root out old individualistic attitudes and is placing his hope for a new kind of society in the Cuban youth, but he places more stress on the cultivation of moral social consciousness than Marx, who would have labeled such preoccupations as utopian. Nonetheless, this strand of the Marxian inheritance has rooted itself in the tradition:

One must not forget that many generations—including the whole generation that was living in our country at the time of the triumph of the Revolution—were completely formed under the influence of capitalist ideas, methods and attitudes. And even within our working class sectors many of these vices existed, many of these concepts were deep-rooted. Of course what Marx said was that in the historic process the workers and the exploited are pitted against their exploiters, that the working class is the class whose social function makes it the standard-bearer and enables it to understand socialism and put it into practice. This is absolutely true, but it is also absolutely true that the exploiters and ruling class exert influence over the

*minds of all the people. And the Revolution has eradicated
a great number of these ideas from the minds of all the
people, but it is specifically in the virgin minds of the new
generation growing up with the Revolution where we find
less of the thinking of the past, where we most clearly
perceive revolutionary ideas.*

*There are many who wondered what would become
of our young people. Many were worried as to whether
these young people, who never suffered the horrors of the
past, who never knew the sacrifices of the past, would be
capable of understanding the Revolution, of being revolutionary, of working and sacrificing. And through our
Cuban experience we can say with deep satisfaction that
we are seeing how an even more revolutionary youth is
growing and developing here . . . What have we seen with
the students in the technological institutes who have gone
into the fields to work for ninety days? We observed an
extraordinary phenomenon. Those young people didn't go
there to work for wages, they didn't go there to work for
money. They went there with a deep awareness that their
efforts were needed for the economic development of the
country. They went there with the deep awareness that it
was necessary for them to participate in that effort, not
only as an economic need, but also as an educational need.*

*And what happened? Something that has had a great
influence upon full-time workers and farmers everywhere
these students have gone. They have had an extremely
positive influence. Why? Because if the workday is eight
hours, our students work 14, 15, 16 and on some
occasions even 18 hours a day.*

*What has happened everywhere with the technologi-
cal students, the junior and senior high school students? At
first we thought it logical to expect such an attitude from
the students of the technological institutes, many of them
of farmer or working class orgin. But how great was the
admiration of all of us when we saw that the senior high
students from the cities, the junior high students, the
students in general, had exactly the same attitude; and,
what's more, that attitude increasingly improved!*

And just as our students reacted this way, so did the

comrades from the army who participated in productive activities, and the comrades from the Ministry of the Interior who worked in these activities.

Thus it can be stated already that huge numbers, hundreds of thousands of young people in this country, are becoming accustomed to and showing themselves capable of working and producing according to entirely new concepts, that huge numbers, hundreds of thousands of young people, are capable of working hard, doubling and even tripling the yield of full-time workers, not with any idea that this work is going to solve their own problems, but rather with the idea that it will solve the problem of all of society, once and for all.

Nevertheless, not everyone in this country is acting that way. We must say that beside the impressive movement of our people, and principally of our young people with their incorporation in productive work, there are those whose ideas and actions are completely apart from collective interests, from collective aspirations.

In our trips through the country we have been impressed by the efforts our young people are making. We have seen women members of the Party who have gone to do agricultural work for two years, working under the scorching midday sun. We have seen columns of young girls, members of the Young Communists or simply part of the people in general, not Party members, also volunteer to work in production for two years.

What is more, we have seen many young people doing very hard work. In southern Havana Province in recent days, we came across an outstanding detachment of youngsters knee-deep in muddy water, cultivating water cress. And in the past only workers who lived in the worst conditions would do that job of cultivating water cress in mud; it was done by Japanese and Chinese immigrants, who were forced to do such work under capitalism. And, nevertheless, we were able to see many young people of this generation doing such work with great enthusiasm, great productivity and great revolutionary spirit. And we have seen numerous instances of this. [33]

Economic development, cooperative awareness, social and cultural equality—these are the ingredients of Castro's brand of socialism. Not until 1965 did he decide to give his state a communist label. When he made the announcement, he did it with a flourish—and a rationale:

The word COMMUNIST has been maligned and distorted for centuries. Communists have existed throughout history; men with communist ideas, men who conceived of a way of life, different from that into which they were born. For example, those who thought in a communistic way in other times were considered Utopian Communists, who, five hundred years ago, aspired in an idealistic manner to establish a type of society that was not possible then, because of the minimal development of the productive forces which man possessed at that time. Because to go back to the type of communism from which primitive man began, to live in a type of primitive communism, would not be possible for man except by means of such a utilization of those forces as would create the material goods and services in quantities more than sufficient to satisfy the needs of man. . . .

The reactionary classes have always used every method to curse and slander new ideas. Thus, all the paper and all the resources at their disposal are not sufficient to slander communist ideas. As if the desire for a society in which man is not the exploiter of man, but a real brother of man; as if the dream of a society in which all human beings are really equal in fact and by law not simply in constitutional clause as in some bourgeois constitutions which say that all men are born free and equal as if that could be true both for the child born in a slum, in a humble cradle, and for the child born in a cradle of gold—as if one could ever state that all men are born free and equal in a society of exploiters and exploited, a society of rich and poor; as if these men were to have the same opportunities in life.

The age-old dream of man—possible today—of a society without exploiters or exploited, has aroused the hatred and rancor of all exploiters. The imperialists—as if they were going to offend us or as if it were an insult—speak of the Communist Government of Cuba just like they [the Spanish] used the word "Mambi" [rebels against the Spanish in the Cuban Civil War of the nineteenth century] as an offense against our liberators. In the same way, they try to use the word "communist" as an insult, and the word "communists" is not an insult but rather an honor for us.

It's the word which symbolizes the aspiration of a great part of humanity, and for it hundreds and hundreds of millions of human beings are concretely working today. Within one hundred years, there won't be a greater glory, nor anything more natural and logical than to be called communists.

We're on the road towards a communist society. And if the Imperialists don't like it, they can lump it. . . .

A new era is emerging in the history of our country, a different form of society, a different form of government. The government of a Party, the Party of the workers— established with the participation of all the masses, so that we may justly and reasonably state that this Party is the vanguard of the workers, and that it is the representative of the workers in our revolutionary workers' democracy.

It will be a thousand times more democratic than bourgeois democracy, because we will establish administrative and political institutions that will call for the constant participation of the masses in the problems of society. This participation will be accomplished through capable organizations, through the Party, on all levels.

And we will continue developing the conscientiousness and the habits necessary for these new forms. And we will not stop. Our people will not stop until they have achieved their final objectives. This step means a lot. It constitutes one of the most outstanding events in this history of our country. It marks the historic moment in which the unifying forces became mightier than the forces that separated and divided them. It marks the historic moment in which a revolutionary people firmly united, in which the sense of duty prevailed over everything else, in which the interest of the homeland overwhelmingly and

definitely prevailed over individual and group interests. It
means that we have reached the highest level of unity and
organization with the most up-to-date, and the most
scientific, and at the same time, the most revolutionary
and human of all political conceptions. [34]

Castro gained much of his understanding of Marxism from Che
Guevara. Guevara emphasized the humanistic side of Marx's
thought and became preoccupied with its ramifications. In his
speeches he tried to point up the moral qualities of the
revolutionary, that a New Man must be developed in Cuba, a
man of total dedication and commitment to his human brothers
and sisters. Neither Guevara nor Castro believed that the people
of their society could develop into the New Man without a
change in all the social and economic structures. Over a period
of time, they expected behavioral patterns to fall in line with
the new social structures and attitudes to correspond to the new
behavior.

For Guevara the New Man's attitudes are infused with
conciencia and *emulacion*, roughly translated, political awareness and exemplary conduct. The awareness refers to the New
Man's motivation, his selflessness and concern for others,
expressed through revolutionary activity. *Conciencia* is the
antithesis of a capitalist, individualist, cutthroat mentality. The
New Man's service extends to an attempt to outdo his comrades
in revolutionary work or study, and this friendly competition
among work brigades is called *emulacion.*

Guevara summarizes his theory of liberation in his already
classic work, *Socialism and Man.* His brand of utopianism has
caught the imagination of all of Cuban society, especially the
youth:

The new society being formed has to compete fiercely
with the past. The latter makes itself felt in the conscious-
ness in which the residue of an education systematically
oriented towards isolating the individual still weighs
heavily, and also through the very character of the
transitional period in which the market relationships of the
past still persist. The commodity is the economic cell of

capitalist society; so long as it exists its effects will make themselves felt in the organization of production and, consequently in consciousness.

Marx outlined the period of transition as a period which results from the explosive transformation of the capitalist system of a country destroyed by its own contradictions. However in historical reality we have seen that some countries, which were weak limbs of the tree of imperialism, were torn off first—a phenomenon foreseen by Lenin.

In these countries capitalism had developed to a degree sufficient to make its effects felt by the people in one way or another; but, having exhausted all its possibilities, it was not its internal contradictions which caused these systems to explode. The struggle for liberation from a foreign oppressor, the misery caused by external events like war whose consequences make the privileged classes bear down more heavily on the oppressed, liberation movements aimed at the overthrow of neo-colonial regimes—these are the usual factors in this kind of explosion. Conscious action does the rest.

In these countries a complete education for social labor has not yet taken place, and wealth is far from being within the reach of the masses simply through the process of appropriation. Underdevelopment on the one hand, and the inevitable flight of capital on the other, make a rapid transition impossible without sacrifices. There remains a long way to go in constructing the economic base, and the temptation to follow the beaten track of material interest as the moving lever of accelerated development is very great.

There is the danger that the forest won't be seen for the trees. Following the will-o'-the-wisp method of achieving socialism with the help of the dull instruments which link us to capitalism (the commodity as the economic cell, profitability, individual material interest as a lever, etc.) can lead into a blind alley.

Further, you get there after having traveled a long distance in which there were many crossroads and it is hard to figure out just where it was that you took the wrong turn. The economic foundation which has been forced has already done its work of undermining the development of consciousness. To build communism, you must build new men as well as the new economic base.

Hence it is very important to choose correctly the instrument for mobilizing the masses. Basically, this instrument must be moral in character, without neglecting, however, a correct utilization of the material stimulus—especially of a social character.

As I have already said, in moments of great peril it is easy to muster powerful responses to moral stimuli; but for them to retain their effect requires the development of a consciousness in which there is a new priority of values. Society as a whole must be converted into a gigantic school. . . .

New Men

In this period of the building of socialism we can see the new man being born. His image is not yet completely finished—it never could be—since the process goes forward hand in hand with the development of new economic forms.

Leaving out of consideration those whose lack of education makes them take the solitary road toward satisfying their own personal ambitions, there are those, even within this new panorama of a unified march forward, who have a tendency to remain isolated from the masses accompanying them. But what is important is that every day men are continuing to acquire more consciousness of the need for their incorporation into society and, at the same time, of their importance as the movers of society.

They no longer travel completely alone over trackless routes toward distant desires. They follow their vanguard consisting of the party, the advanced workers, the advanced men who walk in unity with the masses and in close communion with them. The vanguard has its eyes fixed on the future and its rewards, but this is not seen as something personal. The reward is the new society in which men will have attained new features: the society of communist man.

The road is long and full of difficulties. At times we wander from the path and must turn back; at other times we go too fast and separate ourselves from the masses; on occasions we go too slow and feel the hot breath of those treading on our heels. In our zeal as revolutionists we try to move ahead as fast as possible, clearing the way, but knowing we must draw our sustenance from the masses and that it can advance more rapidly only if we inspire it by our example.

The fact remains a division into two main groups (excluding, of course, that minority not participating for one reason or another in the building of socialism), despite the importance given to moral stimuli, indicates the relative lack of development of social consciousness.

The vanguard group is ideologically more advanced than the mass; the latter understands the new values, but not sufficiently. While among the former there has been a qualitative change which enables them to make sacrifices to carry out their function as an advance guard, the latter go only half way and must be subjected to stimuli and pressures of a certain intensity. That is the dictatorship of the proletariat operating not only on the defeated class but also on individuals of the victorious class. . . .

Liberated Labor

Despite the lack of institutions, which must be corrected gradually, the masses are now making history as a conscious aggregate of individuals fighting for the same cause. Man under socialism, despite his apparent standardization, is more complete; despite the lack of perfect machinery for it, his opportunities for expressing himself and making himself felt in the social organism are infinitely greater.

It is still necessary to strengthen his conscious participation, individual and collective, in all the mechanisms of management and production, and to link it to the idea of the need for technical and ideological education, so that he sees how closely interdependent these processes are and how their advancement is parallel. In this way he will reach total consciousness of his social function, which is equivalent to his full realization as a human being, once the chains of alienation are broken.

This will be translated concretely into the regaining of his true nature through liberated labor, and the expression of his proper human condition through culture and art.

In order for him to develop in the first of the above categories, labor must acquire a new status. Man dominated by commodity relationships will cease to exist, and a system will be created which establishes a quota for the fulfillment of his social duty. The means of production belong to society, and the machine will merely be a trench where duty is fulfilled.

Man will begin to see himself mirrored in his work and to realize his full stature as a human being through the object created, through the work accomplished. Work will no longer entail surrendering a part of his being in the form of labor-power sold, which no longer belongs to him, but will represent an emanation of himself reflecting his contribution to the common life, the fulfillment of his social duty.

We are doing everything possible to give labor this new status of social duty and to link it on the one side with the development of a technology which will create the conditions for greater freedom, and on the other side with voluntary work based on a Marxist appreciation of the fact that man truly reaches a full human condition when he produces without being driven by the physical need to sell his labor as a commodity.

Of course there are other factors involved even when labor is voluntary: Man has not transformed all the coercive factors around him into conditioned reflexes of a social character, and he still produces under the pressures of his society. Fidel calls this moral compulsion.

Man still needs to undergo a complete spiritual rebirth in his attitude towards his work, freed from the direct pressure of his social environment, though linked to it by his new habits. That will be communism. . . .

True Revolutionaries

Within the country the leadership has to carry out its vanguard role, and it must be said with all sincerity that in a real revolution, to which one gives himself entirely and from which he expects no material remuneration, the task of the revolutionary vanguard is at one and the same time glorious and agonizing.

At the risk of seeming ridiculous, let me say that the true revolutionary is guided by a great feeling of love. It is impossible to think of a genuine revolutionary lacking this quality. Perhaps it is one of the great dramas of the leader that he must combine a passionate spirit with a cold intelligence and make painful decisions without contracting a muscle. Our vanguard revolutionaries must idealize this love of the people, the most sacred cause, and make it one and indivisible. They cannot descend, with small doses of daily affection, to the level where ordinary men put their love into practice.

The leaders of the revolution have children just beginning to talk, who are not learning to call their fathers by name; wives, from whom they have to be separated as part of the general sacrifice of their lives to bring the revolution to its fulfillment; the circle of their friends is limited strictly to the number of fellow revolutionists. There is no life outside of the revolution.

In these circumstances one must have a great deal of humanity and a strong sense of justice and truth in order not to fall into extreme dogmatism and cold scholasticism, into an isolation from the masses. We must strive every day so that this love of living humanity will be transformed into actual deeds, into acts that serve as examples, as a moving force.

The revolutionary, the ideological motor force of the revolution, is consumed by his uninterrupted activity which can come to an end only with death until the building of socialism on a world scale has been accomplished. If his revolutionary zeal is blunted when the most urgent tasks are being accomplished on a local scale and he forgets his proletarian internationalism, the revolution which he leads will cease to be an inspiring force, and he will sink into a comfortable lethargy which imperialism, our irreconcilable enemy, will utilize well. Proletarian internationalism is a duty, but it is also a revolutionary necessity. So we educate our people. . . .

Let me attempt some conclusions:

We socialists are freer because we are more complete; we are more complete because we are freer.

The skeleton of our complete freedom is already formed. The flesh and the clothing are lacking. We will create them.

Our freedom and its daily maintenance are paid for in blood and sacrifice.

Our sacrifice is conscious: an installment payment on the freedom that we are building.

The road is long and in part unknown. We understand our limitations. We will create the man of the twenty-first century—we, ourselves.

We will forge ourselves in daily action, creating a new man with a new technology.

Individual personality plays a role in mobilizing and leading the masses insofar as it embodies the highest virtues and aspirations of the people and does not wander from the path.

It is the vanguard group which clears the way, the best among the good, the party.

The basic clay of our work is the youth. We place our hope in them and prepare them to take the banner from our hands. [35]

CONTEMPORARY ANALYSIS

According to a Marxian onlook the new society is in the process of being born within the structures of the old order. Marx identified the new elements with the progressive forces of social institutions. In contemporary society analysis must focus on concrete economic, political, and social movements and on the emergence of consciousness that seem to be progressing towards a de-alienated society. These "moments" of liberation can be

classified within the Marxian schema. In the following questions, some of the appropriate Marxian conceptual units are
framed: How may the *proletariat* be defined as a *progressive
force* today? What kind of *awareness* is necessary for the
beginnings of radical social change? What is the role of a
revolutionary party in helping to raise the awareness of the
people? How can a humane yet effective *revolutionary theory*
be developed? What measure may be used to judge contemporary *social movements*? What makes men *free* to tap their own
creative potential? What models of *community* provide
humanizing, egalitarian structures? How can men exercise
creative control over economic, political, and social processes?
What social movements maximize the *free development of the
individual and social relations*? Can new economic structures
that *preclude alienated labor* be furthered within the larger
capitalist society? Where are the forces united *against alienated
social relations*—against imperialism, racism, authoritarianism,
chauvinism? Will a liberated society result from a solution to
the problems of alienated social relations or only from the
resolution of the basic class conflict between the proletariat and
the ruling class? What political and social structures enhance the
possibilities of *freedom among men*?

The editors of *Socialist Revolution* attempted to delineate
the direction which the progressive forces of the social order
and the consciousness of these forces is taking. They distinguish
betwen secondary conflicts growing around the issues of
imperialism, racism, authoritarianism, and chauvinism, and the
fundamental conflict between the ruling class and the proletariat. Again, their analysis embraces the basic Marxian conceptual units:

> All of these movements—by blacks, women, and youth—
> have already begun to link their opposition to alienated
> social relations with a critique of production. The draft
> resister opposes the allocation of the largest part of the
> Federal budget for military spending. The black militant
> begins to link racism with the utilization of public funds
> for business-oriented urban renewal, rather than for the
> needs of the black community. The women's liberationist
> sees male chauvinism in advertising, styles, and fashions.

The radical teacher opposes the fiscal deprivation of the school; the radical social worker, the fiscal starvation of the welfare budget; the radical scientist, the rape of nature; the radical industrial worker and technician, the production of unsafe, wasteful, useless objects. The opposition begins to mount demands for a reorientation of production—free abortions, free client-controlled child care centers, more classrooms, black-controlled ghetto redevelopment, curbs on the automobile industry, the oil industry.

When critiques of this depth and scope express themselves in action, the ruling class has difficulty containing the proletariat: social democracy and corporate liberalism begin to flounder. The proletariat's posing of alternatives to bourgeois social relations and ideological hegemony demonstrates the bourgeoisie's growing inability to rule on its own terms: through ideology. The coexistence of "orthodox" economic crises—in the form of inflation, unemployment, the fiscal crisis of the state, the imbalance in the international balance of payments— hurries the process along. The ruling class is thus caught between its own failures and the successes of the proletariat. At this point, it will be possible for the contradictions in the secondary institutions to be dissolved into the primary contradiction in production. . . .

Stages of Unconsciousness

A theoretical critique of capitalism, ripped out of the context of practical, oppositionist activity, or vice versa, is at the least, irrelevant, and at the most self-destructive. People in the "movement" today, both the visible movement of organized groups and parties, and the invisible movement of those individuals and small, informal collectives in and out of work who oppose this or that manifestation of advanced capitalism, are moving through various stages of consciousness.

First, there are those whose ideas and practice oppose bourgeois social relations in secondary institutions, those who have acquired a degree of both historical conscious-

*ness and self-consciousness. There are those blacks who say
to whites, "I am not an object. I am a man. I am a
woman"; blacks who are aware that their social condition
is not explicable in terms of their "blackness," but in
terms of their social relations with whites and blacks.
There are those youths who say to their elders, "I am not a
thing. I am a young man. I am a young woman"; youth
who are aware that their social condition is not explicable
in terms of their "age" alone, but also in terms of their
social relations with their elders and other youths. And
there are those women who say to men, "I am not an
object. I am a woman"; women who are aware that their
social condition is not explicable in terms of their sex
alone, but in terms of their social relations with men and
other women. In summary, there are those who have
obtained a degree of historical consciousness* and who are
acting upon it.

    *Second, there are those who are engaged in a
theoretical critique of bourgeois production relations, but
whose practice remains underdeveloped. There are those
blacks who say to whites and blacks, "It is not a question
of race alone, but also of class"; blacks who are aware that
their social condition is not explicable in terms of their
blackness and social relations with whites alone, but also in
terms of their production relations with capital. There are
those youth who say to their elders and to other youths,
"It is not a question of age alone, but also of class." And
there are those women who say to men and other women,
"It is not a question of sex alone, but also of class." In
summary, there are those who have obtained a high degree
of historical consciousness, but not a corresponding degree
of self-consciousness, and who are thus not* acting *on their
historical consciousness.*

    *Third, there are those who are engaged in a practical
critique of bourgeois production relations, but whose
consciousness remains underdeveloped. There are those
who say to themselves in production, "I am not an object.
I am a man. I am a woman"; workers who are emotionally
aware that their condition is not explicable in terms of
their race, age, sex, or social relations in secondary*

*institutions alone, but in terms of their immediate produc-
tion relations. These men and women have attained a high
degree of self-consciousness, but remain unself-conscious
historically. Their practical opposition to capitalism
remains limited. The auto worker who strikes back at the
foreman or company through sabotage, as an* individual,
*engages in a self-deceptive form of struggle, one that is
potentially murderous or suicidal. And the drop-out who
refuses alienated labor altogether also deceives himself, in
that he remains dependent on social labor and social
production, and thus must either flee bourgeois society
altogether or be forced back on "underground" petty
bourgeois or lumpen-proletariat activity—dealing, panhan-
dling, or stealing.*

*Fourth, and last in the morphology of consciousness,
there are those engaged in both a theoretical and practical
critique of the bourgeois mode of production, those who
are mounting an "action critique" against production, as
well as the superstructures. There are those workers who
say to their supervisors, "I am not an object. I am a man. I
am a woman," and who say to other workers, "It is not a
question of you and your supervisor alone; it is a question
of wage labor and capital, a question of alienated labor, a
process that requries your active participation." In summary, there are those who are intellectually and emotionally aware that their social condition is explicable only in
terms of the relations of production, that is, of capitalism
itself, and who are practicing the de-alienation of labor.*

The Primary Struggle

*Today, the movement against racism, male chauv-
inism, imperialism, and authoritarianism is acquiring a
growing consciousness of itself as a historical category, as a
historical subject. This is a promising development for the
socialist revolution. Already there are signs that these
movements may begin to aim their critiques of alienated
social relations at production itself, that there is a growing
understanding among youth, black people, and women
that they cannot successfully fight instrumental and*

oppressive social relations in secondary spheres, so long as they subject themselves to instrumental relations in production. . . .

Socialist revolutionary thought and practice must widen and deepen the historical consciousness and self-consciousness being attained by a growing minority of the proletariat, and acted upon in many ways in the secondary spheres. Revolutionary thought and practice must dissolve the secondary contradictions and force the struggle into the primary contradiction, not the contradiction between wages and profits, which merely reflects *the primary contradiction, but the contradiction in alienated labor as a social relation. This requires the development of theoretical and live alternatives to a social order based on alienated labor—alternatives based on mass participation and planning.*

This also requires the giving back to capital the irritation, anger, and rage that blacks feel toward whites, women toward men, and youth toward age—the rage and anger that at present the proletariat has displaced and turns on itself, but that should be expressed against capital in production.

This requires the opening up of psychic space, emotional space, for the development of new relations within the proletariat, in order that the struggle against capital intensifies, as the proletariat develops a capacity for more solidarity and more trust.

Socialist revolution is a process that negates bourgeois society and creates a new society, a process in which the struggle for humanity is inseparable from the struggle against the bourgeoisie.[36]

LIBERATION: A CHRISTIAN ONLOOK

As we have seen from Mendenhall's account of the Hebrew conquest of Palestine, the content of early Israelite religion focused on mobilizing a group of alienated people, who had withdrawn from oppressive institutions, and unifying them under Yahweh. Later traditions in Israel diluted its strong ecumenicity but even when its faith became ritually and culturally fixed, the religion kept its Exodus experience alive in the midst of alienating forces within and around Israel.

Israelite religion and culture developed a tradition which sought to keep alienation at a minimum within its own community; indeed it was the fostering of community itself that liberated its members. The blessed community is ruled by shalom—i.e., peace, harmony, mutuality, open brotherhood. Shalom exists only among brothers.[37]

Biblical texts offer many examples both of broken community and the joys of shalom. Isaiah rails against the strife and murder in Jerusalem (1:21). Jeremiah loses trust in his brothers (12:6). The Psalms lament the dissolution of the brotherhood (31, 41, 69). Genuine pain is felt by teachers and prophets who are helpless in their efforts to heal the loneliness and alienation of the land. They appeal to their common covenant, their history, their faith. For the prophets shalom meant that men live together in peace, act together in joy, and eat together in a covenant brotherhood.

But the peace and community of Israel was often threatened by outside military might, and its religion played a major role in every conflict. Often patriotism was identified with the Israelite religion. The authors of the books of Maccabees, for example, show the struggle of the lay Jews to overcome the cultural and military oppression brought against them by the Greeks and Hellenizing Jews. The wars and rebellions of Israel, however, had more to do with the desire for shalom than with patriotic sentiments. The people of Israel sought above all God's kingdom of peace and justice. Their religion expressed this need in dozens of ways and supported every effort to fulfill it.

The problem of oppression was no less acute in Palestine at the time of Jesus, whose message of liberation caused a great stir throughout the land. Both during his own lifetime and after his death, his followers looked upon his work and teaching basically as the struggle against the forces of evil, oppression, and alienation. The theme which runs through the book of Mark, the earliest gospel, touches on the cosmic struggle between Jesus and Satan.[38] Jesus is presented as receiving the power of the Spirit to overcome Satan in the central eschatological struggle of history. The exorcism narratives in Mark further dramatize the victory of Jesus over Satan, who stands for all of the historical forces that oppress man. Even the demons themselves reveal the mission of Jesus: "You have come to destroy us," i.e., destroy all the evil powers of the world. In addition, the miracle stories attest to Jesus' ability to surmount physical evil. The sick are cured; the demon-possessed are freed to return to their homes; the hungry are fed; the deaf, dumb, blind, and maimed are made whole. Finally Jesus overcomes Satan's strongest hold on man—death.

The significance of the cosmic struggle is amplified in Luke and Matthew: "But if it is by the finger of God [not by Beelzebub] that I cast out demons, then the kingdom of God has come upon you" (Luke 11:20; Matt. 12:28). Because Jesus exorcises demons, men discover that the kingdom has arrived. The people of Jesus' time link the two events, a powerful exorcist (who could have recieved his strength from Satan) and the coming of the kingdom. The success of Jesus as an exorcist undoubtedly led to his popularity as a teacher.[39] Perrin maintains that the Beelzebub saying is authentic and gives this interpretation: "Certainly the thought of the saying is, 'This is not the work of demons, but of God, and if God is at work in this manner, then you are even now experiencing the New Exodus: the Kingdom of God has come upon you.'"[40] To the Jews the "New Exodus" meant freedom now, liberation, new life, shalom. Events in the ministry of Jesus were to be an experience of the kingdom of God, a situation of confrontation with the forces of evil, an ushering in of shalom and the kingdom—peace, harmony, community.[41]

When did Jesus and his followers expect the kingdom to come? In his lifetime? After his death? Did the time of the coming of the kingdom concern Jesus? How were Jesus' sayings understood by his followers? These questions have supplied the material for volumes of research during this century. Albert Schweitzer began the discussion at the turn of the century by asserting that Jesus preached the imminent coming of the kingdom of God and that he warned men to repent in the face of their impending judgment.[42] Schweitzer believed that Jesus was indifferent to all historical social institutions because of his confidence that God was soon to transform the world. Most contemporary scholars acknowledge their debt to Schweitzer but modify his position in different ways. Kummel and Manson hold that Jesus mistakenly expected the kingdom to come in his time; Schnackenburg agrees that Jesus was looking for the imminent coming of the kingdom but that his expectation can be interpreted in such a way that he was not mistaken. Glasson and J. A. T. Robinson drastically reduce the eschatological element in the message of Jesus. Others—Dodd, Perrin, Bultmann, Bornkamm, Kasemann, Conzelmann, Fuchs, James M. Robinson—place stress on the existential presence of the kingdom in Jesus' own time but differ on the question of the eschatological arrival of the world-transformation.[43] For the latter group, man's liberation is associated with the coming of the kingdom, sometimes in a personal way, sometimes with social consequences.

Among the sayings of Jesus both kinds of texts, those that announce a present reality and those that proclaim a future about to arrive, are authentic. Since the new order becomes present for all to see—devils are cast out, the sick are healed, the poor have the gospel preached to them—the message of Jesus cannot be understood in an exclusively futuristic sense. Judgment is falling on the old order with every deed of Jesus. The kingdom should not be thought of only in terms of the final apocalypse: "Being asked by the Pharisees when the kingdom of God was coming, he answered them, 'The kingdom of God is not coming with signs to be observed; nor will they say, "Lo, here it is!" or "There!" for behold, the kingdom of God is in the midst of you'" (Luke 17:20-21).

Perrin believes this saying to belong to the earliest stratum of biblical tradition. He concludes from it that the words "in the midst of you" or "among you" mean "the kingdom is a matter of human experience! It does not come in such a way that it can be found by looking at the march of armies or the movement of heavenly bodies; it is not to be seen in the coming of messianic pretenders. Rather it is to be found wherever God is active decisively within the experience of an individual, and men have faith to recognize this for what it is."[44]

Perrin carries this interpretation through much of his exegesis. In his treatment of the Lord's Prayer, he sees the early disciples praying for the kingdom to come and in this prayer and fellowship of the table experiencing the kingdom "in their midst." The message and ministry of Jesus is understood as pointing to the experience of the present as an anticipation of the future. Perrin reminds us that the biblical notion of time is not strictly linear, but one in which an occasion is given meaning by the content that fills it. If the present is filled with the reality of the kingdom, then the kingdom has come and it is a pledge, a promise, of a more meaningful fulfillment in the future. Biblical experience is a now and a not yet. For Perrin, Jesus' preaching of the kingdom was an experiential confrontation, calling man to respond to a challenge to live the kingdom now in a new and radical manner.[45] For the proper response to his challenge Jesus promised nothing less than liberation, i.e., the coming of the kingdom, which contains an individual but also a social dimension.

The question remains, of course, to what social, liberating reality did Jesus challenge his disciples? Once again it is important to understand the social, religious, and political background of Jesus' world. We have seen that from the time of his boyhood, Jesus lived in turbulent and revolutionary days. The country was overpopulated and suffered under two independent systems of taxation, Roman and religious. The Romans took taxes from crops, imports, consumer items, roads, bridges, and even levied poll taxes; Jews were also assessed tithes, first-fruits, redemption money for the first-born, and the temple tax. The tax burden in Palestine amounted to about 30 to 40 percent, a sizeable figure considering the fact that the country was agricultural and not a modern wealthy industrial nation.[46] The Romans occupied the land and grew rich from oppressive taxation and social control. The Jewish religious establishment would not undermine the occupying armies as long as its own institutions were tolerated and its own property increased.

Jesus was obviously aware of the political and social oppression of his country. His program of liberation was both political and religious, and he rejected both an exclusively political and an exclusively religious solution. He did not subscribe to the Pharisees' religious understanding, which would encourage the Jewish people to concern themselves only with keeping the law and to wait for God to bring an end to Roman oppression. Nor did he directly engage in revolutionary activity against the Roman authorities, though he might have been sympathetic to the movement. He showed profound disdain for Herod Antipas, whom he called the "Fox," and for the Herodian followers of the king. Jesus disliked all forms of wanton power: "You know that those who are supposed to rule over the Gentiles lord it over them, and their great men exercise authority over them. But it shall not be so among you" (Mark 10:42-43). In Jesus' eyes soft living went with excessive power; in speaking of John the Baptist he asked his followers: "Why then did you go out? To see a man clothed in soft raiment? Behold, those who wear soft clothing are in the houses of kings!" (Matt. 11:8).

Jesus was a political realist. He knew that the political, social, and religious establishments of his day were so entrenched that he could not attack them head-on. He did cause some trouble for the sacerdotal aristocracy by overturning the tables of the moneychangers and traders, the control of which was a source of great power and influence.[47] And he made it known that the emperor's authority was subordinate to God's. But Jesus' program was only indirectly revolutionary in that he proposed a new model of society, which itself would eventually replace oppressive old structures one by one until God completely transforms the world on the Last Day. The very composition and social goals of the group were potentially threatening to the political powers which confronted his followers.

Jesus was interested in the problems of his own day; his own teaching and deeds indicate that he did not recommend that his followers adopt a quietist policy of waiting for God to reform the world. Moreover, he did not simply moralize to his listeners; he believed that times had become ripe for their decision to respond to the arrival of the kingdom among them. Perrin shows that in Jesus' message "there is nothing about standards of conduct or moral judgments; there is only the urgent call to recognize the challenge of the proclamation and to respond to it."[48] Jesus preached a message of "Liberation Now"; his hour was the right time to respond. The consequences and ramifications of his message were far-reaching and complex.

Jesus defined the nature of the kingdom he proclaimed in dozens of the most ancient sayings and parables of the gospel, but most of all in the "acted parable" of his life. Whatever Jesus said to his followers, the most certain fact Christian tradition has passed to us is the fact of his death on the cross. That is, Jesus did something that threatened the authorities of his day to the extent that they put him to death. The occasion could have been his attack on the Jewish hierarchy and the trading system, as Brandon suggests.[49] Perrin holds that Jesus' most universally offensive act was his regular table fellowship with "tax collectors and sinners," the Jews who were most despised by their fellows for their collusion with the Romans. That Jesus should not only sit at table with the outcasts of his society—Jews who had turned Gentile—but especially to do it in the name of the Kingdom of God would have been too much for Jewish morals to bear at that critical time in its history, according to Perrin.[50] But Jesus chose his table-fellows precisely because of their revolutionary diversity and social implications. If all men responded to the times and the challenge of Jesus, largescale changes would have taken place on the social, religious, and political scene. The threat was plain; Jewish authorities apparently decided to seize their opportunity to try to dispose of him at the time of the cleansing of the Temple, but Jesus had sealed his own fate before this event. The Jewish leaders had to act to keep the exclusivist quality of their nationalist and religious hope intact.

To support his argument, Perrin points to two very old and undoubtedly authentic sayings of Jesus: "For John came neither eating nor drinking, and they say, 'He has a demon'; the Son of man came eating and drinking, and they say, 'Behold, a glutton and a drunkard, a friend of tax collectors and sinners!'" (Matt. 11:18-19). And: "I tell you, many will come from east and west and sit at table with Abraham, Isaac, and Jacob in the kingdom of heaven" (Matt. 8:11). In the first text Jesus was criticized both for eating with "tax collectors" and "sinners" and for enjoying himself with them. The second is an eschatological saying and refers to the universalist banquet at the final kingdom, which Jesus anticipates by linking his own table fellowship with it. He is acting as though the kingdom were already present in his action. The joy of the table fellowship celebrated the anticipation of a wider future uni-versalism.[51]

Of course, Jesus ate with his disciples and with other kinds of outcasts, along with the very small number of "tax collectors and sinners." If he ate with tax collectors, who had been representatives of the oppressing class, he also proclaimed the good news to the poor and oppressed. Other representatives of the suffering majority and outcasts—formerly blind, lame, leprous, deaf—joined the fellowship of the table. The people who inspired the parables of the prodigal son, the lost sheep, and the lost coin were members of the new community. Thus Jesus began and continued his ministry by setting up a new community which was to represent an alternative to the social oppression and alienation of the people of his society. It was both a political and religious undertaking: political because he brought together people of different castes, social groupings, and religious outlooks (consider the faith imputed to the Samaritan leper, the Syrophoenician woman, and the Gentile soldier) into a new, energizing, joyous, and communal relation-ship, religious because the response of the participants to Jesus inaugurated the kingdom in their midst. Shalom became a new, heightened reality. Within the new community alienative, oppressive hostility dissolved; outside it, the members were threatened.

The society which Jesus proclaimed was built on entirely new structures: "No one sews a piece of unshrunk cloth on an old garment; if he does, the patch tears away from it, the new from the old, and a worse tear is made. And no one puts new wine into old wineskins; if he does, the wine will burst the skins and the wine is lost, and so are the skins; but new wine is for fresh skins" (Mark 2:21-22). Jesus wanted to make a new start, socially and religiously. The new cloth, the new skin is none other than the arrival of the kingdom, first of all in the experience of men. It seems quite likely that the experience of the kingdom, with all its overtones of shalom and community, would lead its participants to more intensive political activity in the world around them. Liberated freedom is its own diffusion.

The people in this fellowship did not spend all their time at table with Jesus. They were sent out, two by two, as the evangelists noted, to share the good news: that all the signs of the kingdom were present—demons exorcized, blind seeing, captives freed, etc. Quietism was not characteristic of the new community. Their faith consisted in an active and ready response to Jesus' challenge to overcome the alienating circumstances of their lives. The seventy who were sent out returned with joy (Luke 10:17), having been empowered to preach the new way of life of the kingdom. The rewards promised to those who took up the challenge of Jesus were reaped in their new life style. The enthusiasm of this earliest Christian community indicated their belief that "pre-history" had run its course and the dawn of a new day had arrived.

Perrin believes that the most characteristic feature of earliest Christianity lies in the continuation of the communal meals.[52] Their meaning was more social and political than theological in that they had not yet taken on any eucharistic significance. They simply continued the practice of Jesus, and the community recorded in Acts is presented as holding goods and property in common (4:32-35). The Lord's Supper may or may not have been an outgrowth of these meals. St. Paul later taught that when one eats at the Lord's Supper he is incorporated into the unity of the Body of Christ,[53] a theological consideration that very well could have stemmed from the table fellowship that was a kingdom experience.

In Paul's teaching the political reality becomes a theological truth, perhaps because of Christianity's position in a hostile empire and the ineffectiveness of lower class Christians' social and political power: "Therefore, if anyone is in Christ, he is a new creation; the old has passed away, behold the new has come. All this is from God, who through Christ reconciled us to himself and gave us the ministry of reconciliation" (2 Cor. 5:17-18). Jews and Greeks, slaves and freemen, male and female are now united in Christ especially in the banquet they share in his name: "For he is our peace who . . . has broken down the dividing wall of hostility . . . that he might create in himself one new man in place of the two" (Eph. 2:14-15).

In very few centuries Christianity would become *the* establishment, but the fellowship of Christian communities has carried a hidden dynamism throughout the centuries to overcome oppression, exploitation, and alienation:

*"He has scattered those who in the thought of their hearts
are arrogant;
He has taken down potentates from their thrones and
exalted the lowly;
The hungry he has filled with good things and the rich he
has sent away empty" (Luke 1:51-53).*

Where the eschatological characteristics of the kingdom—
freedom, peace, justice, reconciliation, community, shalom—are
emerging in the world through the heightened awareness and
activity of men, there is the church. There is also the
anticipation of a more complete future fulfillment.

A comparison of Marxian and Christian onlooks towards
liberation again shows striking similarities. Both traditions base
their theories of liberation on the concept of community, in
Marxian terms *Gemeinwesen*, individual fulfillment through the
common being of men. Marx began with the assumption that
man's essential species-life called for communal development
but that economic and social structures cause alienation and
prohibit human growth. Jesus' ministry rested on a similar
assumption, and he foresaw the dissolution of alienation in his
society through the initiation of new social relationships.
Rather than organize a direct attack on the oppressive structures, as the Zealots attempted to do, Jesus subverted the
foundations of these institutions. He understood the signs of
the times to be favorable for his undertaking and challenged his
listeners to respond to the challenge of the kingdom, so that a
new life might unfold before them. Marx saw the emergence of
the proletariat as the portent of the coming revolution when
men would be able to enter into wholly new relationships with
each other and the world. In a sense both Jesus and Marx
understood that a "privileged class" whose own interests
became identical with all of mankind was a necessary precursor
of the new society.

Once more, then, political theology may benefit from a
Marxian analysis with its conceptual units concerning the
liberating tendencies of society. This set of units, however,
takes on additional connotations when derived from Marxian
theoreticians of the Socialist states. The latter, influenced by

Engels' interpretation of Marx,[54] maximized the voluntaristic thrust of the Marx corpus. Because of great economic and social obstacles each of these leaders met in his state, awareness was conceived of as being induced in the proletariat by an "advanced class" or the Party, rather than as simply coming about through the life situation of the proletariat itself. These units, conditioned by historical circumstances, may or may not be helpful in the work of political theology.

Prior to any analytical undertaking, however, the political theologian must place himself in an historical situation, attempt to determine the alienating and the liberating forces of his own life, and respond to their challenge. This kind of decision can be made only in the context of an ecclesial community.

Notes

1. "Preface to *The Critique of Political Economy*" in *Selected Works*, Vol. I (Moscow: Foreign Languages, 1962), p. 363.
2. "Letters to Weydemeyer" in *Selected Correspondence* (New York: International, 1962), p. 57.
3. *Early Writings* (New York: McGraw-Hill, 1964), p. 52.
4. *Ibid.*, pp. 55-56, 58.
5. *The Poverty of Philosophy* (New York: International, 1967), pp. 173-175.
6. Frederick Engels, *Socialism: Utopian and Scientific* (New York: International, 1935), pp. 70-71.
7. *Cf. Early Writings*, p. 153.
8. *Ibid.*, pp. 155, 157-158.
9. *Ibid.*, p. 159.
10. *Ibid.*, pp. 193-194.
11. Karl Marx and Frederick Engels, *The German Ideology* (New York: International, 1966), pp. 70, 74-75.
12. *Early Writings*, p. 176.
13. "Inaugural Address of the Working Men's International Association" in *Selected Works*, Vol. I., p. 383.
14. *Cf. Early Writings*, pp. 181 ff.
15. "Critique of the Gotha Programme" in *Selected Works*, Vol. II, p. 24.

16. *Anti-Duhring* (Moscow: Foreign Languages, 1954), pp. 407-409, 411, 412.
17. *Capital*, Vol. III (New York: International, 1967), pp. 436-437).
18. *Ibid.*, p. 820.
19. *Capital*, Vol. I, p. 530.
20. *Early Writings*, pp. 24-26, 29-31.
21. "Draft and Explanation of the Program of the Social-Democratic Party" in *Lenin on the Proletarian Party of a New Type* (Peking: Foreign Languages, 1960), pp. 15-16.
22. *Selected Works*, Vol 7 (Moscow: Progress, 1963), p. 278.
23. *State and Revolution* (New York: International, 1943), p. 82.
24. *Collected Works*, Vol. 31 (Moscow: Progress, 1966), pp. 292-296.
25. "The Foolish Old Man Who Moved the Mountains" in *Selected Readings from the Works of Mao Tse-Tung* (Peking: Foreign Languages, 1967), p. 261.
26. "Where Do Correct Ideas Come From," *Selected Readings*, pp. 405-406.
27. "On the Question of Agricultural Cooperation," *Selected Readings*, pp. 326-327, 333-334.
28. "Notes in *Socialist Upsurge in China's Countryside*," *Selected Readings*, p. 347.
29. "Speech at the Chinese Communist Party's National Conference on Propaganda Work," *Selected Readings*, p. 388-389.
30. "On the People's Democratic Dictatorship," *Selected Readings*, p. 308-310.
31. Sept. 26, 1960, printed by the Fair Play for Cuba Committee, New York.
32. "May Day Speech," May 1, 1966, printed by the Stenographic Department of the Cuban Revolutionary Government, Havana.
33. "Speech made on the 14th Anniversary of the Attack on Moncada Garrison," July 26, 1967, Havana.
34. "Speech made at the Presentation of the Members of the Central Committee of the Communist Party," 1965, Havana.

35. Ernesto C. Guevara, *Socialism and Man* (New York: Pathfinder Press, 1968), pp. 7-8, 10-14, 20-22.
36. *Socialist Revolution*, I, No. 2, (March-April, 1970), pp. 25, 27-30, 31-32.
37. *Cf.* Johns Pedersen, *Israel: Its Life and Culture*, Vol. I-II (London: Oxford University, 1926), pp. 264-335 for an extended treatment of the meaning of shalom.
38. *Cf.* James M. Robinson, *The Problem of History in Mark* (London: SCM, 1968).
39. See Norman Perrin, *Rediscovering the Teaching of Jesus* (New York: Harper and Row, 1967), pp. 63-68. Perrin attests to a consensus of critical opinion which holds that Jesus acted as an exorcist during his lifetime.
40. *Ibid.*, p. 67.
41. *Ibid.*.
42. *The Quest of the Historical Jesus* (London: A. and C. Black, 1910).
43. See W. G. Kummel, *Promise and Fulfillment* (London: SCM, 1957), pp. 54-87; also T. W. Manson, *The Teaching of Jesus* (Cambridge: Cambridge University Press, 1935), pp. 234-284; R. Schnackenburg, *God's Rule and Kingdom* (New York: Herder and Herder, 1963), pp. 195-214; and T. F. Glasson, *The Second Advent* (London: Epworth, 1963), J. A. T. Robinson, *Jesus and His Coming* (London: SCM, 1957), C. H. Dodd, *The Parables of the Kingdom* (New York: Scribners, 1961). The final group of scholars are discussed in Perrin, *The Kingdom of God in the Teaching of Jesus* (Philadelphia: Westminster, 1963), pp. 112-124.
44. *Rediscovering the Teaching of Jesus*, p. 74.
45. *Ibid.*, pp. 204-205.
46. F. C. Grant, *The Economic Background of the Gospels*, quoted in Sherman E. Johnson, *Jesus in His Own Times* (London: A. and C. Black, 1958), p. 103.
47. *Cf.* S. C. F. Brandon, *Jesus and the Zealots* (Manchester: Manchester University Press, 1967), pp. 331-333.
48. *Rediscovering the Teaching of Jesus*, p. 109.
49. *Jesus and the Zealots*, p. 335.
50. *Rediscovering the Teaching of Jesus*, p. 103.
51. *Ibid.*, pp. 105-108.

52. *Ibid.*, p. 104. See also Rudolf Bultmann, *Theology of the New Testament*, Vol. I (New York: Scribners, 1951), pp. 57-58.
53. *Cf.* Ernst Kasemann, *Essays on New Testament Themes* (London: SCM, 1960), pp. 108-135.
54. *Cf.* Iring Fetscher, *Karl Marx und der Marxismus* (Munchen: R. Piper, 1967), pp. 132 ff.

CHAPTER FOUR

Ecclesial Praxis

EARLY CHRISTIAN COMMUNITIES

The preceding chapters call for an examination of the praxis of Christian ecclesial communities, but before getting into that we should emphasize the tentative quality of our interpretation of the Christian onlook. For example, contemporary biblical research[1] generally affirms that our understanding of Jesus has been related to us through a variety of later community traditions, which looked upon Jesus within the context of their own specific needs, problems, and aspirations. At the same time, as we have inferred in the last chapter, a great number of authentic "sayings" and occurrences can be established from the tradition of eyewitnesses or parallel texts outside the Gospels themselves. Although it may not be possible to set up a chronology of Jesus' ministry, we *can* point up significant episodes of his life, activities, and sayings, which tend to uncover his intent. This procedure may indeed produce many different portraits of Jesus, since history is largely a matter of selective data-gathering, but it is the only methodology open to those who wish to base their interpretation on historical foundations.

A similar historical difficulty arises when we consider the nature of the earliest ecclesial communities or churches. It is difficult to put one's finger on a uniform self-image or praxis in early Christianity. Hans Küng points out that Jesus was not interested in founding a church during his ministry.[2] This is to say that he did not organize a select group of people separated from the larger masses he preached to. His table fellowship, even his call of the Twelve who represented the whole of Israel, had quite the opposite effect of establishing an "open" community. His followers and their communal life related more to the beginnings of the kingdom than to any kind of religious organized society. The basic requirement seemed to be a radical decision to accept his message of salvation; the effect was the experience of peace and joy, realized in the present time but looking to a superabundant realization in the time to come.

It is not surprising, then, that "the notion of the Church in the New Testament is so varied and the understanding of what Christ has done so diverse, that the historian has no good reason to speak of a single and universal Church in the New Testament. What we find in the Scriptures is the creation of local communities."[3] Diverse, local ecclesial communities of table fellowship continued after the death of Jesus. The membership of the communities sought to incorporate the spirit of the kingdom which Jesus preached as they looked forward to its completion in hope. Their activity, religious or social, was open-ended. Perrin argues that early Christian fellowship meals flourished for a time before any theological meaning could be attributed to them and points to testimony from The Acts of the Apostles (2:46), the epistles, and the *Didache*.[4]

But table fellowship eventually developed into the *Ekklesia*. Küng shows that the word *Ekklesia* in the New Testament refers to a community, a congregation, a church.[5] There is an interesting connection between the New Testament usage of the word as a meeting of the people and its Greek origins which indicate a political meeting.[6] The term of course came to refer to a cultic group and included the sense of congregating together for a religious purpose. The praxis of the communities remained open-ended but radiated confidence that they represented the eschatalogical community of salvation: joyous table fellowship, openness to every stratum of society, service to one another, love extended even to their enemies, the eschewing of power and prestige, the common use of money and goods, and all the while confounding the political powers of the day by their strange behavior. Christians anticipated the fullness of the kingdom by projecting its beginnings to the world around them. The New Testament records these communities in various stages of development, but at least a generation from the time of Jesus lapsed before these communities changed their character from signs of the kingdom to semi-exclusivist churches. Scripture presents a uniform picture, however, of two types of their praxis: *koinonia*—fellowship, commonality in their relationships, and *diakonia*—service, mission, and ministry among themselves and to the world around them. Their composition was ecumenical, admission open. The commonality extended to life styles, goals, accountability ("Confess your sins to one another" James 5:16). Since they were a cultic community, their praxis was religious; since their presence and activity challenged the social and economic systems of privilege of the day, their praxis was also indirectly political. That is, their activity had political consequences even if the early Christians did not directly enter the political arena.

CONTEMPORARY ECCLESIAL COMMUNITIES

The characteristic thrust of H. Richard Niebuhr's *The Meaning of Revelation* lies in its presentation of Christianity as "permanent revolution."[7] Niebuhr warns against substituting religion, revelation, the church or Christian morality for God himself, so that we always avoid absolutizing the relative forms of Christianity in a way that reifies the faith. Christian theology and specific organizational forms of the Christian church are historically conditioned; the Christian faith demands a permanent revolution out of these static forms.

In a later essay Niebuhr applies this notion in a special way to the church.[8] Historical forms of the church are seen as emerging organizations that arise to meet specific temporal needs. Niebuhr gives some churches a "Christian" label only as a "family name"—rather than as a "descriptive adjective." Christian theologies, rites, organizational forms have a multitude of contributing sources; and even economic and scientific influences have helped to shape the Christian heritage. There is no such thing as a pristine Christian church. At the same time,

many secular societies exhibit a large measure of the spirit of
Christianity; it is difficult to put one's finger on the presence of
what Niebuhr terms the Church with a capital C, the "universal
fellowship of reconciliation." Churches, with small c's, are
emergent realities, all of which are partial representatives of the
Church, which will make itself fully known in the future
kingdom.

The model of the churches we will describe below is based
upon the fragmentary knowledge we have of Jesus' fellowship
communities, and upon some of the activity recorded about the
early Christian communities. Contemporary ecclesial communities will enjoy no more of an absolute character than the table
fellowship groups of the first century. The praxis of contemporary ecclesial communities obviously is dependent on
a different historical situation from that of the first century;
different yet the same, for there are still strong alienating forces
in the world, still efforts at liberation. Ecclesial communities
need not replace existing church structures, though they are
meant to provide a legitimate alternative to them and may in
the future influence older church forms.

Norman Gottwald has traced contemporary Christian
church-culture interaction and patterns from their origins in
ancient Israel and has given the name "crypto-church" to the
ecclesial groups that may not be directly related to the larger
church organization but nonetheless seem to be doing God's
work in the world. He states, "Our whole way of discerning
'church' in ancient Israel and in the present context has had a
double character. 'Church' always has a historical, communal
character, marked by specific memories and symbols (centrally
the Torah or Jesus Christ). 'Church' also always has a dynamic,
eventful character, marked by specific discoveries of God's
action in the present and commitment to it (the precise way in
which Torah or Jesus confronts us). 'Church' has continuity and
contextuality, tradition and novelty, assurance and precariousness, visibility and invisibility. 'Church' is historically shaped
and history-shaping."[9]

The "contextuality," "novelty," "precariousness," "invisibility," and "history-shaping" aspects of the "crypto-church"
are distinguishing marks of ecclesial communities. Gottwald
further explains:

For a mature doctrine of the church today, full place must be given to the church within culture, the crypto-church, *or the* anonymous church, *in which God is as validly and actively at work as in the historically or covenantly defined church. This is not to say that the distinctions between historic church and crypto-church are unimportant, any more than it is appropriate to erase distinctions between the covenantal and the noncovenantal religions. It is to insist, however, that the crypto-church must be reckoned with as a major instrument of God, one that the church in its historic embodiment cannot ignore and with which it must increasingly ally itself for various kinds of immediate and long-range study and action. Social action as something that a church committee or individual members do on the periphery of the congregation will give way to the conception of social action as something God and men do in concert throughout human life; some activities will be initiated from within the institutional church, but many more will arise in culture on other institutional foundations, and with all of them the church must come to theological and practical terms as a congregation and not simply as individual believers.*[10]

Ecclesial communities are built on "other institutional foundations." They share a commitment perspective with other Christians, however, so that their roots are not entirely secular. With this background, then, the following tentative notions are intended to describe a few of the qualities that, on the basis of our discussion thus far, are important for contemporary ecclesial communities.

1. *Contemporary ecclesial communities should grow ecumenically out of small house, neighborhood, occupational, professional or ad hoc collectives; equality and mutuality should characterize the relationship of the participants.*

Ecumenicity refers not only to religious or nonreligious beliefs but also to class, racial, and ethnic composition. "Publicans and sinners" today can refer to anyone who does not have a binding stake in the establishment—intellectuals, manual laborers, hippies, students, etc.—whether or not they work within it. The community is to be a sign of the future society which will erase the divisions that plague the social order today—political divisions, social divisions, economic divisions, religious divisions, etc. The composition of the group bespeaks a commitment to an open society; its very existence becomes a sacrament to the world. Personal religious beliefs or doctrinaire political ideologies are not to be set up as criteria for membership. Members hold a common commitment (See 2 below), but their shared tactical theories (or common ideology) develop only in the course of their praxis, experience, and theoretical analysis.

The relationships of the people in the community are to be equal ones. Ecclesial communities must begin with the understanding that mutuality is a condition of growth. Equal relationships do not assure human development but they are an indispensable start in that direction. The paternalism that has marked the churches of the past and that is responsible for an elite which makes decisions for the rest of its members has to give way to a fully egalitarian democracy. Elitism, frequently justified in the interests of efficiency, is actually counterproductive, for its results destroy the possibility of community. Elitism is a form of alienation: top separated from bottom and vice versa; a caste divided from the people in a subtle form of class rule. Even liberal democracy, in and out of the churches, manages to preserve a system of privilege for the few.

Decisions in ecclesial communities are to be made by all, preferably by consensus; therefore, the size of the groups should not become too large. Participants do not look to priests or ministers to provide divine insights about what is best for the rest of the community and its projects. Everyone is entrusted with equal voice since each person possesses a unique experience and background that enables him to contribute to the welfare and program of the community. Neither are men necessarily gifted with more leadership qualities than women. No one person is set apart in a privileged or paternalistic capacity from the other members of the group, although one might preside temporarily and all might take on special functions. Communal responsibility, ecumenicity, and mutuality become the basic ingredients of personal liberation within the group itself.

Collectives should not become rigidly uniform in membership, size, activity, or life styles. Some will resemble traditional parishes and perhaps be linked with the organized church. Others will be based in neighborhoods, at factories, in apartment complexes. Some will spring from professional groups. Family groups or communes could increase the effectiveness of the community because of the closeness of the membership.

Although a network of collectives may strengthen their external impact by coordinated planning, no one group should be given precedence of authority over the others. Decisions are made by the network in the same manner of participatory consensus that operates within each collective.

Participation by each member of the group, then, creates "community" and an environment, "from each according to his ability, to each according to his needs." Each individual's contribution is a repayment for what he receives from other members of the community. Activity and reflection, support and receptivity spark the beginnings of a liberated society in a community that mirrors a vision of the kingdom. The "liberated zone" of ecclesial communities tends to encompass more and more space within itself.

2. *Contemporary ecclesial communities should embody a commitment to the humanization of oppressive social structures.*

The credibility of political theology rests upon the praxis and experience of its practitioners. Commitment determines praxis; praxis determines commitment. On the one hand, members of ecclesial communities commit themselves to work in the direction of the historical forces which they believe are tending towards the humanization of society. On the other hand, their praxis itself deepens their commitment and raises their historical consciousness and self-awareness.

Commitment and praxis go together. Ecclesial communities are not born in a vacuum. People come together to do something, to share a common vision. Their strategies, tactics, ideologies, and methodologies might differ, for they are venturing into uncharted regions. Fundamentally the members of ecclesial communities are committed to the concept of a liberated, egalitarian society, both for their own communities and for the larger social order. They want to move from a state of relative alienation to a state of relative liberation. As we have seen, Christian tradition provides a foundation for the commitment; other traditions are equally firm in the conviction.

Christianity's historical position on such a radical "this-worldly" commitment has been ambivalent. For centuries the Christian faith has been viewed as the bulwark of the status quo in western civilization, but in this generation more than a meager sampling of Christian participation is present in the ranks of most social movements and some radical causes. Ecclesial communities will consolidate the efforts of individuals in the churches and focus on an essential task: the de-alienation and humanization of social structures.

In both Marxian and Christian thinking men are able to develop their real and authentic being only within communities, among the egalitarian and humanizing influence of other men. In Marxian terms, man's species-life can be formed only in community, in his *Ekklesia* in Christian terms. Marx understood, however, that isolated communities, however humanizing, could not survive in the larger society when old oppressive, elitist class structures robbed communal microcosms of the possibility of complete fulfillment. The viability of ecclesial communities depends logically on the emancipation of the whole of society and instrumentally on their contribution towards the emancipation of the whole. Today it is not enough to retreat into monastic simplicity or rural communes. No community will be completely free until the rest of the social structures are liberated, until exploitation and alienation at every level of society are erased. The commitment to set about this task is the commitment to do what many Jewish and Christian apocalyptic writers thought only God would do—bring on the kingdom.

The primary difficulty of ecclesial communities comes in the formulation of a program that will in some small way implement their commitment.

3. *Specific tactics for the transformation of oppressive economic, political, and social structures will depend on concrete analysis of these structures.*

This analysis is the contribution of political theology. Again analysis is derived from praxis and influences future praxis in a way that maintains a dialectical relationship between theory and praxis. Strategies and tactics become quickly outdated with changing circumstances and priorities. Alienation and exploitation continually take new forms and must be dealt with by continually new tactics. The questions raised in the "contemporary analysis" sections of Chapter Two and Chapter Three provide a starting point for theoretical analysis. But even after analysis has been made, specific local conditions will require specific modes of operation and tactics for addressing immediate issues must be formulated differently than long-range programs. Yet it is essential that long-range programs and short-range tactics be interrelated.

The people in ecclesial communities will work outside the group in various occupations, or perhaps in the same occupation. Their theory will come from actual praxis inside the social structures they are presuming to judge. Therefore in ecclesial communities there is no "centralism" that makes professional revolutionaries out of an elite segment of the community. Priests and ministers become workers or members of professions and occupations, not only to work for the humanizing of these occupations, but also to bring varied experiences back to their ecclesial groups. Without institutional and ecclesial praxis, along with continual societal analysis, ideological abstractions could begin to stifle the work of the community.

Ecclesial communities do not envision themselves as a vanguard party, an elitist group that presumes to speak for the rest of society. They may work either inside or outside of institutional frameworks to bring about a de-alienation of the work process and an abolition of class relationships. Although ecclesial communities may work in association with other groups in a network of collectives, activity should be decentralized, directed to specific economic or political areas. An egalitarian mode of social relations is the goal, within individual institutions and, finally, within all of society. Decentralized tactics maximize the possibility of success or partial success, and furnish educational experience in specific areas—workers achieving equality with managers, women with men, proletariat with ruling class. The liberated zone is then a localized sociological entity consisting of humanized relationships, not a spatial, geographical zone.

THE RELEVANCE OF MARX AND ENGELS

We have already seen the broad similarity between Marx's concept of the proletariat whose emancipation is correlated with the emancipation of all of humanity and Jesus' call for a new community which would ultimately serve the same purpose. Those who would work out of ecclesial communities share Marx's assumption that the liberation of people from oppressive social structures will occur when they develop the awareness that impels them to liberate themselves. Ecclesial communities purpose to work with other men to achieve greater historical and personal self-awareness so that everyone in society eventually takes complete control of his life.

A second point pertinent to the strategies of ecclesial communities deals with Marx's notion of the advent of a socialized society. Two selections quoted in Chapter Three indicate that Marx believed that the new society would undergo gradual institutional transformation before the final political transformation: the short selection on cooperatives and the excerpt from the third volume of *Capital* on stock companies. In the latter he showed that capitalist ownership is passing from private individual hands to the hands of corporate, i.e., collective, stock companies. This is a transitional phase of capitalism, and could easily lead to the time when the workers themselves will control their own factories. Marx points to the cooperative association as another example of the gradual replacement of private ownership and management by social ownership and management. These are only small indicators, but in both cases workers are considered to be taking gradual steps towards the final transformation of society.

Marx drew a somewhat similar conclusion in the "Inaugural Address" about the possibility of gradualism in political matters. He claimed that social production began to be controlled in behalf of the proletariat's interests for the first time with the enactment of the Ten Hour's Bill.[11] Of course, Marx insists that total emancipation will not arrive until the proletariat achieves complete political control, but the process can begin piecemeal in a decentralized way.

Engels offered historical precedent for this perspective

when he observed that the bourgeoisie had taken power from the feudal autocracy little by little economically, then finally in the political realm:

Originally an oppressed estate liable to pay dues to the ruling feudal nobility, recruited from serfs and villeins of every type, the burghers conquered one position after another in their continuous struggle with the nobility, and finally, in the most highly developed countries, took power in its stead: in France, by directly overthrowing the nobility; in England, by making it more and more bourgeois, and incorporating it as the ornamental head of the bourgeoisie itself. And how did it accomplish this? Simply through a change in the "economic order," which sooner or later, voluntarily or as the outcome of struggle, was followed by a change in the political conditions. The struggle of the bourgeoisie against feudal nobility is the struggle of the town against the country, of industry against landed property, of money economy against natural economy; and the decisive weapon of the burghers in this struggle was their economic power, constantly increasing through the development first of handicraft industry, at a later stage progressing to manufacturing industry, and through the extension of commerce.[12]

Both Marx and Engels, then, fit in with the work of ecclesial communities which strive to increase awareness through "revolutionary" reforms, always with an eye to the final goal of complete transformation and humanization, which may precipitate a large-scale social struggle between the ruling class and the proletariat.

The obvious danger of this approach to radical social change is that partial reforms are always in danger of co-optation, that is, of being utilized to preserve the status quo and the system of privilege. The reforms need to be honestly assessed at every step.

There is a third Marxian parallel that seems to apply to the task of ecclesial communities: contemporary commitment groups represent the same interests which Marx ascribed to the working class of his day.[13] Marx himself associated with the European labor movement at the 1864 formation of the First International, an international federation of affiliated working-class organizations and parties. The International was not the organized Communist Party, nor did a select cadre of Marx's comrades operate as a secret society within the International. In contrast to Marx and Engels' earlier conceptions expressed in the *Communist Manifesto* placing the Communist League as a vanguard organization with a higher theoretical awareness than working-class groups, the International embraced a variety of organizations: "English trade unions, the French, Belgian, Italian and Spanish Proudhonists and the German Lassall-eans."[14] Every affiliated organization was to individually develop its own theoretical program.[15] The groups were united by their common opposition to the oppression of the existing order. Marx struggled to uphold this pluralism in the International, especially against Bakunin, who wanted to control the organization by means of a secret society, as long as his association with it endured. His "General Rules of the International Working Men's Association" provide something of a charter for ecclesial communities today:

Considering,
    That the emancipation of the working classes must be conquered by the working classes themselves; that the struggle for the emancipation of the working classes means not a struggle for class privileges and monopolies, but for equal rights and duties, and the abolition of all class rule;
    That the economical subjection of the man of labour to the monopoliser of the means of labour, that is, the sources of life, lies at the bottom of servitude in all its forms, of all social misery, mental degradation, and political dependence;
    That the economical emancipation of the working classes is therefore the great end to which every political movement ought to be subordinate as a means;
    That all efforts aiming at that great end have hitherto failed from the want of solidarity between the manifold divisions of labour in each country, and from the absence

*of a fraternal bond of union between the working classes
of different countries;*
    *That the present revival of the working classes in the
most industrial countries of Europe, while it raises a new
hope, gives solemn warning against a relapse into the old
errors, and calls for the immediate combination of the still
disconnected movements;*
For These Reasons—
    *The International Working Men's Association has
been founded. It declares:*
    *That all societies and individuals adhering to it will
acknowledge truth, justice, and morality, as the basis of
their conduct towards each other and towards all men,
without regard to colour, creed, or nationality;*
    That it acknowledges no rights without duties, no
duties without rights. . . .
    *This constitution of the proletariat into a political
party is indispensable to ensure the triumph of the social
Revolution and of its ultimate goal: the abolition of
classes.*
    *The coalition of the forces of the working class,
already achieved by the economic struggle, must also serve,
in the hands of this class, as a lever in its struggle against
the political power of its exploiters.*
    *As lords of the land and of capital always make use of
their political privileges to defend and perpetuate their
economic monopolies and to enslave labour, the conquest
of political power becomes the great duty of the proletariat. . . .*[16]

Marx shows that groups of every variety must unite in the
struggle against alienation and oppression, and that political
power is not a tool that should be discarded as "nonrevolutionary."

LENIN

Marx's model for the revolutionary transformation of society
envisaged the active work of organizations and parties cooperat-

ing with the working classes in their respective societies. But Marx never actually led a revolution as did Lenin and Mao. In pre-Revolutionary Russia Lenin believed that circumstances required him to reshape Marx's model to suit what he thought were the needs of his land. Lenin conceived the Party as a vanguard of the working class, as a vehicle to raise the latter's consciousness and to provoke a political crisis that would enable his group to take power. Lenin did not think that any transformation of society was possible until the Party took over the reins of government and enabled the proletariat to control the means of production.

Lenin's position rested on the assumption that his Party had to be organized, centralized, and disciplined into cadres in order to counteract the underdeveloped consciousness of the working class of his time. In his famous 1902 work on the subject, *What Is to Be Done?*, he stressed the importance of professional revolutionaries who would act as balance in behalf of the proletariat against repressive police activity. In this declaration Lenin clearly shows the elitist quality of his Party, which was organized to direct the masses rather than to work with them.

However, in 1905 a spontaneous rebellion of the Russian workers—one carried out without directions from his Party—caused Lenin to reformulate his conception. He moved from the elitist notions of subordination of the masses to the Party, of lower echelons to higher bodies of the Party, and of a small disciplined revolutionary group, towards a mass Party and a democratization of its structures:[17] "The new form of organization, or rather the new form of the basic organizational nucleus of the workers' party, must be definitely much broader than were the old circles. Apart from this, the new nucleus will most likely have to be a less rigid, more 'free,' more 'loose' organization. . . ."[18] Lenin called for freedom of discussion and the right of minority opinion to exist within the Party, but insisted on unity of action, which would not be determined by the Central Committee but rather by the Party Congress of all factions. This was his idea of "democratic centralism," which incorporates freedom of discussion with unity of action. Problems arise when a person or a committee gain enough power in the Party to make unilateral decisions about the amount of free discussion or opposing ideological doctrine that is to be permitted. Unilateral tendencies are usually present in a system of democratic centralism, as subsequent events in Russia have indicated. At any rate, when Tsarism reestablished itself in Russia in 1908, the monolithic, dogmatic, elitist traits of the Party reappeared and generally have characterized its activity since that time.

It is important to realize that Lenin did not always hold to an elitism in the Party's relationship to the rest of society. Much of his theory contains valuable insights for any small collective interested in effecting radical social change, more so even than Marx's own theory, since Marx did not grapple with the practical problems of changing political, economic, and social relationships in a particular situation. For example, even in his manifesto for an elitist party, *What Is to Be Done?*, Lenin shows great solidarity with the people he and his Party presumed to educate politically; and he was not paternalistic in his language. He lays out specific tactics of political education for the members of his group, encouraging them to act as theoreticians, propagandists, agitators (in the sense of forcing issues before oppressors and oppressed), and organizers. This selection presupposes that cadre members engage in intensive study of the class activity of the society, of overt and covert exploitation, corruption, and oppression. *What Is to Be Done?* offers excellent hints for the beginnings of political work in ecclesial communities:

The question now arises: What does political education mean? Is it sufficient to confine oneself to the propaganda of working-class hostility to autocracy? Of course not. It is not enough to explain to the workers that they are politically oppressed (any more than it was to explain to them that their interests were antagonistic to the interests of the employers). Advantage must be taken of every concrete example of this oppression for the purpose of agitation (in the same way as we began to use concrete examples of economic oppression for the purposes of agitation). And inasmuch as it manifests itself in various spheres of life and activity, in industrial life, civic life, in personal and family life, in religious life, scientific life, etc., etc., is it not evident that we shall not be fulfilling our task of developing the political consciousness of the workers if we do not undertake the organisation of the political exposure of autocracy in all its aspects? In order to agitate over concrete examples of oppression, these examples must be exposed (in the same way as it was necessary to expose factory evils in order to carry on economic agitation). . . .

Is it true that in general, the economic struggle "is the most widely applicable method" of drawing the masses into the political struggle? It is absolutely untrue. All and sundry manifestations of police tyranny and autocratic outrage, in addition to the evils connected with the economic struggle, are equally "widely applicable" as a means of "drawing in" the masses. The tyranny of the Zemstvo chiefs [landowners], the flogging of the peasantry, the corruption of the officials, the fight against the famine-stricken and the suppression of the popular striving towards enlightenment and knowledge, the extortion of taxes, the persecution of the religious sects, the severe discipline in the army, the militarist conduct towards the students and the liberal intelligentsia—all these and a thousand other similar manifestations of tyranny, though not directly connected with the "economic" struggle, do they not, in general, represent a less "widely applicable" method and subject for political agitation and for drawing the masses into the political struggle? The very opposite is the case. Of all the innumerable cases in which the workers suffer (either personally or those closely associated with them) from tyranny, violence, and lack of rights, undoubtedly only a relatively few represent cases of police tyranny in the economic struggle as such. Why then should we beforehand restrict the scope of political agitation by declaring only one of the methods to be "the most widely applicable," when Social-Democrats have other, generally speaking, not less "widely applicable" means? . . .

Broader Struggle

Revolutionary Social-Democracy always included, and now includes, the fight for reforms in its activities. But

*it utilises "economic" agitation for the purpose of present-
ing to the government, not only demands for all sorts of
measures, but also (and primarily) the demand that it cease
to be an autocratic government. Moreover, it considers it
to be its duty to present this demand to the government,
not on the basis of the economic struggle alone, but on the
basis of all manifestations of public and political life. In a
word, it subordinates the struggle for reforms to the
revolutionary struggle for liberty and for Socialism, in the
same way as the part is subordinate to the whole. . . .*

*As a matter of fact, it is possible to "raise the activity
of the masses of the workers" only provided this activity is
not restricted entirely to "political agitation on an
economic basis." And one of the fundamental conditions
for the necessary expansion of political agitation is the
organisation of all-sided political exposure. In no other
way can the masses be trained in political consciousness
and revolutionary activity except by means of such
exposures. Hence, to conduct such activity is one of the
most important functions of international Social-Democracy as a whole, for even in countries where political
liberty exists, there is still a field for work of exposure,
although in such countries the work is conducted in a
different sphere. For example, the German party is
strengthening its position and spreading its influence,
thanks particularly to the untiring energy with which it is
conducting a campaign of political exposure. Working-class
consciousness cannot be genuinely political consciousness
unless the workers are trained to respond to all cases of
tyranny, oppression, violence, and abuse, no matter what
class is affected. . . .*

Our Philistinism

*Why is it that the Russian workers as yet display so
little revolutionary activity in connection with the brutal
way in which the police maltreat the people, in connection
with the persecution of the religious sects, with the
flogging of the peasantry, with the outrageous censorship,
with the torture of soldiers, with the persecution of the*

most innocent cultural enterprises, etc.? Is it because the "economic struggle" does not "stimulate" them to this, because such political activity does not "promise palpable results," because it produces little that is "positive"? To advance this argument, we repeat, is merely to shift the blame to the shoulders of others, to blame the masses of the workers for our own philistinism. We must blame ourselves, our remoteness from the mass movement; we must blame ourselves for being unable as yet to organise a sufficiently wide, striking, and rapid exposure of these despicable outrages. When we do that (and we must and can do it), the most backward worker will understand, or will feel, that the students and religious sects, the muzhiks and the authors are being abused and outraged by the very same dark forces that are oppressing and crushing him at every step of his life, and, feeling that, he himself will be filled with an irresistible desire to respond to these things and then he will organise cat-calls against the censors one day, another day he will demonstrate outside the house of the provincial governor who has brutally suppressed a peasant uprising, another day he will teach a lesson to the gendarmes in surplices who are doing the work of the Holy Inquisition, etc. As yet we have done very little, almost nothing, to hurl universal and fresh exposures among the masses of the workers. Many of us as yet do not appreciate the bounden duty that rests upon us, but spontaneously follow in the wake of the "drab everyday struggle," in the narrow confines of factory life. . . .

The Workers Speak

The "economic struggle between the workers and the employers and the government," about which you make as much fuss as if you had made a new discovery, is being carried on in all parts of Russia, even the most remote, by the workers themselves who have heard about strikes, but who have heard almost nothing about Socialism. The "activity" you want to stimulate among us workers by advancing concrete demands promising palpable results, we are already displaying, and in our everyday, petty trade-

union work, we put forward concrete demands, very often without any assistance from the intellectuals whatever. But such activity is not enough for us; we are not children to be fed on the sops of "economic" politics alone; we want to know everything that everybody else knows; we want to learn the details of all aspects of political life and to take part actively in every political event. In order that we may do this, the intellectuals must talk to us less on what we already know, and tell us more about what we do not know and what we can never learn from our factory and "economic" experience, that is, you must give us political knowledge. You intellectuals can acquire this knowledge, and it is your duty to bring us that knowledge in a hundred and a thousand times greater measure than you have done up till now; and you must bring us this knowledge, not only in the form of arguments, pamphlets and articles which sometimes—excuse my frankness!—are very dull, but in the form of live exposures of what our government and our governing classes are doing at this very moment in all spheres of life. Fulfil this duty with greater zeal, and talk less about "increasing the activity of the masses of the workers"! We are far more active than you think, and we are quite able to support by open street fighting demands that do not even promise any "palpable results" whatever! You cannot "increase" our activity, because you yourselves are not sufficiently active. Be less subservient to spontaneity, and think more about increasing your own activity, gentlemen! ...

The workers can acquire class political consciousness only from without, that is, only outside of the economic struggle, outside of the sphere of relations between workers and employers. The sphere from which alone it is possible to obtain this knowledge is the sphere of relationships among all classes and the state and the government—the sphere of the inter-relations between all classes. For that reason, the reply to the question: What must be done in order that the workers may acquire political knowledge? cannot be merely the one which, in the majority of cases, the practical workers, especially those who are inclined towards Economism, usually content themselves with, i.e., "go among the workers." To bring political knowledge to the workers the Social-Democrats must go among all classes of the population, must dispatch units of their army in all directions. . . .

Not Another Trade Unionist

Take the type of Social-Democratic circle that has been most widespread during the past few years, and examine its work. It has "contact with the workers"; it issues leaflets—in which abuses in the factories, the government's partiality towards the capitalists, and the tyranny of the police are strongly condemned—and rests content with this. At meetings of workers, there are either no discussions or they do not extend beyond such subjects. Lectures and discussions on the history of the revolutionary movement, on questions of the home and foreign policy of our government, on questions of the economic evolution of Russia and of Europe, and the position of the various classes in modern society, etc., are extremely rare. Of systematically acquiring and extending contact with other classes of society, no one even dreams. The ideal leader, as the majority of the members of such circles picture him, is something more in the nature of a trade-union secretary than a Socialist political leader. Any trade-union secretary, an English one, for instance, helps the workers to conduct the economic struggle, helps to expose factory abuses, explains the injustice of the laws and of measures which hamper the freedom of strikes and the freedom to picket, to warn all and sundry that a strike is proceeding at a certain factory, explains the partiality of arbitration courts which are in the hands of the bourgeois classes, etc., etc. In a word, every trade-union secretary conducts and helps to conduct "the economic struggle against the employers and the government." It cannot be too strongly insisted that this is not enough to constitute Social-Democracy. The Social-Democrat's ideal should not be a trade-union secretary, but a tribune of the people, able to react to every manifestation of tyranny and oppression, no matter where it takes place, no matter what stratum or class of the people it affects; he must be able to group all these manifestations into a single picture of police violence and capitalist exploitation; he must be able to take advantage of every petty event in order to explain his Socialistic convictions and his Social-Democratic demands to all, in order to explain to all and everyone the world historical significance of the struggle of the emancipation of the proletariat. . . .

Let us return, however, to the, elucidation of our thesis. We said that a Social-Democrat, if he really believes it is necessary to develop the political consciousness of the proletariat, must "go among all classes of the people." This gives rise to the questions: How is this to be done? Have we enough forces to do this? Is there a base for such work among all the other classes? Will this not mean a retreat, or lead to a retreat from the class point-of-view? We shall deal with these questions.

We must "go among all classes of the people" as theoreticians, as propagandists, as agitators, and as organisers. No one doubts that the theoretical work of Social-Democrats should be directed toward studying all the features of the social and political position of the various classes. But extremely little is done in this direction compared with the work that is done in studying the features of factory life. In the committees and circles, you will meet men who are immersed, say, in the study of some special branch of the metal industry, but you will hardly ever find members of organisations (obliged, as often happens, for some reason or other to give up practical work) especially engaged in the collection of material concerning some pressing question of social and political life which could serve as a means for conducting Social-Democratic work among other strata of the population. In speaking of the lack of training of the majority of present-day leaders of the labour movement, we cannot refrain from mentioning the point about training in this connection also, for it is also bound up with the "economic" conception of "close organic contact with the proletarian struggle." The principal thing, of course, is propaganda and agitation among all strata of the people.

The Western-European Social-Democrats find their work in this field facilitated by the calling of public meetings, to which all are free to go, and by the parliament, in which they speak to the representatives of all classes. We have neither a parliament, nor the freedom to call meetings; nevertheless we are able to arrange meetings of workers who desire to listen to a Social-Democrat. We must also find ways and means of calling meetings of representatives of all and every other class of the population that desire to listen to a Democrat; for he who forgets that "the Communists support every revolutionary movement," that we are obliged for that reason to emphasize general democratic tasks before the whole people, without for a moment concealing our Socialistic convictions, is not a Social-Democrat. He who forgets his obligation to be in advance of everybody in bringing up, sharpening, and solving every general democratic question, is not a Social-Democrat. . . .

Total Exposure Needed

Only a party that will organise real all-national exposures can become the vanguard of the revolutionary forces in our time. The word "all-national" has a very profound meaning. The overwhelming majority of the non-working class exposers (and in order to become the vanguard, we must attract other classes) are sober politicians and cool business men. They know perfectly well how dangerous it is to "complain" even against a minor official, let alone against the "omnipotent" Russian government. And they will come to us with their complaints only when they see that these complaints really have effect, and when they see that we represent a political force. In order to become this political force in the eyes of outsiders, much persistent and stubborn work is required to increase our own consciousness, initiative, and energy. For this, it is not sufficient to stick the label "vanguard" on "rearguard" theory and practice.

But if we have to undertake the organisation of the real all-national exposure of the government, then in what

*way will the class character of our movement be ex-
pressed?—the over-zealous advocates of "close organic
contact with the proletarian struggle" will ask us. The
reply is: In that we Social-Democrats will organise these
public exposures; in that all the questions that are brought
up by the agitation will be explained in the spirit of Social-
Democracy, without any deliberate or unconscious distor-
tions of Marxism; in the fact that the party will carry on
this universal political agitation, uniting into one inseparable whole the pressure upon the government in the name
of the whole people, the revolutionary training of the
proletariat—while preserving its political independence—
the guidance of the economic struggle of the working class,
the utilisation of all its spontaneous conflicts with its
exploiters, which rouse and bring into our camp increasing
numbers of the proletariat!*[19]

Praxis leads to theory, which provides a cognitive base for
further activity. Agitation means more than causing trouble; it
means causing people to think:

*The programme must formulate our basic views, exactly
establish our immediate political tasks, point out those
immediate demands which must mark out the range of
agitational activity and give it unity, broaden and deepen
it, raising agitation from the particular, from fragmentary
agitation for small, separate demands to agitation for the
whole body of Social-Democratic demands. Now, when
Social-Democratic activity has already roused a consider-
ably wide circle of socialist-intellectuals and conscious
workers, it is urgently necessary to consolidate the links
between them with a programme and thus give them all a
firm basis for further, wider activity.*[20]

Ecclesial communities must constantly be in touch with the
people they work with in the larger society. The road to a
better society begins where people, within ecclesial groups and
outside them, get together to discuss how mutual needs can
better be satisfied:

*We, on the other hand, consider that only events in which
the actors are the masses themselves, which are born out of
their sentiments and are not staged "with a special aim" by
one or the other organization, are able to have a really
seriously "agitational" (arousing), and not only arousing,
but (and this is much more important) an educational
effect. We think that a whole hundred assassinations of
tsars will never have such an arousing and educational
effect as will the mere participation by tens of thousands
of the working people in meetings discussing their vital
interests and the connection between politics and those
interests—as participation in a struggle that really raises
ever more new "untouched" strata of the proletariat to a
more conscious life, to a wider revolutionary struggle.*[21]

Alliances have to be made with similar groups. Communication
networks have to be established so that collectives with similar
goals can map out common strategies. Effective political and
social action results from the cooperation of many groups:
"The idea of building communist society exclusively with the
hands of the Communists is childish, absolutely childish. The
Communists are drops in the ocean, drops in the ocean of the
people."[22] And even more to the point:

*One of the biggest and most dangerous mistakes of
Communists (as generally of revolutionaries who have
successfully accomplished the beginning of a great revolution) is the idea that a revolution can be made by
revolutionaries alone. On the contrary, to be successful
every serious revolutionary work requires the understanding and translation into action of the idea that revolutionaries are capable of playing the part only of the
vanguard of the truly virile and advanced class. A vanguard
performs its task as vanguard only when it is able to avoid
becoming divorced from the masses it leads and is able
really to lead the whole mass forward. Without an alliance
with non-Communists in the most varied spheres of
activity there can be no question of any successful
communist constructive work.*[23]

Significant social change takes place usually after years of planning and work. During this time "revolutionary" commitment and an image of the final goal are necessary ingredients of an ultimately successful struggle:

And we solemnly and firmly promise each other that we shall be prepared for every sacrifice, that we shall remain steadfast and resolute in this most difficult fight, the fight against the force of habit, and that we shall work for years and decades without sparing ourselves. We shall work for the eradication of that accursed law "every man for himself and the devil take the hindmost,"? for the eradication of the habit of regarding labour only as a thing of compulsion and justified only when paid in accordance with certain labour standards. We shall work to inculcate in people the habit, to implant in the everyday life of the masses the law "all for one and one for all," "from each according to his ability, to each according to his needs," to introduce, gradually but undeviatingly, communist discipline in communist labour.[24]

Often ecclesial communities will engage in a "caring ministry." Immediate problems of hunger, health, education and specific problems of the youth or aged will sometimes take precedence over more subtle long-range planning. This kind of activity will occupy an important place on the agenda:

I shall quote a few examples from the experience of the work of some of the youth organisations so as to illustrate how this training in communism should proceed. Everybody is talking about abolishing illiteracy. You know that a communist society cannot be built in an illiterate country. It is not enough for the Soviet government to issue an order, or for the Party to issue a particular slogan, or to assign a certain number of the best workers to this task. The young generation itself must take up this work. Communism means that the youth, the young men and women who belong to the Youth League, should say: this is our job; we abolish illiteracy, so that there shall be no illiterates among our young people. We are trying to get the rising generation to devote their activities to this work. You know that we cannot rapidly transform an ignorant and illiterate Russia into a literate country. But if the Youth League sets to work on the job, and if all young people work for the benefit of all, the men and women, it will be entitled to call itself a Young Communist League. It is also a task of the League, not only to acquire knowledge itself, but to help those young people who are unable to extricate themselves by their own efforts from the toils of illiteracy. Being a member of the Youth League means devoting one's labour and efforts to the common causes. That is what a communist education means. Only in the course of such work do young men and women become real Communists. Only if they achieve practical results in this work will they become Communists.

Take, for example, work in the suburban vegetable gardens. Is that not a real job of work? It is one of the tasks of the Young Communist League. People are starving; there is hunger in the factories. To save ourselves from starvation, vegetable gardens must be developed. But farming is being carried on in the old way. Therefore, more class-conscious elements should engage in this work, and then you will find that the number of vegetable gardens will increase, their acreage will grow, and the results will improve. The Young Communist League must take an active part in this work. Every League and League branch should regard this as its duty.

The Young Communist League must be a shock force, helping in every job and displaying initiative and enterprise. The League should be an organisation enabling any worker to see that it consists of people whose teachings he perhaps does not understand, and whose teachings he may not immediately believe, but from whose practical work and activity he can see that they are really people who are showing him the right road.

If the Young Communist League fails to organise its work in this way in all fields, it will mean that it is reverting to the old bourgeois path. We must combine our education with the struggle of the working people against the exploiters, so as to help the former accomplish the tasks set by the teachings of communism.

The members of the League should use every spare hour to improve the vegetable gardens, or to organise the education of young people at some factory, and so on. We want to transform Russia from a poverty-stricken and wretched country into one that is wealthy. The Young Communist League must combine its education, learning, and training with the labour of the workers and peasants, so as not to confine itself to schools or to reading communist books and pamphlets. Only by working side by side with the workers and peasants can one become a genuine Communist. It has to be generally realised that all members of the Youth League are literate people and at the same time are keen at their jobs. When everyone sees that we have ousted the old drill-ground methods from the old schools and have replaced them with conscious discipline, that all young men and women take part in subbotniks [volunteer work groups], and utilise every suburban farm to help the population—people will cease to regard labour in the old way.

It is the task of the Young Communist League to organise assistance everywhere, in village or city block, in such matters as—and I shall take a small example—public hygiene or the distribution of food. How was this done in the old, capitalist society? Everybody worked only for himself and nobody cared a straw for the aged and the sick, or whether housework was the concern only of the women, who, in consequence, were in a condition of oppression and servitude. Whose business is it to combat this? It is the business of the Youth Leagues, which must say: we shall organise detachments of young people who will help to assure public hygiene or distribute food, who will conduct systematic house-to-house inspections, and work in an organised way for the benefit of the whole of society, distributing their forces properly and demonstrating that labour must be organised.

The generation of people who are now at the age of fifty cannot expect to see a communist society. This generation will be gone before then. But the generation of

> *those who are now fifteen will see a communist society,*
> *and will itself build this society. This generation should*
> *know that the entire purpose of their lives is to build a*
> *communist society. In the old society, each family worked*
> *separately and labour was not organised by anybody*
> *except the landowners and capitalists, who oppressed the*
> *masses of the people. We must organise all labour, no*
> *matter how toilsome or messy it may be, in such a way*
> *that every worker and peasant will be able to say: I am*
> *part of the great army of free labour, and shall be able to*
> *build up my life without the landowners and capitalists,*
> *able to help establish a communist system.* [25]

Small gains will be made by ecclesial communities and every
medium should be utilized to illustrate the difference between
life as it is and life as it could be, both in and out of the
collectives. Propaganda is a necessity that can be employed for
the good of the people. When a better way of life is known and
experienced, it is more likely to be embraced and to project
itself as a wider possibility. Many examples can be cited:

> *Take the position of women. In this field, not a single*
> *democratic party in the world, not even in the most*
> *advanced bourgeois republic, has done in decades so much*
> *as a hundredth part of what we did in our very first year in*
> *power. We really razed to the ground the infamous laws*
> *placing women in a position of inequality, restricting*
> *divorce and surrounding it with disgusting formalities,*
> *denying recognition to children born out of wedlock,*
> *enforcing a search for their father, etc., laws numerous*
> *survivals of which, to the shame of the bourgeoisie and of*
> *capitalism, are to be found in all civilised countries. We*
> *have a thousand times the right to be proud of what we*
> *have done in this field. But the more thoroughly we have*
> *cleared the ground of the lumber of the old, bourgeois*
> *laws and institutions, the clearer it is to us that we have*
> *only cleared the ground to build on but are not yet*
> *building.*
>
> *Notwithstanding all the laws emancipating woman,*
> *she continues to be a domestic slave, because petty*

housework crushes, strangles, stultifies, and degrades her, chains her to the kitchen and the nursery, and she wastes her labour on barbarously unproductive, petty, nerve-racking, stultifying, and crushing drudgery. The real emancipation of women, real communism, will begin only where and when an all-out struggle begins (led by the proletariat wielding the state power) against this petty housekeeping, or rather when its wholesale transformation into a large-scale socialist economy begins.

Our Practical Failures

Do we in practice pay sufficient attention to this question, which in theory every Communist considers indisputable? Of course not. Do we take proper care of the shoots of communism which already exist in this sphere? Again the answer is no. Public catering establishments, nurseries, kindergartens—here we have examples of these shoots; here we have the simple, everyday means, involving nothing pompous, grandiloquent, or ceremonial, which can really emancipate women, really lessen and abolish their inequality with men as regards their role in social production and public life. These means are not new; they (like all the material prerequisites for socialism) were created by large-scale capitalism. But under capitalism they remained, first a rarity, and secondly—which is particularly important—either profit-making enterprises, with all the worst features of speculation, profiteering, cheating and fraud, or "acrobatics of bourgeois charity," which the best workers rightly hated and despised.

There is no doubt that the number of these institutions in our country has increased enormously and that they are beginning to change in character. There is no doubt that we have far more organising talent among the working and peasant women than we are aware of, that we have far more people than we know of who can organise practical work, with the cooperation of large numbers of workers and of still larger numbers of consumers, without that abundance of talk, fuss, squabbling, and chatter about plans, systems, etc., with which our big-headed "intellec-

tuals" or half-baked "Communists" are "affected." But we do not nurse these shoots of the new as we should.

Look at the bourgeoisie. How very well they know how to advertise what they need! See how millions of copies of their newspapers extol what the capitalists regard as "model" enterprises, and how "model" bourgeois institutions are made an object of national pride! Our press does not take the trouble, or hardly ever, to describe the best catering establishments or nurseries, in order, by daily insistence, to get some of them turned into models of their kind. It does not give them enough publicity, does not describe in detail the saving in human labour, the conveniences for the consumer, the economy of products, the emancipation of women from domestic slavery, the improvement in sanitary conditions, that can be achieved with exemplary communist work and extended to the whole of society, to all working people.

Exemplary production, exemplary communist sub-botniks, exemplary care and conscientiousness in procuring and distributing every pound of grain, exemplary catering establishments, exemplary cleanliness in such-and-such a worker's house, in such-and-such a block, should all receive ten times more attention and care from our press, as well as from every workers' and peasants' organisation, than they receive now. All these are shoots of communism, and it is our common and primary duty to nurse them. . . . We must give very great thought to the significance of the "communist subbotniks," in order that we may draw all the very important practical lessons that follow from this great beginning.

Not Every Enterprise a Commune

The first and main lesson is that this beginning must be given every assistance. The word "commune" is being handled much too freely. Any kind of enterprise started by Communists or with their participation is very often at once declared to be a "commune," it being not infrequently forgotten that this very honourable title must be won by prolonged and persistent effort, by practical achievement in genuine communist development.

That is why, in my opinion, the decision that has matured in the minds of the majority of the members of the Central Executive Committee to repeal the decree of the Council of People's Commissars, as far as it pertains to the title "consumers' communes," is quite right. Let the title be simpler—and incidentally, the defects and short-comings of the initial stages of the new organisational work will not be blamed on the "communes," but (as in all fairness they should be) on bad Communists. It would be a good thing to eliminate the word "commune" from common use, to prohibit every Tom, Dick, and Harry from grabbing at it, or to allow this title to be borne only by genuine communes, which have really demonstrated in practice (and have proved by the unanimous recognition of the whole of the surrounding population) that they are capable of organising their work in a communist manner. First show that you are capable of working without remuneration in the interests of society, in the interests of all the working people, show that you are capable of "working in a revolutionary way," that you are capable of raising productivity of labour, of organising the work in an exemplary manner, and then hold out your hand for the honourable title "commune"!

In this respect, the "communist subbotniks" are a most valuable exception; for the unskilled labourers and railwaymen of the Moscow-Kazan Railway first demon-strated by deeds that they are capable of working like Communists, and then adopted the title of "communist subbotniks" for their undertaking. We must see to it and make sure that in future anyone who calls his enterprise, institution, or undertaking a commune without having proved this by hard work and practical success in prolonged effort, by exemplary and truly communist organisation, is mercilessly ridiculed and pilloried as a charlatan or a windbag.[26]

In the final analysis, when the odds are figured on the likeli-hood of significant social change, pessimism often afflicts the hardiest revolutionary. The temptation lies before any group to retreat and isolate itself from the developments of the society around it. Discouraging events caused Lenin to form a strictly centralized and disciplined Communist Party. We should not overlook the reasons for this development, nor fail to profit from the values of discipline in our own collectives. Ecclesial communities cannot afford to underestimate the task or fail to calculate the cost:

What the opposition [the German Communist Party] has come to is the repudiation of the party principle and of party discipline. And this is tantamount to completely disarming the proletariat for the benefit of the bourgeoisie. It is tantamount to that petty-bourgeois diffuseness, instability, incapacity for sustained effort, unity and organised action, which if indulged in, must inevitably destroy every proletarian revolutionary movement. . . .

They [small proprietors] can (and must) be remoulded and re-educated only by very prolonged, slow, cautious organisational work. They encircle the proletariat on every side with a petty-bourgeois atmosphere, which permeates and corrupts the proletariat and causes constant relapses among the proletariat into petty-bourgeois spinelessness, disunity, individualism, and alternate moods of exaltation and dejection. . . . The dictatorship of the proletariat is a persistent struggle—sanguinary and bloodless, violent and peaceful, military and economic, educational and administrative—against the forces and traditions of the old society. The force of habit of millions and tens of millions is a most terrible force. Without an iron party tempered in the struggle, without a party enjoying the confidence of all the honest elements in the given class, without a party capable of watching and influencing the mood of the masses, it is impossible to conduct such a struggle successfully. It is a thousand times easier to vanquish the centralised big bourgeoisie than to "vanquish" millions and millions of small proprietors, while they, by their ordinary, everyday, imperceptible, elusive, demoralising activity achieve the very results which the bourgeoisie need and which restore the bourgeoisie. Whoever weakens ever so little the iron discipline of the party of the proletariat (especially during the time of dictatorship) actually aids the bourgeoisie against the proletariat.[27]

MAO TSE-TUNG

The writings of Mao Tse-Tung on the Chinese Communist Party and the experience from which these writings were produced offer another backdrop for the activity of ecclesial communities. First a comparison between Lenin's notion of the Party and Mao's should be made. As we have seen, Lenin prescribed an elitist, separatist organization, especially during the early years of the twentieth century in Russia and then during his tenure after the Revolution when rapid industrialization was called for. In Lenin's mind, organization and discipline were just as necessary for achieving technological competence as they were for winning the Revolution. Therefore, the Party had to play the role of a vanguard who would educate, lead, and prod the masses to greater heights.

Although Mao sometimes takes an orthodox, Leninist line in regard to the Party, he has manifested a far more pragmatic attitude towards it. For him the Party never operates with its own political goals outside of the social, military, or economic goals of society. From 1922 to 1927 the "Party" simply represented the leadership of the Kuomintang, and after that time it was identified with the leadership of the Red Army. At the time of the final revolutionary takeover in 1949, the Party intended to facilitate the economic and social transformation of China. It was to be the link between the state machinery and the masses keeping the state from becoming alienated from the people.[28] Party members were to internalize the universal qualities of the proletariat in order to carry out their task.

An essay Mao wrote in 1949 concerning the role of the Party in relation to outside groups shows a little more than revolutionary fervor. Mao insists that "it is better to have several parties" than one.[29] The Party is only one instrument among others called upon to build a socialist nation. Stuart Schram, the noted English Sinologist, goes so far as to claim: "Taking as he does a fundamentally utilitarian view of the Party, Mao has repeatedly revised his ideas in the course of the past twenty years, in the light of the contribution which, in his judgment, this particular form of organization was actually making to the revolutionary transformation of China."[30] Schram shows that Mao has shifted from an orthodox Leninist position on Party leadership to a more pragmatic model whenever orthodox methods did not work in his country: "organization and leadership as opposed to spontaneous action by the masses, the working classes as opposed to the peasantry, the technical and managerial elite as opposed to rank-and-file ingenuity, material factors as opposed to moral factors."[31]

This utilitarian element carries into Mao's speeches and writings. Therefore the study of selections from Mao's writings can be profitable for members of ecclesial communities. Like Lenin Mao has had to grapple with actual conditions in a society engaged in fundamental social change over a long period. The parallel strand from his writings deals with the role of the Party in the revolutionary process.[32]

The Party, of course, represents the proletariat, speaks for it, and reflects its needs. But the Maoist "proletarian" Party has never been confined to the working class, although it has always been given the universal, transcendental qualities Marx applied to that class. The proletarian spirit in the Party represents a synthesis of the worker-peasant-soldier masses. The cadre is to be utterly selfless and potentially capable of doing all things well. Whoever measured up to these high standards could be admitted to the Party, regardless of his family origins. If a person comes to the fore in the struggle to transform Chinese society, he is automatically Party timber. Mao has placed less and less faith in "objective conditions" causing people to adopt revolutionary awareness. He has preferred to place those who have manifested revolutionary attitudes and commitment in the privileged class and in the Party that represents it. Marx looked to the proletariat's objective immiserization, their growing ability to organize the work process, and their increasing technical knowledge, rather than to moral qualities in the continuing emancipation of society. Lenin and Stalin considered these material factors to be exclusively possibilities of the working class. Not so Mao.

With this background it is easy to understand that the

Mao-inspired Chinese Cultural Revolution leveled its principal attack on bureaucratic elements in the Party, which had, little by little under Liu Shao-ch'i, been setting themselves up as final policy arbiters in the country. The Cultural Revolution reestablished the Maoist principle that "the Communist Party is simply an assemblage of like-minded people, and not an entity with a definite structure, still less an organization having an existence and a significance of its own."[33] Ecclesial communities could hardly find a better description of themselves. They gather in groups of people who share a commitment, identify with the oppressed in society, and work selflessly for the total transformation of the social order. They are not, like the Leninst Party or the Triumphal Church, a privileged caste.

A long selection from Mao's writings best communicates the flavor of his thought. The following excerpt considers the internal quality of a commitment group, its relationships with society at large, and the official face it presents to the world. Perhaps the most constant danger to any ecclesial group is its tendency to become insular, exclusivist, separated from the world, sectarian, and finally dogmatic. A unity of theory and practice, a coherent total understanding of the needs of society, and a sincere attempt to communicate with the world will offset the tendency:

> Why must there be a revolutionary party? There must be a revolutionary party because the world contains enemies who oppress the people and the people want to throw off enemy oppression. . . .
>
> Then is there or is there not any problem still facing our Party? I say there is and, in a certain sense, the problem is quite serious.
>
> What is the problem? It is the fact that there is something in the minds of a number of our comrades which strikes one as not quite right, not quite proper.
>
> In other words, there is still something wrong with our style of study, with our style in the Party's internal and external relations and with our style of writing. By something wrong with the style of study we mean the malady of subjectivism. By something wrong with our style in Party relations we mean the malady of sec-

*tarianism. By something wrong with the style of writing
we mean the malady of stereotyped Party writing. All
these are wrong, they are ill winds, but they are not like
the wintry north winds that sweep across the whole sky.
Subjectivism, sectarianism, and stereotyped Party writing
are no longer the dominant styles, but merely gusts of contrary wind, ill winds from the airraid tunnels. [Laughter]
It is bad, however, that such winds should still be blowing
in the Party. We must seal off the passages which produce
them. Our whole Party should undertake the job of sealing
off these passages, and so should the Party School. These
three ill winds, subjectivism, sectarianism, and stereotyped
Party writing, have their historical origins. Although no
longer dominant in the whole Party, they still constantly
create trouble and assail us. Therefore, it is necessary to
resist them and to study, analyse and elucidate them.*

*Fight subjectivism in order to rectify the style of
study, fight sectarianism in order to rectify the style in
Party relations, and fight Party stereotypes in order to
rectify the style of writing—such is the task before us. . . .*

Subjectivism

*There is only one kind of true theory in this world,
theory that is drawn from objective reality and then
verified by objective reality; nothing else is worthy of the
name of theory in our sense. Stalin said that theory
becomes aimless when it is not connected with practice.
Aimless theory is useless and false and should be discarded.
We should point the finger of scorn at those who are fond
of aimless theorizing. . . .*

*It follows that to combat subjectivism we must
enable people of each of these two types to develop in
whichever direction they are deficient and to merge with
the other type. Those with book-learning must develop in
the direction of practice; it is only in this way that they
will stop being content with books and avoid committing
dogmatist errors. Those experienced in work must take up
the study of theory and must read seriously; only then will*

they be able to systematize and synthesize their experience
and raise it to the level of theory; only then will they not
mistake their partial experience for universal truth and not
commit empiricist errors. Dogmatism and empiricism alike
are subjectivism, each originating from an opposite pole.
Hence there are two kinds of subjectivism in our
Party, dogmatism and empiricism. Each sees only a part
and not the whole. If people are not on guard, do not
realize that such one-sidedness is a shortcoming and do not
strive to overcome it, they are liable to go astray.

However, of the two kinds of subjectivism, dogmatism is still the greater danger in our Party. For
dogmatists can easily assume a Marxist guise to bluff,
capture, and make servitors of cadres of working-class and
peasant origin who cannot easily see through them; they
can also bluff and ensnare the naive youth. If we overcome
dogmatism, cadres with book-learning will readily join
with those who have experience and will take to the study
of practical things, and then many good cadres who
integrate theory with experience, as well as some real
theorists, will emerge. If we overcome dogmatism, the
comrades with practical experience will have good teachers
to help them raise their experience to the level of theory
and so avoid empiricist errors. . . .

Remnants of Sectarianism

Let me now speak about the question of sectarianism.

Having been steeled for twenty years, our Party is no
longer dominated by sectarianism. Remnants of sectarianism, however, are still found both in the Party's
internal relations and in its external relations. Sectarian
tendencies in internal relations lead to exclusiveness
towards comrades inside the Party and hinder inner-Party
unity and solidarity, while sectarian tendencies in external
relations lead to exclusiveness towards people outside the
Party and hinder the Party in its task of uniting the whole
people. Only by uprooting this evil in both its aspects can
the Party advance unimpeded in its great task of achieving

unity among all Party comrades and among all the People of our country.

What are the remnants of inner-Party sectarianism? They are mainly as follows:

First, the assertion of "independence." Some comrades see only the interests of the part and not the whole; they always put undue stress on that part of the work for which they themselves are responsible and always wish to subordinate the interests of the whole to the interests of their own part....

Those who assert this kind of "independence" are usually wedded to the doctrine of "me first" and are generally wrong on the question of the relationship between the individual and the Party. Although in words they profess respect for the Party, in practice they put themselves first and the Party second. What are these people after? They are after fame and position and want to be in the limelight. Whenever they are put in charge of a branch of work, they assert their "independence." With this aim, they draw some people in, push others out, and resort to boasting, flattery, and touting among the comrades, thus importing the vulgar style of the bourgeois political parties into the Communist Party....

We must oppose the tendency towards selfish departmentalism by which the interests of one's own unit are looked after to the exclusion of those of others. Whoever is indifferent to the difficulties of others, refuses to transfer cadres to other units on request, or releases only the inferior ones, "using the neighbour's field as an outlet for his overflow," and does not give the slightest consideration to other departments, localities or people—such a person is a selfish departmentalist who has entirely lost the spirit of communism. Lack of consideration for the whole and complete indifference to other departments, localities, and people are characteristics of a selfish departmentalist. We must intensify our efforts to educate such persons and to make them understand that selfish departmentalism is a sectarian tendency which will become very dangerous, if allowed to develop....

Stereotyped Party Writing

Let us now analyse stereotyped Party writing and see where its evils lie. Using poison as an antidote to poison, we shall imitate the form of the stereotyped eight-section essay and set forth the following "eight legs," which might be called the eight major indictments.

The first indictment against stereotyped Party writing is that it fills endless pages with empty verbiage. Some of our comrades love to write long articles with no substance, very much like the "footbindings of a slattern, long as well as smelly." Why must they write such long and empty articles? There can be only one explanation: they are determined the masses shall not read them. Because the articles are long and empty, the masses shake their heads at the very sight of them. How can they be expected to read them? Such writings are good for nothing except to bluff the naive among whom they spread bad influences and foster bad habits. . . .

The second indictment against stereotyped Party writing is that it strikes a pose in order to intimidate people. . . .

The third indictment against stereotyped Party writing is that it shoots at random, without considering the audience. . . .

The saying "to play the lute to a cow" implies a gibe at the audience. If we substitute the idea of respect for the audience, the gibe is turned against the player. Why should he strum away without considering his audience? What is worse, he is producing a Party stereotype as raucous as a crow, and yet he insists on cawing at the masses. When shooting an arrow, one must aim at the target; when playing the lute, one must consider the listener; how, then, can one write articles or make speeches without taking the reader or audience into account? Suppose we want to make friends with a person, whoever he may be; can we become bosom friends if we do not understand each other's hearts, do not know each other's thought? It simply will not do for our propaganda workers to rattle on without investigating, studying, and analysing their audience.

The fourth indictment against stereotyped Party writing is its drab language that reminds one of a piehsan [literally, a shrunken little wretch; it is an all-inclusive term referring to tramps, loafers, beggers, thieves, vagabonds, etc.]. Like our stereotyped Party writing, the creatures known in Shanghai as "little piehsan" are wizened and ugly. If an article or speech merely rings the changes on a few terms in a classroom tone without a shred of vigour or spirit, is it not rather like a piehsan, drab of speech and repulsive in appearance? If someone ehters primary school at seven, goes to middle school in his teens, graduates from college in his twenties and never has contact with the masses of the people, he is not to blame if his language is poor and monotonous. But we are revolutionaries working for the masses, and if we do not learn the language of the masses, we cannot work well. At present many of our comrades doing propaganda work make no study of language. Their propaganda is very dull, and few people care to read their articles or listen to their talk. . . .

The fifth indictment against stereotyped Party writing is that it arranges items under a complicated set of headings, as if starting a Chinese pharmacy. Go and take a look at any Chinese pharmacy, and you will see cabinets with numerous drawers, each bearing the name of a drug—tonical, foxglove, rhubarb, saltpetre . . . indeed, everything that should be there. This method has been picked up by our comrades. In their articles and speeches, their books and reports, they use first the big Chinese numerals, second the small Chinese numerals, third the characters for the ten celestial stems, fourth the characters for the twelve earthly branches, and then capital A, B, C, D, and then small a, b, c, d, followed by the Arabic numerals, and what not! . . .

The sixth indictment against stereotyped Party writing is that it is irresponsible and harms people wherever it appears. All the offences mentioned above are due partly to immaturity and partly to an insufficient sense of responsibility. Let us take washing the face to illustrate the point. We all wash our faces every day, many of us more than once, and inspect ourselves in the mirror afterwards

by way of "investigation and study" [loud laughter], for
fear that something may not be quite right. What a great
sense of responsibility! If we wrote articles and made
speeches with the same sense of responsibility, we would
not be doing badly. Do not present what is not presen-
table. Always bear in mind that it may influence the
thoughts and actions of others. . . .

The seventh indictment against stereotyped Party
writing is that it poisons the whole Party and jeopardizes
the revolution. The eighth indictment is that its spread
would wreck the country and ruin the people. These two
indictments are self-evident and require no elaboration. In
other words, if stereotyped Party writing is not trans-
formed but is allowed to develop unchecked, the conse-
quences will be very serious indeed. The poison of
subjectivism and sectarianism is hidden in stereotyped
Party writing, and if this poison spreads it will endanger
both the Party and the country. [34]

The "eight-legs" referred to by Mao in this selection is an
allusion to classical Chinese literature which Mao caricatures
because of its elitism—e.g., close attention to fancy calligraphy
rather than content. Party writing must be related to the people
in a unity of theory and practice. The unity of theory and
practice is a fundamental Marxian motto—fundamental not only
because the principle assumes contact between cadre and people
but also because it assumes a mutuality and equality of
interrelationships. A Maoist "proletarian" style might prove to
be a worthwhile model even for ecclesial communities:

To teach the masses, newspaper workers should first of all
learn from the masses. You comrades are all intellectuals.
Intellectuals are often ignorant and often have little or no
experience in practical matters. You can't quite under-
stand the pamphlet "How to Differentiate the Classes in
the Rural Areas" issued in 1933; on this point, the
peasants are more than a match for you, for they
understand it fully as soon as they are told about it. Over
180 peasants in two districts of Kuohsien County met for
five days and settled many problems concerning the

distribution of land. If your editorial department were to discuss those problems, I am afraid you would discuss them for two weeks without settling them. The reason is quite simple; you do not understand those problems. To change from lack of understanding to understanding, one must do things and see things; that is learning. Comrades working on the newspapers should go out by turns to take part in mass work, in land-reform work for a time; that is very necessary. When not going out to participate in mass work, you should hear a great deal and read a great deal · about the mass movements and devote time and effort to the study of such material. Our slogan in training troops is, "Officers teach soldiers, soldiers teach officers, and soldiers teach each other." The fighters have a lot of practical combat experience. The officers should learn from the fighters, and when they have made other people's experience their own, they will become more capable. Comrades working on the newspapers, too, should constantly study the material coming from below, gradually enrich their practical knowledge and become experienced. Only thus will you be able to do your work well, will you be able to shoulder your task of educating the masses.[35]

Ecclesial communities have a commitment to the truth, truth which is often elusive but is never discovered somewhere outside the "interests of the people." A continual pursuit of the truth always entails mistakes, but these in turn act as catalysts in a renewed search for what is good for the people. Criticism, self-criticism, struggle, conflict, and tension are positive values for Mao, before and after the Cultural Revolution; they can also act as values for ecclesial communities:

Another hallmark distinguishing our Party from all other political parties is that we have very close ties with the broadest masses of the people. Our point of departure is to serve the people whole-heartedly and never for a moment divorce ourselves from the masses, to proceed in all cases from the interests of the people and not from one's self-interest or from the interests of a small group, and to identify our responsibility to the people with our responsi-

*bility to the leading organs of the Party. Communists must
be ready at all times to stand up for the truth, because
truth is in the interests of the people; Communists must be
ready at all times to correct their mistakes. because
mistakes are against the interests of the people. Twenty-
four years of experience tell us that the right task, policy
and style of work invariably conform with the demands of
the masses at a given time and place and invariably
strengthen our ties with the masses, and the wrong task,
policy and style of work invariably disagree with the
demands of the masses at a given time and place and
invariably alienate us from the masses. The reason why
such evils as dogmatism, empiricism, commandism, tailism,
sectarianism, bureaucracy and an arrogant attitude in work
are definitely harmful and intolerable, and why anyone
suffering from these maladies must overcome them, is that
they alienate us from the masses. Our congress should call
upon the whole Party to be vigilant and to see that no
comrade at any post is divorced from the masses. It should
teach every comrade to love the people and listen
attentively to the voice of the masses; to identify himself
with the masses wherever he goes and, instead of standing
above them, to immerse himself among them; and,
according to their present level, to awaken them or raise
their political consciousness and help them gradually to
organize themselves voluntarily and to set going all
essential struggles permitted by the internal and external
circumstances of the given time and place. Commandism is
wrong in any type of work, because in overstepping the
level of political consciousness of the masses and violating
the principle of voluntary mass action, it reflects the
disease of impetuoisty. Our comrades must not assume
that everything they themselves understand is understood
by the masses. . . .*

*In a word, every comrade must be brought to
understand that the supreme test of the words and deeds
of a Communist is whether they conform with the highest
interests and enjoy the support of the overwhelming
majority of the people. Every comrade must be helped to
understand that as long as we rely on the people, believe*

firmly in the inexhaustible creative power of the masses and hence trust and identify ourselves with them, we can surmount any difficulty, and no enemy can crush us while we can crush any enemy.

Conscientious practice of self-criticism is still another hallmark distinguishing our Party from all other political parties. As we say, dust will accumulate if a room is not cleaned regularly, our faces will get dirty if they are not washed regularly. Our comrades' minds and our Party's work may also collect dust, and also need sweeping and washing. The proverb "Running water is never stale and a door-hinge is never wormeaten" means that constant motion prevents the inroads of germs and other organisms. To check up regularly on our work and in the process develop a democratic style of work, to fear neither criticism nor self-criticism, and to apply such good popular Chinese maxims as "Say all you know and say it without reserve," "Blame not the speaker but be warned by his words" and "Correct mistakes if you have committed them and guard against them if you have not"—this is the only effective way to prevent all kinds of political dust and germs from contaminating the minds of our comrades and the body of our Party. The reason for the great effectiveness of the rectification movement, the purpose of which was "to learn from past mistakes to avoid future ones and to cure the sickness to save the patient," was that the criticism and self-criticism we carried out were honest and conscientious, and not perfunctory and distorted. As we Chinese Communists, who base all our actions on the highest interests of the broadest masses of the Chinese people and who are fully convinced of the justice of our cause, never balk at any personal sacrifice and are ready at all times to give our lives for the cause, can we be reluctant to discard any idea, viewpoint, opinion or method which is not suited to the needs of the people? Can we be willing to allow political dust and germs to dirty our clean faces or eat into our healthy organisms? Countless revolutionary martyrs have laid down their lives in the interests of the people, and our hearts are filled with pain as we the living think of them—can there be any personal interest, then, that we would not sacrifice or any error that we would not discard?[36]

The theme of "unity-criticism-unity" is frequent in the works of Mao. People who work together closely in a collective gradually develop a mutual trust and are not threatened by criticism. They start and finish each discussion with unity. Interchange in an ecclesial community becomes liberating because it takes place in a noncompetitive, nonexploitive environment. Freedom flourishes in a creative tension with disciplined unity:

In advocating freedom with leadership and democracy under centralized guidance, we in no way mean that coercive measures should be taken to settle ideological questions or questions involving the distinction between right and wrong among the people. All attempts to use administrative orders or coercive measures to settle ideological questions or questions of right and wrong are not only ineffective but harmful. We cannot abolish religion by administrative decree or force people not to believe in it. We cannot compel people to give up idealism, any more than we can force them to believe in Marxism. The only way to settle questions of an ideological nature or controversial issues among the people is by the democratic method, the method of discussion, of criticism, of persuasion and education, and not by the method of coercion or repression. . . .

This democratic method of resolving contradictions among the people was epitomized in 1942 in the formula "unity, criticism, unity." To elaborate, it means starting from the desire for unity, resolving contradictions through criticism or struggle and arriving at a new unity on a new basis. In our experience this is the correct method of resolving contradictions among the people. In 1942 we used to resolve contradictions inside the Communist Party, namely, the contradictions between the dogmatists and the great majority of the membership, and between dogmatism and Marxism. The "Left" dogmatists had resorted to the method of "ruthless struggle and merciless blows" in inner-Party struggle. This method was incorrect. In criticizing "Left" dogmatism, we discarded this old method and adopted a new one, that is, one of starting from the desire for unity, distinguishing between right and wrong through criticism or struggle and arriving at a new unity on a new basis. This was the method used in the rectification movement of 1942. Thus within a few years, by the time the Chinese Communist Party held its Seventh National Congress in 1945, unity was achieved throughout the Party, and as a consequence the great victory of the people's revolution was won. The essential thing is to start from the desire for unity. For without this desire for unity, the struggle is certain to get out of hand. Wouldn't this be the same as "ruthless struggle and merciless blows"? And what Party unity would there be left? It was this very experience that led us to the formula: "unity, criticism, unity." Or, in other words, "learn from past mistakes to avoid future ones and cure the sickness to save the patient."[37]

Liberation is a long process. For Mao liberation in a geographical, spatial sense is only the beginning of liberation in a temporal, sociological, psychological sense. Simplicity and continual learning are the Maoist key to a liberated zone in any society:

The Chinese revolution is great, but the road after the revolution will be longer, the work greater and more arduous. This must be made clear now in the Party. The comrades must be helped to remain modest, prudent and free from arrogance and rashness in their style of work. The comrades must be helped to preserve the style of plain living and hard struggle. We have the Marxist-Leninist weapon of criticism and self-criticism. We can get rid of a bad style and keep the good. We can learn what we did not know. We are not only good at destroying the old world, we are also good at building the new. Not only can the Chinese people live without begging alms from the imperialists, they will live a better life than that in the imperialist countries.[38]

In contrast to the institutional organizations of an alienated social order, a commitment community should energize the personalities of its members. Unfortunately it takes little time for the problems of the society at large to infect the environment of ecclesial groups. Continual effort, therefore, must be made to dispose of mental and emotional "baggage":

In order to win new victories we must call on our Party cadres to get rid of the baggage and start up the machinery. "To get rid of the baggage" means to free our minds of many encumbrances. Many things may become baggage, may become encumbrances, if we cling to them blindly and uncritically. Let us take some illustrations. Having made mistakes, you may feel that, come what may, you are saddled with them and so become dispirited; if you have not made mistakes, you feel that you are free from error and so become conceited. Lack of achievement in work may breed pessimism and depression, while achievement may breed pride and arrogance. A comrade with a short record of struggle may shirk responsibility on this account, while a veteran may become opinionated because of his long record of struggle. Worker and peasant comrades, because of pride in their class origin, may look down upon intellectuals, while intellectuals, because they have a certain amount of knowledge, may look down upon worker and peasant comrades. Any specialized skill may be capitalized on and so may lead to arrogance and contempt of others. Even one's age may become ground for conceit. The young, because they are bright and capable, may look down upon the old; and the old, because they are rich in experience, may look down upon the young. All such things become encumbrances or baggage if there is no critical awareness. An important reason why some comrades are very lofty, isolating themselves from the masses and making repeated mistakes, is that they carry such baggage. Thus, a prerequisite for maintaining close links with the masses and making fewer mistakes is to examine one's baggage, to get rid of it and so emancipate the mind.

"To start up the machinery" means to make good use of the organ of thought. Although some people carry no

*baggage and have the virtue of close contact with the
masses, they fail to accomplish anything because they do
not know how to think searchingly or are unwilling to use
their brains to think much and think hard. Others refuse to
use their brains because they are carrying baggage which
cramps their intellect.* [39]

Freedom in a group should combine with a discipline which
gives it effectiveness and strength. In 1937 the Chinese
Communists were ensconced in Yenan. The Japanese were
launching a full-scale invasion of China, and Mao was concentra-
ting on building the kind of disciplined Party which could lead
the resistance. Discipline, however, even at this critical stage,
did not mean acquiescence to authority for the sake of
authority. Both during this era and thirty years later during the
Cultural Revolution, Mao placed a premium on speaking out
and tried to make it an essential part of the creative
organization. It is amazing how applicable the following
selection is in postindustrial, twentieth-century society:

Liberalism manifests itself in various ways.

*To let things slide for the sake of peace and
friendship when a person has clearly gone wrong, and
refrain·from principled argument because he is an old
acquaintance, a fellow townsman, a schoolmate, a close
friend, a loved one, an old colleague or old subordinate. Or
to touch on the matter lightly instead of going into it
thoroughly, so as to keep on good terms. The result is that
both the organization and the individual are harmed. This
is one type of liberalism.*

*To indulge in irresponsible criticism in private instead
of actively putting forward one's suggestions to the
organization. To say nothing to people to their faces but
to gossip behind their backs, or to say nothing at a meeting
but to gossip afterwards. To show no regard at all for the
principles of collective life but to follow one's own
inclination. This is a second type.*

*To let things drift if they do not affect one
personally; to say as little as possible while knowing*

perfectly well what is wrong, to be worldly wise and play safe and seek only to avoid blame. This is a third type.

Not to obey orders but to give pride of place to one's own opinions. To demand special consideration from the organization but to reject its discipline. This is a fourth type.

To indulge in personal attacks, pick quarrels, vent personal spite or seek revenge instead of entering into an argument and struggling against incorrect views for the sake of unity or progress or getting the work done properly. This is a fifth type.

To hear incorrect views without rebutting them and even to hear counter-revolutionary remarks without reporting them, but instead to take them calmly as if nothing had happened. This is a sixth type.

To be among the masses and fail to conduct propaganda and agitation or speak at meetings or conduct investigations and inquiries among them, and instead to be indifferent to them and show no concern for their well-being, forgetting that one is a Communist and behaving as if one were an ordinary non-Communist. This is a seventh type.

To see someone harming the interests of the masses and yet not feel indignant, or dissuade or stop him or reason with him, but to allow him to continue. This is an eighth type.

To work half-heartedly without a definite plan or direction; to work perfunctorily and muddle along—"So long as one remains a monk, one goes on tolling the bell." This is a ninth type.

To regard oneself as having rendered great service to the revolution, to pride oneself on being a veteran, to disdain minor assignments while being quite unequal to major tasks, to be slipshod in work and slack in study. This is a tenth type.

To be aware of one's own mistakes and yet make no attempt to correct them, taking a liberal attitude towards oneself. This is an eleventh type.

We could name more. But these eleven are the principal types.

They are all manifestations of liberalism.
Liberalism is extremely harmful in a revolutionary
collective. It is a corrosive which eats away unity,
undermines cohesion, causes apathy and creates dissension.
It robs the revolutionary ranks of compact organization
and strict discipline, prevents policies from being carried
through and alienates the Party organizations from the
masses which the Party leads. It is an extremely bad
tendency.
     Liberalism stems from petty-bourgeois selfishness; it
places personal interests first and the interests of the
revolution second, and this gives rise to ideological,
political and organizational liberalism.[40]

The agenda of ecclesial communities is necessarily broad. Some
issues, however, are basic to the immediate survival of oppressed
groups. Until the larger society catches up with the needs of all
the people, these concerns must be met by commitment groups:

I earnestly suggest to this congress that we pay close
attention to the well-being of the masses, from the
problems of land and labour to those of fuel, rice, cooking
oil and salt. The women want to learn ploughing and
harrowing. Whom can we get to teach them? The children
want to go to school. Have we set up primary schools? The
wooden bridge over there is too narrow and people may
fall off. Should we not repair it? Many people suffer from
boils and other ailments. What are we going to do about it?
All such problems concerning the well-being of the masses
should be placed on our agenda. We should discuss them,
adopt and carry out decisions and check up on the results.
We should help the masses to realize that we represent
their interests, that our lives are intimately bound up with
theirs. [41]

Ecclesial communities obviously assume a position of leadership
in society, but must constantly guard against elitism. How a
group exercises leadership becomes a crucial issue when
bureaucratism sets in; e.g., during China's Cultural Revolution.
The word "revolutionary" takes on frightful connotations when

it is applied to groups that set themselves above the rest of society and decide that they are the vanguard that will bring on the "revolution":

1. There are two methods which we Communists must employ in whatever work we do. One is to combine the general with the particular; the other is to combine the leadership with the masses.
2. In any task, if no general and widespread call is issued, the broad masses cannot be mobilized for action. But if persons in leading positions confine themselves to a general call—if they do not personally, in some of the organizations, go deeply and concretely into the work called for, make a break-through at some single point, gain experience and use this experience for guiding other units—then they will have no way of testing the correctness or of enriching the content of their general call, and there is the danger that nothing may come of it. . . .
3. However active the leading group may be, its activity will amount to fruitless effort by a handful of people unless combined with the activity of the masses. On the other hand, if the masses alone are active without a strong leading group to organize their activity properly, such activity cannot be sustained for long, or carried forward in the right direction, or raised to a high level. The masses in any given place are generally composed of three parts, the relatively active, the intermediate and the relatively backward. The leaders must therefore be skilled in uniting the small number of active elements around the leadership and must rely on them to raise the level of the intermediate elements and to win over the backward elements. A leading group that is genuinely united and is linked with the masses can gradually be formed only in the process of a great struggle, and not in isolation from it.
4. In all the practical work of our Party, all correct leadership is necessarily "from the masses, to the masses." This means: take the ideas of the masses (scattered and unsystematic ideas) and concentrate them (through study turn them into concentrated and systematic ideas), then go to the masses and propagate and explain these ideas until

*the masses embrace them as their own, hold fast to them
and translate them into action, and test the correctness of
these ideas in such action. Then once again concentrate
ideas from the masses and once again go to the masses so
that the ideas are persevered in and carried through. . . .*

5. *The concept of a correct relationship between the
leading group and the masses in an organization or in a
struggle, the concept that correct ideas on the part of the
leadership can only be "from the masses, to the masses,"
and the concept that the general call must be combined
with particular guidance when the leadership's ideas are
being put into practice—these concepts must be propa-
gated everywhere during the present rectification movement in order to correct the mistaken viewpoints among
our cadres on these questions. Many comrades do not see
the importance of, or are not good at, drawing together
the activists to form a nucleus of leadership, and they do
not see the importance of, or are not good at, linking their
nucleus of leadership closely with the masses, and so their
leadership becomes bureaucratic and divorced from the
masses. Many comrades do not see the importance of, or
are not good at, summing up the experience of mass
struggles, but fancying themselves clever, are fond of
voicing their subjectivist ideas, and so their ideas become
empty and impractical. Many comrades rest content with
making a general call with regard to a task and do not see
the importance of, or are not good at, following it up
immediately with particular and concrete guidance, and so
their call remains on their lips, or on paper or in the
conference room, and their leadership becomes bureaucratic. . . .*

6. *Take the ideas of the masses and concentrate
them, then go to the masses, persevere in the ideas and
carry them through, so as to form correct ideas of
leadership—such is the basic method of leadership.*

7. *In relaying to subordinate units any task (whether
it concerns revolutionary war, production or education,
the rectification movement, check-up on work or the
examination of cadres' histories; propaganda work, organizational work or anti-espionage, or other work), a higher*

*organization and its departments should in all cases go
through the leader of the lower organization concerned so
that he may assume responsibility; in this way both
division of labour and unified centralized leadership are
achieved. . . .*
   *8. In any given place, there cannot be a number of
central tasks at the same time. At any one time there can
be only one central task, supplemented by other tasks of a
second or third order of importance. . . .*
   *9. Details concerning methods of leadership are not
dealt with here; it is hoped that comrades in all localities
will themselves do some hard thinking and give full play to
their own creativeness on the basis of the principles here
set forth. The harder the struggle, the greater the need for
Communists to link their leadership closely with the
demands of the vast masses, and to combine the general
calls closely with particular guidance, so as to smash the
subjectivist and bureaucratic methods of leadership completely.*[42]

Note particularly the fourth point that Mao discusses—"from
the masses, to the masses." It represents the method of political
theology; political theologians engage in societal praxis, through
which they derive theoretical analysis, then return to the social
situation with their theory, which is tested, etc.
   A common "revolutionary" commitment characterizes
ecclesial communities. When the commitment exists to the
degree that it completely shapes a person's existence, its impact
moves all the members of his group. Dr. Norman Bethune, who
went to China during its war with Japan, as the head of a medical team to help the Chinese, was a man of such commitment.
Mao praises Bethune mainly for his desire to use his expertise
to serve people rather than for his own prestige. He holds
Bethune up as a model of dedication for the people:

*Comrade Bethune's spirit, his utter devotion to others
without any thought of self, was shown in his boundless
sense of responsibility in his work and his boundless
warmheartedness towards all comrades and the people.
Every Communist must learn from him. There are not a*

*few people who are irresponsible in their work, preferring
the light to the heavy, shoving the heavy loads on to others
and choosing the easy ones for themselves. At every turn
they think of themselves before others. When they make
some small contribution, they swell with pride and brag
about it for fear that others will not know. They feel no
warmth towards comrades and the people are cold,
indifferent and apathetic. In fact such people are not
Communists, or at least cannot be counted as true
Communists. No one who returned from the front failed
to express admiration for Bethune whenever his name was
mentioned, and none remained unmoved by his spirit. In
the Shansi-Chahar-Hopei border area, no soldier or civilian
was unmoved who had been treated by Dr. Bethune or had
seen how he worked. Every Communist must learn this
true communist spirit from Comrade Bethune. . . .*

*Comrade Bethune and I met only once. Afterwards
he wrote me many letters. But I was busy, and I wrote him
only one letter and do not even know if he ever received it.
I am deeply grieved over his death. Now we are all
commemorating him, which shows how profoundly his
spirit inspires everyone. We must all learn the spirit of
absolute selflessness from him. With this spirit everyone
can be very useful to the people. A man's ability may be
great or small, but if he has this spirit, he is already
noble-minded and pure, a man of moral integrity and
above vulgar interests, a man who is of value to the
people.*[43]

During most of Christian history, believers have satisfied their
need for a "sacred" experience within the confines of the
organized churches. But now the meaning of "sacred" is
beginning to include a sense of a communal secular mission to
create a better world, and "crypto-churches" are growing from
this consciousness, sometimes with no reference to the traditional churches at all. These new churches, traditional or not,
can afford to absorb the Marxian and Communist experience of

such a revolutionary endeavor. Of course, no complete set of tactics could ever be laid out for particular ecclesial communities in their specific circumstances. History moves too quickly for any theoretician, especially one who is applying the theory of another culture, to be exactly relevent to his own working context. Tentative models and insights can be savored or employed, however, as we have tried to indicate from the Marxian corpus of writings. The Marxian goal of an egalitarian, self-determining society and the Marxian style of constant empirical discovery through struggle are links to the work of ecclesial communities despite differences in cultural or economic development.

Permanent revolution is another conceptual element useful in both the Marxian and Christian camps. As Niebuhr has shown, *metanoia*, continuous conversion, is an essential quality of the Christian faith. Our notions of God, the church, doctrines, our most cherished beliefs and modes of morality must be continuously de-absolutized, reformed, and reformulated so that they do not become lifeless idols, likewise the strategies and tactics of ecclesial communities. Collective social action must know metanoia, struggle, the tentative nature of its process.

Marx laid the foundations of the theory of permanent revolution in his philosophy of praxis. He placed no absolute value on any period or era of history. He simply indicated that men made their own world and that every generation stood on the shoulders of former periods. He further noted and described various forces struggling with one another in his own time. Both before and after their revolutions, Lenin and Mao (and Castro too, but his theory is sketchy and limited to a postrevolutionary, consciousness-raising strategy) have placed major stress on the praxis of their constituents. They also have displayed a remarkable variety of strategies and tactics in the pursuit of their goals, often changing directions at unlikely moments because of the influence of historical events or movements. Although the leaders of socialist states have not tolerated what they have considered counter-revolutionary activity and have absolutized many relative Marxian dogmas, they have at the same time exhibited much tactical flexibility. This latter characteristic provides an opening for Christian groups with similar onlooks.

Ecclesial groups here described are "Christian" only in the sense that their members are open to Jesus and his message. Most of the participants will be influenced by the biblical and Christian tradition and will have experienced the community of organized Christian churches. It is probable that most will have become engaged in ecclesial groups because of the impact of the symbols, beliefs, myths, and experiences of their earlier membership in churches. Consequently the life style of the groups will be influenced by the Christian heritage.

In this chapter we have been concerned chiefly with establishing political activity as a legitimate concern for ecclesial communities. If ecclesial communities are to give insight to the organized churches, their contribution will probably be made primarily in the realm of political commitment. But some traditional theological concepts—God, evil, celebration—are also important for ecclesial communities. They form an indispensable dimension of the work of political theology.

Notes

1. Although the question of the historical Jesus goes back to Reimarus and Schweitzer, interest in the problem of the Jesus of history was intensified by Rudolf Bultmann a generation ago and since that time few New Testament scholars have been able to avoid the controversy. See R. H. Fuller, *The New Treatment in Current Study* (New York: Scribners, 1962) and J. M. Robinson, *A New Quest of the Historical Jesus* (London: S.C.M., 1959). Jack T. Sanders points up the problem of "modernizing" Jesus in "The Question of the Relevance of Jesus for Ethics Today," *Journal of the American Academy of Religion*, 38, (June 1970), 131-146.

2. Hans Küng, *The Church* (New York: Sheed and Ward, 1967), p. 72.

3. Gregory Baum, *The Credibility of the Church Today* (New York: Herder and Herder, 1968), p. 131. Baum's statement

is a summary of the opinion of Ernst Käsemann, who presented it at the 1963 Montreal Faith and Order Conference.

4. *Rediscovering the Teaching of Jesus* (New York: Harper and Row, 1967), p. 104.
5. *The Church*, pp. 79-88.
6. *Ibid.*, p. 82.
7. New York, Macmillan, 1946, pp. ix, 118, 172 ff., 182.
8. The Hidden Church and the Churches in Sight," *Religion in Life*, 15 (1946) 106-117.
9. Norman Gottwald, *The Church Unbound* (Philadelphia: J. B. Lippincott, 1967), p. 154.
10. *Ibid.*, p. 160-161.
11. *Selected Works*, Vol. I, p. 382.
12. *Anti-Duhring* (Moscow: Foreign Languages, 1954), pp. 226-227.
13. *Cf.* Monty Johnstone, "Marx and Engels and the Concept of the Party," *The Socialist Register, 1967* (New York: Monthly Review Press), pp. 131 ff.
14. Engels' Preface to the German edition of the *Communist Manifesto*, 1890, *Selected Works*, Vol. I, p. 30.
15. Johnstone, *art. cit.*, p. 131.
16. *Selected Works*, Vol. I, pp. 386-389.
17. This argument is advanced by Marcel Liebman in *Le Leninisme et la Revolucion* (Paris: Editions du Seuil, 1970) and condensed in *Monthly Review* 21 (April 1970) 57-75.
18. V. I. Lenin, "The Reorganization of the Party," quoted in Liebman, *Monthly Review*, p. 60.
19. New York, N.W. International, 1969, pp. 57-59, 67-69, 71-72, 76-80, 85-86.
20. V. I. Lenin, "Draft Programme for our Party," from *The Revolutionary Proletarian Party of a New Type* (Peking: Foreign Languages, 1960), p. 7.
21. V. I. Lenin, "New Events and Old Questions," *The Revolutionary Proletarian Party*, p. 41.
22. V. I. Lenin, "Political Report of the Central Committee of the Russian Communist Party," *The Revolutionary Proletarian Party*, p. 45.
23. V. I. Lenin, "On the Significance of Militant Materialism," *ibid.*

24. V. I. Lenin, "The First Subbotnik," *The Revolutionary Proletarian Party*, p. 53.
25. V. I. Lenin, "The Task of the Youth Leagues," *Collected Works*, Vol. 31 (Moscow: Progress, 1966), pp. 296-299.
26. V. I. Lenin, "A Great Beginning," *Collected Works*, Vol. 29 (Moscow: Progress, 1965), pp. 427-428, 430-432.
27. V. I. Lenin, *"Left-Wing Communism," An Infantile Disorder* (New York: International, 1940), pp. 28-29.
28. *Cf.* Franz Schurmann, *Ideology and Organization in Communist China* (Berkeley: University of California, 1966), pp. 11-14.
29. "On the Ten Great Relationships," in *Mao*, a collection of documents edited by Jerome Ch'en (Englewood Cliffs: Prentice-Hall, 1969), p. 77.
30. Stuart Schram, "The Party in Chinese Communist Ideology," *The China Quarterly*, No. 38 (April-June 1969), p. 11.
31. *Ibid.*
32. *Cf.* Schurmann, pp. 103-128 and Schram, pp. 15 ff.
33. Schram, p. 20.
34. "Rectify the Party's Style of Work" and "Oppose Stereotyped Party Writing," *Selected Readings from the Works of Mao Tse-Tung* (Peking: Foreign Languages, 1967), pp. 171-172, 176-180, 182, 191-198.
35. "A Talk to the Editorial Staff of the Shansi-Suiyuan Daily," *Selected Readings*, p. 290.
36. "Let the Whole Party Unite and Fight to Accomplish Its Tasks!," *Selected Readings*, pp. 255-257.
37. "On the Correct Handling of Contradictions Among the People," *Selected Readings*, pp. 355-356.
38. "Preserve the Style of Plain Living and Hard Struggle," *Selected Readings*, pp. 295-296.
39. "Get Rid of the Baggage and Start Up the Machinery," *Selected Readings*, pp. 249-250.
40. "Combat Liberalism," *Selected Readings*, pp. 109-110.
41. "Be Concerned with the Well-Being of the Masses," *Selected Readings*, p. 44.
42. "Some Questions Concerning Methods of Leadership," *Selected Readings*, pp. 234-238.
43. "In Memory of Norman Bethune," *Selected Readings*, pp. 146-147.

CHAPTER FIVE

The Christian Dimension

At the end of this examination of the possible uses of an analytical and tactical Marxian perspective for political theology, it is necessary to look at the specifically Christian theological contribution to political theology. What value is there in a political *theology*, even if one admits a similarity between Marxian and Christian onlooks? What does Christianity add to the empirical dimension? Why not leave religion to the private sphere and engage in political activity without theological baggage?

A preliminary point has to be underscored once again: men do not act, much less act publicly and politically, outside of the influence of belief systems and symbols. The foundation of political activity is a "fiduciary framework," theistic or not; and it has been my contention that many Christian teachings and symbols inspire political activity in principle and can lead to a Marxian view of social change in particular. Of course, the Christian tradition is rich symbolically and can provoke a variety of interpretations and activities. Even attempts to uncover the intent and ministry of Jesus must be regarded as tentative because of conflicting evidence and varied early traditions. For example, it is quite possible to hold, as Schweitzer did,[1] that Jesus did not preach an encompassing ethical doctrine (and even less a theory of social change), but simply exhorted his followers to await with him the transformation of the world by God. It is possible then to respond to the Christian tradition by accepting Jesus' call for a radical surrender to God and by hoping that God will soon intervene into the world to cure its ills. But to admit in this way that Christianity can support a variety of belief and ethical patterns does not alter the fact that it has at times provided the symbolic impetus for radical social change, nor does it weaken the claim that some of the same symbols may today perform a similar function.[2] Here we will discuss briefly three of the basic Christian concepts which directly influence an ecclesial group's style of political activity.

GOD

It is clear that our notion of God can lead us to an active or to a passive relationship to the social processes. As we have seen, God was viewed as the divine protector of political unity and permanence during much of Western history. The king or emperor often assumed divine authority in the handling of his subjects, most of whom did not presume to question or change the arrangement, especially in the name of the Christian religion. This concept of authority, stability, and political order has carried into our own times. In the minds of many Christians, "God, country, and home" still evoke images which make it difficult to separate divine from human authority.

Even when rationalist philosophical forces began to secularize culture and the political processes, Christianity possessed a ready-made substitute for an ontocratic model of the world. The Augustinian model enabled Christians to take refuge in their ecclesiastical institutions where they could establish their individual relationships with God. Neither the ontocratic nor the Augustinian model promoted political, much less revolutionary, activity in Christian societies. Insofar as Christians were taught to find their salvation in otherworldly realms, Marx could rightly criticize Christianity.

Marx, however, did not imitate the militant atheism of some of his contemporaries. He simply insisted that religion is the natural result of an alienated social order, and he criticized Feuerbach for not investigating why mankind tended to alienate its finest qualities onto God. He thought that religion would disappear when the material causes of man's alienation disappeared; Feuerbach and the Young Hegelians, he felt, were beating a near-dead horse in their obsession for hastening the demise of religion. When a new socialist world order replaced the present perverted one, religion, the "spiritual odor" of the latter, would pass away.

I have already mentioned Ernst Bloch, one contemporary Marxist who believes that Christianity can become a revolutionary force in the world, that its symbols need no longer express the sigh of an oppressed mankind. Bloch is convinced that man's religious consciousness, his religious hope, will be active in or out of a socialist society. He even assigns to this religious hope the same quality which Marx ascribes to revolutionary consciousness—the power to actualize itself in new social forms. Bloch's presuppositions are atheistic; he believes in nothing outside of man and man's religious instincts, which he understands in their revolutionary dimensions. He takes us a dialectical step away from Marx's criticism of religion as a symptom of an alienated world, and he does so using a revisionist Marxian analysis. But if Bloch is satisfied to use religious symbols in this progressive, yet atheistic, sense, the question of whether religious symbols can be used in a progressive *and theistic* sense remains open.

The problem can be stated in another way: can theistic religion, with its predominantly otherworldly and reactionary history, play a revolutionary or liberating role within the social process? Recent biblical scholarship has pointed to at least one solid affirmative example in the biblical tradition: premonarchic Israel. In Chapter Two I cited Mendenhall's thesis that oppressed minorities in Palestine joined the Hebrews who escaped from Egypt at the end of the second millennium B.C. Yahweh, the God of the Hebrews, became the central symbol for all who threw off various forms of social, political, and economic oppression. Norman Gottwald has further theorized that a union of Israelite tribes subsequent to the exodus took place "as a conjunction among lower class rebels and refugees from Canaanite feudalism and Egyptian imperialism, on the one hand, and of semi-nomadic pastoralists aspiring to agricultural sedentation, on the other hand."[3] The exodus experience of the

Bible actually is a condensed version of two centuries of "permanent revolution" in Palestine, according to Gottwald. The cult of Yahweh assured the tribes of a unity which protected them from outside oppression and also safeguarded their autonomy and mutual egalitarianism. Mono-Yahwism is the term which Gottwald employs to indicate the source of Israel's communal egalitarianism and the central symbol responsible for the achievement of a "self-governing association of farmers, constituting basically a single liberated class of agricultural procedures."[4]

Religious institutions in practically all of the ancient world had the primary function of supporting a monarchy and aristocracy. Mono-Yahwism in Israel was a notable exception. No single officer ruled Israel, since Yahweh alone was permitted supreme power, and although religious prescriptions became extensive, "they were regarded, on the whole, as preferable to the extractions of wealth and manpower and the sacrifices of autonomy and free production required by kings and nobles."[5] Israelite families and clans organized tribal councils of elders which made the critical decisions of defense, provided for survival in famine, or judged significant legal disputes. Smaller issues were taken care of within the family or clan. A superordinate religious consciousness of liberation so affected the day-by-day social practice of political decentralization that it became reflected in Israelite religious law. Mono-Yahwism was born in the context of the experience of alienation in Near Eastern society—exploitation, class domination, feudalistic social structures and imperialism.

Gottwald also shows that mono-Yahwism was the symbolic device used to develop a progressively classless society in premonarchic Israel. Utilizing Max Weber's definition of class, he points out that the Israelite religion contained the "basic mechanisms for leveling class differences" because all Israelites enjoyed approximately the same opportunities for a supply of goods, external living conditions, and personal experiences. The pastoralist population of Israel at that time, in the beginning a "lower class," had the opportunity to become agriculturist and could easily settle into an agricultural mode of life. In any case, the less well-situated pastoralists were protected from economic exploitation by the tenets of mono-Yahwism. Since there were no significant economic differences among the population of Israel, economic class domination was not possible, although it was a sad fact of existence in all surrounding territories. Israelite law, selected and permeated by Yahwistic motives, "aimed deliberately at maintaining relatively equal strength and wealth among the clans and families conceived as brothers in community. There were specific proscriptions of economic practices which might lead to deprivation of some sub-units in Israel at the expense of others."[6] Although virtually every aspect of Israelite life had religious overtones, a very small fraction of its wealth was demanded for its religious cult. Yahwism was not cause of widespread poverty for the laymen, nor the source of riches for the Levitical priesthood.

In summary, mono-Yahwism was correlated to and, in a sense, responsible for liberating institutions in Israel; social power was distributed among extended families and clans, political power was distributed among tribes or clan clusters, and religious power was invested in a professional Levitical priesthood, supported and checked by the tribes. This decentralization and communal egalitarianism, Gottwald notes, formed the unique identity of Israelite Yahwism. Indeed in his opinion, "Yahwism was so integral to its [Israel's] formative life and so crucial a factor in its unity that the empirical achievement of the community depended upon its ability to symbolize itself as the people of Yahweh. . . . The object of the divine activity is an entire people egalitarianly conceived and the struggle of a people in motion to bring its endeavor at egalitarian unity to fruition."[7] Yahweh was in fact characterized in the premonarchic Israelite community by his liberating qualities. He stood in direct opposition to the gods of Israel's neighbors, whose service involved repressive class domination and exploitation of the masses through the union of religion and monarchy.

Professor Gottwald does not draw out the possibilities of premonarchic Israel for contemporary theology, but theologians of our generations have been at pains to indicate that the Christian God, as well as the Yahweh of premonarchic Israel, can set "people in motion." Karl Barth might have unwittingly set the stage for this new theological activity with his famous

commentary, *The Epistle to the Romans.* [8] Barth reacted strongly
to the tendencies of nineteenth-century liberal theology, which
stressed God's presence immanently in the world and in the
individual believer. Barth's emphasis came on the absolute
Otherness of God, his separateness from any human category.
He discounted claims of natural revelation and the philosophy
of religion; these he considered idolatrous efforts. The ineffable
God makes himself known to man only through his revelation
in his Word. Thus Barth was responsible for a powerful blow to
a metaphysical notion of God which ties men to a closed, static
conception of society and the world. If man is related to God at
all, said Barth, it is not in terms of ontological categories but
rather in terms of God's grace and man's faith.

A Barthian theological understanding has helped contemporary theologians see that men tend to substitute their own
"goods" for God himself. [9] Faith now is often represented by
causes, commitments, and institutions which have come to
consume the total energies of man: "The religious and also the
political institutions of the West have long been officially
monotheistic, so that we do not easily regard ourselves as
polytheists, believers in many gods, or as henotheists, loyal to
one god among many. Using the word 'god' without definition,
we regard ourselves as either theists or atheists. But if we
confine our inquiry to the forms of faith, then it seems more
true to say that monotheism as value dependence and as loyalty
to One beyond the many is in constant conflict among us with
the two dominant forms: a pluralism that has many objects of
devotion, and a social faith that has one object, which is,
however, only one among many." [10]

Niebuhr indicates that the oldest kind of faith seems to be
henotheistic, a social faith in the family or tribe above all other
loyalties. But because many people become disillusioned by
closed societies which promise so much and produce so little,
they turn to polytheistic forms of faith, dividing their loyalties
among many causes and commitments: Christian, Jewish,
American, Russian, democratic, republican, socialist, capitalist,
Presbyterian, Catholic, left-wing, right-wing, etc.

Christianity has a special proclivity for henotheism because
of the temptation of its adherents to place their complete trust
and faith in their churches, doctrines, rites, moral codes. The
church becomes the object of a henotheistic faith; its doctrines

are seen as the source of all truth and goodness; its programs are viewed as the most highly moral of undertakings. But any cause which usurps the total loyalty of men, however highminded its purpose, is henotheistic, including what many groups term "revolutionary" praxis. This notion in no way detracts from the value of temporal causes, commitments, or loyalties. It simply locates the position of Christian political theology.

A Christian theologian does not approach the problem of God and social change from the vantage point of a metaphysician, a social scientist, a revolutionary, or least of all, of a neutral observer. First of all, he sees God as the "One beyond the many,"[11] beyond nations, classes, churches, causes, ideologies. In Barthian terms, God cannot be identified with any human category. Second, Christian faith is a practical trust and hope that there is One who goes beyond the many and is present to the world and its destiny. Third, the Christian understanding of history includes an attempt to realize how God is present to the world, but Christians cannot reach beyond the history itself. God is the One beyond the many.

This seems to place the political theologian at a serious disadvantage. How can he claim theological support for his enterprise if no connection can be made between God and social change? The answer is no easier than the problem of revelation, the problem of what we can know about God's dealings with man. God is One beyond the many, but the historical Christian community has compiled a record book of its religious experiences, which we have understood to contain many political overtones. Niebuhr looks at revelation as the experiences of a community that illumine its entire history.[12] The stories and symbols of Scripture and the significant events of Christian history take on a universal meaning for all Christians. At the moment of their occurrence the events seem to possess no special meaning; afterwards they become stories, tradition, revelation—the Word, the reflection of God's activity in the world. When the Christian community recalls these stories, it understands them in a wider application to include its own hopes for liberation and fulfillment, or its own rigidity in sin:

"First of all, interpreting our present, we use the life and death of Christ as a parable and as an analogy. The scribes and Pharisees now sit in Peter's seat, and in the churches of

> *St. Paul priests plot defense against the disturber of the*
> *people; moneychangers and those who sell human victims*
> *for vain sacrifices conspire with Pilates who wash their*
> *bloody hands in public; poor unreasoning soldiers commit*
> *sins which are not their own; betrayals and denials take*
> *place in every capital; and so, out of cumulative self-deceit*
> *and treachery, out of great ignorance, out of false fears*
> *and all the evil imaginations of the heart, crosses are*
> *constructed not only for .thieves but for the sons of*
> *God.* "[13]

God is the One beyond the many. Men are left to find his images and reflections in their midst: creation, sonship, sin, judgment, redemption, grace, final liberation. Creation and sonship are linked in the Bible: "The link is given with man's origin: because God creates man as son, that is the creature which by nature is to correspond to his creative call, he creates at the same time the world as his, man's world. Therefore, in the two passages where Paul speaks of man's sonship, he also calls him the heir (Romans 8:17; Gal. 4:7)."[14] Creation means that men take on the work of making history, not according to any preordained, metaphysical plan, but in the struggle and ambiguities of an open-ended, tentative, finite world. The Christian understanding of creation necessitates man's responsible freedom in an open future.

It is easy to grasp the implications for political theology. According to a contemporary theology of secularity, man is not a product of a divinely propelled and ordered universe, but the creator of his own world in freedom and finitude. This is secularity—a restoration to man's original created state of responsibility for the world. He is freed from metaphysical encasements that determine his future, freed from ideologies that burden him with a fixed pattern of life, freed from religious securities that undermine a strong faith, freed to create the world with responsibility. Jesus' proclamation of the gospel dispelled the power of the mythical sacred societies and nature. Christianity ended a sacralized, closed society and introduced a secular, historical perspective on the world.

Friedrich Gogarten, to whom I am indebted for this understanding of secularization, puts it this way:

"Secularization has historicized the world—this is the meaning of secular existence—and now . . . [secular man] and the world are exposed to the future. Confronted with shapeless darkness which threatens the present form of his and the world's existence with dissolution and annihilation, he perceives the demand for wholeness and unity, but he can never know it, except in the form of questioning ignorance. This threat from the future which simultaneously contains the possibility for shaping things anew, provides the demand for wholeness with its authoritative foundation."[15]

However, man is constantly tempted to escape the dynamic world process. This is his sin, the situation from which he must be redeemed. He cannot save himself; events must occur in his life which restore him to the grace of historical openness whenever he encloses himself in the false security of a pseudo divinely-ordained, fixed system. Redemption is the iconoclastic grace of God's judgment on closed systems and the restoration to an open, provisional existence. Christian communities look at history and relate its redemptive events to the redemptive ministry of Jesus Christ.

God is the One beyond the many. Our faith in him tries to reach beyond the void, occasionally slips to a faith in the gods, and finally has to settle for a feeble retrospective groping for his signs in history. We are charged to make the world: "all things are lawful" (1 Cor. 10:23) for men who freely take up the task.[16] When we do, it is not long before we have worked our way into comfortable, secure, privileged positions:

"We justify ourselves before men as churches and as other groups because of the nobility of our ideals. We disguise our transgressions by a vast self-deceit, and when the law too obviously disagrees with our wishes and vices we correct it, inventing new moralities, designed not to make possible the performance of our duty but its evasion. Then we call our greed the sacred right of liberty, our covetousness liberation from slavery, our economic warfare peace, our sentimentalities love, our callousness scientific attitude, our isolation love of peace, our wars

*crusades, our unwillingness to accept responsibility mon-
asticism, our compromises churchmanship. And our workday self-justification and self-deception is given academic
rationalization in theological and philosophical treatises
bearing titles of 'Christian Ethics' and 'Moral Philosophy.'* "[17]

Then we are shaken from our smugness, inertia, conformity, arrogance. Men see through our devices which we call
ideals, confront our irrelevance or irresponsibility, accuse us in
our accumulating riches and greed. We lose a war, suffer a
recession, watch our country become polarized, observe the
dwindling membership of the churches. We are redeemed when
we recognize our guilt and begin the work of creation anew
with those who will join us. Our faith tells us that God's grace
enables us to transcend our fixed patterns of action and to open
ourselves up to the new possibilities of the future. Our Christian
community has understood the events of history as God's
judgment on our present and his offering us redemption
through Jesus Christ if we break out of our rigidity.

God is futurity, but not an eschatological goal to be
reached at the end of a long and weary journey. He is no
otherworldly model with which we can measure our utopian
planning. Much less does he represent an "innerworldly" ideal
future. God does not step into man's province of the world in
order to take over the work which he has entrusted to man.

God is futurity in the sense that he is beyond the present,
beyond the many, yet acts in the present, crushing man's
fondest stabilized images of himself and his world and pushing
him into the insecure but free future. Christianity's history is a
cycle of man's passing from responsibility to irresponsibility
and back again to responsibility, from freedom to unfreedom to
his recapturing of freedom, from liberation to alienation to the
new struggle for liberation. The recurring events that have
brought men to their senses are termed "the grace of God" by
Christians. God's redemptive activity does not interfere with
man's creative activity. Redemption is the way God indicates
his presence to man, not his usurpation of man's responsibility
to make the future. The Bible is a book of God's revelation, the
story of man's understanding that God is present to the world,

that he comes from beyond to enable man to see the destructiveness of man's own present.

Political theology rests on the contemporary theological understanding which highlights man's freedom in the making of his world and also his salvation from irresponsibility and rigidity. The tentative, probing, dynamic character of Christian faith is what makes its political activity potentially creative. Christian symbolic impulses representing God should not be dismissed as irrelevant to social change despite the atheistic analysis of Ernst Bloch.

EVIL AND SIN

The Christian anthropology of sin and evil deals with the condition of man variously described as concupiscence, proneness to evil, dividedness, disintegration, etc. Man's experience attests to his dividedness, his alienation from himself and others. Concupiscence refers to the same kind of disparate conflict in man: "an interior pluralism of man in all his dimensions, levels, and impulses of such a kind that man, insofar as he is (in his deepest self) a free and personal being, can never adequately and radically integrate it in the one decision of freedom (for or against God)."[18]

Since man is exposed to the dividedness and alienation in society, it is likely that he should absorb social pathology into himself. Rahner interprets the statements of traditional theology about concupiscence in man as statements about the secular world.[19] An economic philosophy of competition, and institutionalized racism that keeps minority groups from select neighborhoods, schools, and jobs, an opulent society which unabashedly and patently carries huge pockets of poverty within it, and a value orientation that extols a materialistic "good life" above all other human priorities are bound to infect the individual living in that society.

But the Christian view of evil, concupiscence, and sin in man cannot ascribe evil to the influence of social structures alone. Christianity does not absolve men from their responsibility for wars, class and racial hatreds, colonialist and individual greed, and the selfish refusal to love other men. The world may well infect men with social evils, but in their own freedom individuals confirm a particular way of life for themselves.

Many psychologists would concur with the Christian position that concupiscence, a plurality of conflicting tendencies, is built into the heart of man. Rollo May refers to individual "natural functions which have the power to take over the whole person" as the "daimonic" in man.[20] He sees in man creative and destructive desires which are permanently linked: "The daimonic is the urge in every being to affirm itself, assert itself, perpetuate and increase itself. The daimonic becomes evil when it usurps the total self without regard to the integration of that self, or to the unique forms and desires of others and their need for integration. It then appears as excessive aggression, hostility, cruelty—the things about ourselves that horrify us most, and which we repress whenever we can or, more likely, project on to others. But these are the reverse side of the same assertion which empowers our creativity."[21] His point is that the daimonic is built into man; the destructive is the reverse of the creative; the negative presupposes the positive. May finds a human problem where all the elements of the daimonic are not in open dialogue, when one element takes power over the whole person.

Christianity looks at the same phenomenon and asserts that human nature is prone to sin. Scripture is replete with examples. The prophets, especially Amos, use the word *pesha*, sin, to speak of different kinds of "transgressions"—inhumanity, cruelty, social injustice, violation of contracts, bribing, greed, lust, hypocrisy (*cf.* Amos 1,2,5). The most complete treatment of sin in the New Testament is in Paul's Epistle to the Romans. Paul first emphasizes that all men are in the state of sin because they have constantly rejected God's overtures to them. In the fifth chapter he personalizes sin as a tyrant who rules over all of human history and who is responsible for death in the world. Paul weaves in the Adam story to further illustrate man's need of redemption. Jesus, of course, is the New Adam.

Men in every age, before and after Jesus, tell their own story of their dividedness, of their conspiracies with evil forces in the world, and truly admit that evil has managed to root itself in the best of their species. Christianity has made this aspect of the human predicament a part of its religion, and its many traditions have shaded in a rich variety of meanings regarding the nature of sin. Since the world offers an infinite supply of idols for man to glorify and absolutize, and since the structures of society draw men into ever-changing forms of dehumanization, it is not strange that the last word about evil and sin has not been said.

An awareness of evil and man's consequent pursuit of it has political overtones. This awareness leads to a healthy skepticism about absolute remedies—proposed by either establishment politicians or radical militants. If their religious mandate warns Christians to accept political, economic, religious, and social structures in relative terms only and to work to eliminate those which dehumanize man, the same mandate tells them that no final cataclysmic "revolution" will solve every problem dividing men from each other and themselves. On theological grounds the Christian understanding of evil and sin necessitates a constant "criticism and self-criticism" of group, party, church, society, state, no one of which has been exempt from seeking power for its own ends. It is difficult for a Christian to believe in a privileged class, free from every taint of evil, ready to bring on the new dawn of peace and joy.

Marxism does not adequately deal with the question of evil. It is true that Marx himself defined alienation in terms of the dividedness and fragmentation of man because of the institution of private property and the social division of labor. Further, he speaks of the mystified consciousness that results from a capitalist economic system. And it is true that Marxist leaders have insisted that capitalism has crippled the human growth of people in a way that inhibits their full cooperation with each other. Mao sees criticism and self-criticism as important keys to the continual development of the socialist state. But Marxists generally assume that the true proletariat is capable of achieving a totally developed consciousness and that the "permanent revolution" will dissolve with the state when society blooms into full-fledged communism.

Herein lies the critical difference between Marxism and Christianity. Christianity holds that a permanent revolution will always be necessary because of the limitations of human nature and the evil attached to this finitude. Permanent revolution, or continual conversion, includes both the recognition of a sinful state of affairs (closed, rigid complacency) and the radical reorientation of a life of conversion as preached by John the Baptist. Jesus issues a similar demand (*cf.* Matt. 3:8), and the Christian community has traditionally linked conversion with the impact of God's grace (*cf.* Romans 2:4).

In Christianity the tendency to allow one group, environ- ment, style of life, or ideology to rule over the whole person, excluding the rest of the pluralist world of man, represents the concupiscential proclivity to sin. To hold that there is only one way to live, one religion to embrace, one ideology to follow, one science to learn, one country to serve, one road to "revolution," etc. is to hold naive, destructive, sinful proposi- tions. To fall into apathetic inaction, to become indifferent to the lot and future of mankind, to refuse to accept the unintegrated ambiguity and plurality of human existence, or to yield to the absolutizing of preferred plans or courses of action, in Christian eyes, is to bear sinful fruit.

CELEBRATION

Christians hold that Jesus Christ is the measure of their salvation from the state of sin. It is through Jesus that men can conquer the evil in themselves and in the world, however tentatively and provisionally. There have been many particular interpretations of this doctrine, but the redemptive grace of Jesus has always been the key to Christian salvation. Grace is present when divisions and isolation are overcome. Atonement means at-one-ment. Paul describes salvation as the situation in which "there is neither Jew nor Greek, there is neither slave nor free, there is neither male nor female; for you are all one in Christ Jesus" (Gal. 3:28; *cf.* Col. 3:11 and 1 Cor. 12:13). The power of the grace of Jesus brings with it a new community, a new life, peace (Eph. 2:14).

The table fellowships of Jesus provided a model for later descriptions of grace and community. Paul clarified the the- ological dimensions of Jesus' work, especially in his letters to the Ephesians and Colossians. Paul proclaims that the wall of division among men has been abolished by Jesus Christ (Eph. 2:13-18). The wall Paul refers to in Ephesians 2:14 might be the wall separating Gentiles from Jewish worshipers at the Temple in Jerusalem, the wall around Jerusalem, or the angel guard around the promised land (*cf.* Gen. 32:1-2). At any rate, it is a wall dividing men from men, insiders from outsiders; when the wall is broken down through Jesus, man's peace in grace is established with God.

This understanding had the same practical effect on the celebrations of the early Christian communities as it did during the fellowship meals of Jesus' time: "And do not get drunk with wine, for that is debauchery; but be filled with the Spirit, addressing one another in psalms and hymns and spiritual songs, singing and making melody to the Lord with all your heart, always and for everything giving thanks in the name of our Lord Jesus Christ to God the Father" (Eph. 5:18-20). Christians found it natural to celebrate their new life and community in "eucharists," thanksgiving meals, and "agape" meals, love feasts; they seemed to become so enthusiastic about their celebrations that Paul had to warn them against drunkenness. The newly-founded relationships in the early Christian communities had a liberating effect, which inspired a quality of love that was to become a special characteristic of Christianity. For Christians, people coming together in unity, love, and celebration is Christ, or Christ's Spirit, or grace. The conquering of their disintegration and dividedness is best understood in terms of human community.

It is in celebration that all the elements of the Christian worldview come together—God, sin, salvation, affirmation, community. In celebration the fragmentary aspects of man's life are integrated into a meaningful whole; symbols, play, ritual, psychological release, affirmation, music, dance, congregating, and myth revitalize and liberate the human personality. Johan Huizinga's *Homo Ludens* underlines the importance of celebration and play.[22] Celebration is not simply a question of having fun; it is the ritual social creation of life meaning and its expression, the "living principle of all civilization," in the absence of which "civilization is impossible."[23]

Christian celebration in the established churches has been sapped of much of its potential power to vitalize congregations. Social conformity and habit continue to push listless and passive worshipers to church for streamlined, efficient, dull liturgies that are quick and painless. Others receive solace from traditional forms where they are still enacted. Still others have placed their hopes in liturgical renewal. But even this movement has been content to trim around the edges of old styles, propping up old structures with contemporary music, different language, and an occasional gimmick. Celebrations in the Christian churches notably lack spontaneity, congregational interchange, freedom of movement and expression, and above all, festivity.

Ecclesial communities have the opportunity to create new forms of celebration and perhaps recapture the quintessence of Christianity in the process. Celebration is not an extra. It sums up, embodies, and recharges a person's life commitment in festive terms. In *The Feast of Fools* Harvey Cox mentions three ingredients of festivity: conscious excess, celebrative affirmation, and juxtaposition.[24] Excess means "overdoing it" in food, drink, emotions, clothes, and expression. Affirmation means "saying yes to life" in all its joys and sorrows, accomplishments and failures, hopes and disappointments. The juxtaposition is in the contrast between the toil and drabness of everyday life and the exceptional quality of the celebration. A day of celebration is a feast day, big or little, and it links the participants to the memories of a past faith commitment and the hopes of future promises. The essential quality of a festive celebration is its joy. A good celebration sends the people home with an inner glow.

The smaller size and closer relationships of ecclesial communities aid them in adding new dimensions to their celebrations. So does their relation to secular culture. Rock music, dance, street theater, "rap" sessions, films, pop art, jazz and multimedia forms of expression can naturally be integrated into the celebration of groups which identify the sacred with the secular. Secular culture is set apart for a "sacred" purpose—to energize a community's existence, purpose and future.

Celebrations in ecclesial communities will become just that—celebrations. In *Man at Play* Hugo Rahner speaks of the "Playing of God," the "Playing of Men," and even the "Playing of the Church."[25] He quotes Cyril of Alexandria's and Jerome's commentaries on Zechariah 8:5 ("and the streets of the city shall be full of boys and girls playing") both of which claim the text is alluding to the playing of the church.[26] Taking his lead from Jerome, Rahner formulates a motto for his chapter, "The Playing of the Church": "In the Church the joy of the spirit finds expression in bodily gesture."[27] This principle applies in a special way to dancing: "The dance is a sacral form of play because it is, first and foremost, an attempt to imitate in the form of gesture and rhythm something of that free-soaring motion which God as creative principle has imparted to the cosmos."[28] Rahner offers an array of patristic texts to support his thesis on dance, but we have only to recall "the dancing of Miriam before the people of Israel when they had been freed from their bondage in Egypt, the dancing of David before the ark of the covenant, and Solomon's impressive ordering of the singers in his temple."[29]

Celebration is one of the primary energizing sources of any community, a point Huizinga makes very often; for ecclesial groups it plays a role similar to the table fellowship of Jesus' community. The celebratory life style of a commitment community challenges the rigid, dehumanizing structures of the larger society. According to Harvey Cox, those who embrace a "theology of juxtaposition"[30] celebrate the discontinuity of *the present from the past* in their affirmation of a God who will not allow men to be satisfied with their religious memories, the discontinuity of *the present from the present* in their affirmation of a God who comes to judge petrified, static social structures, and the discontinuity of *the present from the future* in their affirmation of a God who represents an undisclosed humanized future. Celebration does not attempt to resolve the conflicts among past, present, and future; it glories in the tension and plays with it. In so doing the community offers a radical alternative to established ways of behavior and outlooks on life. By adopting a celebratory life style, by experimenting with new forms of social relationships and religious affirmation, an ecclesial community can break the weak links holding together ossified and rigid patterns of the social order.

Celebration also feeds the political imagination of ecclesial groups. It offsets an exclusively empirical analysis of social forces by contributing a salutary utopianism to the process of social change. Cox calls this kind of social vision "political fantasy": "Political fantasy goes beyond the mere political imagination. It is not content to dream up interesting twists within existing societal patterns. It envisions new forms of social existence and operates without first asking whether they are 'possible.' Utopian thinking is to the *polis*, the corporate human community, what fantasy is to the individual person. It provides images by which existing societies can be cracked open and recreated. It prevents societies, like thought systems, from becoming 'closed and ossified.' "[31] Celebration possesses a natural symbol system for political fantasy. It reminds us that the future is indeed open and anything *can* happen because it *is* happening.

The title and motif of *The Feast of Fools* comes from an annual medieval feast at which all the traditional establishment figures were lampooned in comic caricature. Kings, bishops, "superiors" of every type had their pomposity deflated by the people of the realm. It was a celebration that evened things out, if only briefly. Celebration can perform a similar function today, perhaps even include some of the guerilla theater's penchant for mimicry of the establishment. A contemporary feast of fools may find new targets in the dour-faced militants who take themselves too seriously. Celebration must restore balance to a community and those who focus too narrowly on the "work of the revolution" have to be brought to themselves—even literally by being presented with caricatures of themselves.

No pattern or specific order for celebrations need be outlined. Some will take the form of small festive meals with music, dancing, conversation, perhaps a guest to "rap" with or an old W. C. Fields film to enjoy. Others will develop on the spot in the middle of work projects, demonstrations, solidarity meetings. Sometimes an event, a rally, a march will turn into a celebratory experience. Other celebrations will rely on traditional religious symbols, images, rituals. All types can be uplifting, meaningful occasions of renewal. The tradition of celebration in Christianity is an indispensable part of the life of an ecclesial community.

One is reminded here of Marx's treatment of the liberated senses of man in a communist society and of his discussion of man's need to gather socially (as quoted, for instance, in "The Conquest of Alienation," Chapter Three). Marx assumed that creative social labor would become its own "celebration," meaning, and source of pleasure. But he did not consider the question of celebration in an alienated society; he probably would have relegated Christian celebration to that class of activity which diverts revolutionary potential into socially acceptable channels. As we have seen, however, Christian celebration can actually include revolutionary implications. It interprets the past and present and hopes for a more humanized future. Its liturgy brims with praise for the "wonderful works of God," prays for man's response to the grace of creative responsibility, and gives thanks for deeper human community. Socialist societies lack a religious dimension in their politically oriented community celebrations. Politics and economics do not exhaust the entire meaning of man's human life. Celebration should include the mystery, the transcendent, the parts of man's life beyond the present and the knowable future. This is what Christian celebration can express and give a revolutionary dimension.

THE CHRISTIAN-MARXIST DIALOGUE

The Christian-Marxist dialogue in recent years has performed at least one important function: it has assured Marxists that, in Bonhoeffer's words, man and religion have "come of age." For Christian theologians God is no longer a miracle-worker who intervenes in the world to perform man's work for him. The burden of building the world has been placed on man's shoulders, let us hope, once and for all. Neither is God any longer a device that is used to explain suffering, evil, death, weakness, the secrets of nature, or the future. "Man has come of age." Christian man has learned to live autonomously in the world that has been given to him to develop. If man does not improve society, Christianity now teaches, no one will, and it is for man to work out the details of this enterprise. If the world is threatened by man's folly or insanity, man is now willing to face up to the threat by himself—without calling down a divine agent to set things back on their normal course. If suffering, alienation, and evil seem to drive man to the state of despair, only his hope and hard work will begin to liberate him from social difficulties. God, Christians now know, will not step in to do what we should do.

The problem with the Christian-Marxist dialogue is that even after settling the question of religious alienation, the discussion has remained on a highly abstract and theoretical level. Harvey Cox put it this way:

> *"Given the immense relief we all feel at the emergence of a Christian-Marxist dialogue, to complain about the agenda at this point may seem at first like bickering. But questions must be raised nevertheless. Roger Garaudy is a good example. He wins theological friends just a bit too easily. He suggests that the dialogue should center not on class struggle or revolution but on such problems as transcendence, subjectivity, and the meaning of love. Christians find themselves all too comfortable when they hear such phrases. Isn't this just what we discuss all the time, and haven't we proved to ourselves and others that we can discuss them endlessly? Why not have a Christian-Marxist dialogue? The reason that Garaudy is attractive to Christians is that he is talking about* our *traditional agenda."*[32]

Now that the preliminaries have been dispensed with, that is, now that each side has ceased demonizing the opposition, philosophers and theologians and activists of varying ideologies are eager to get on with some dialogue that might reverberate in the social order. There are similar problems in all societies of the world; a dialogue must get down to specifics even if proposed solutions will be tentative. The hope is that Marxism and Christianity will complement each other in a theoretical analysis of existing societies developed from the most humanizing praxis of both sides' experience.

For example, one problem that has enormous ramifications and is central to both Marxist and Christian experience is the relation of community and the individual. Individual freedom is connected with a complex of issues, but at the heart of them all is the question of how men should relate to one another in community. In the West the liberal theory that places primacy on the individual's right to his own happiness— including, of course, his right to pursue wealth privately—has scarcely been seriously criticized, while in communist states extreme measures of mass collectivization have been justified in the name of progress. Is there a way out of this critical impasse? Can the experience of each society be of help to the other?

Christianity has dealt with this problem no less than Marxism, if in less specific terms. Marxists have enjoyed the advantage of historical experimentation even if the results have not always merited our accolades. Christians in an unsettled capitalist society stand to learn much from Marxists who have been suffering through a venture of incalculable importance. At the same time Christians can try to understand their own central doctrine of love and respect for the individual in new ways.

This is not the place to level another attack on communist societies for running roughshod over individual rights, or even to accuse the Marxists of a monolithic understanding of man's social nature; it is quite obvious that there can be more than one kind of society which conforms to the species-life of man. We in the West should begin to explore what the concepts of political community and common destiny *could* mean if *every* member of our society were made a *full* participant of the community, and if people of other lands and cultures were given the same opportunity. Only in such a world will the Christian ideal of the sacredness of the individual be vindicated. Christians can talk to Marxists on this question with empathy and concern.

There are some questions which Christians have to work out for themselves before they go to conferences with Marxists—for example, are they serious enough about social change to struggle for it rather than just talk about it? Does class struggle imply class hate? And there are philosophical and religious experiences they should be willing to offer to Marxists as possible contributions to socialist culture: their understanding of personal life-space, the importance of an interior life, etc.

The crucial question, of course, remains in the political realm. Is it possible to form a common front throughout capitalist and socialist countries against alienation, oppression, and dehumanization? Can the "revolutionaries" in both camps learn to trust each other? Both the Marxian and the Christian tradition possess trenchant complementary significances which relate to changing the world. We can no longer afford to neglect each other.

Notes

1. Albert Schweitzer, *The Quest of the Historical Jesus* (London: A. and C. Black, 1910), p. 364.
2. See Rosemary Ruether's excellent analysis of the motif of messianic expectation in Western history, *The Radical Kingdom* (New York: Harper and Row, 1970) for an impressive description of the revolutionary underpinnings of the Christian faith.
3. "A Sociology of the Religion of Liberated Israel, 1250-1000 B.C." Unpublished manuscript, 1970. For class use in the Graduate Theological Union, Berkeley, California.
4. *Ibid.*
5. *Ibid.*
6. *Ibid.*
7. *Ibid.*
8. Trans. by Edwyn C. Hoskyns, 6th ed. (London: Oxford University Press, 1968).
9. For a powerful treatment of this idea see H. Richard Niebuhr, *Radical Monotheism and Western Culture* (New York: Harper, 1960).
10. *Ibid.*, p. 24.
11. *Ibid.*, p. 32.
12. H. Richard Niebuhr, *The Meaning of Revelation* (New York: Macmillan, 1960), p. 93.
13. *Ibid.*, p. 91.
14. Friedrich Gogarten, *Despair and Hope for Our Time* (Philadelphia: Pilgrim, 1970), p. 59.
15. *Ibid.*, p. 151. For a further development of Gogarten's secularization theology see *Der Mensch zwischen Gott und Welt* (Stuttgart: Friedrich Vorwerk, 1956).
16. *Despair and Hope*, pp. 80 ff.
17. Niebuhr, *The Meaning of Revelation*, p. 124.
18. Karl Rahner, "Theological Reflections on the Problem of Secularization," *Theological Renewal*, Vol. 1 (Montreal: Palm, 1968), p. 187.
19. *Ibid.*, p. 188.
20. Rollo May, *Love and Will* (New York: Norton, 1969), p. 123.

21. *Ibid.*
22. Johan Huizinga, *Homo Ludens: A Study of the Play Element in Culture* (New York: Beacon, 1955).
23. *Ibid.*, pp. 100-101.
24. Harvey Cox, *The Feast of Fools* (Cambridge, Massachusetts: Harvard University Press, 1969), pp. 22-24.
25. Hugo Rahner, *Man at Play* (London: Burns and Oates, 1965).
26. *Man at Play*, pp. 50-51.
27. *Ibid.*, p. 52.
28. *Ibid.*, p. 67
29. *Ibid.*, p. 75.
30. *Feast of Fools*, pp. 131-138.
31. *Ibid.*, pp. 82-83.
32. "The Marxist-Christian Dialogue: What Next?" in *Marxism and Christianity*, ed. Herbert Aptheker (New York: Humanities, 1968), pp. 24-25.

Appendix

Bibliography

Alvineri, Shlomo. *The Social and Political Thought of Karl Marx.* Cambridge: Cambridge University Press, 1969.

Anchor Bible: John. Commentary by Raymond Brown. Vol. 1. Garden City: Doubleday, 1966.

St. Augustine. *City of God.* Garden City: Doubleday, 1958.

Barth, Karl. *The Epistle to the Romans.* Trans. by Edwin C. Hoskyns. London: Oxford University Press, 1960, 6th ed., 1968.

Baum, Gregory. *The Credibility of the Church Today.* New York: Herder and Herder, 1968.

Bloch, Ernst. *Das Prinzip Hoffnung.* 3 Bande. Frankfurt: Suhrkamp, 1959.

————. "Man as Possibility." *Cross Currents* (Summer 1968) 273-282.

————. *Man on His Own.* New York: Herder and Herder, 1970.

Brandon, S. C. F. *Jesus and the Zealots.* Manchester: Manchester University Press, 1967.

Castro, Fidel. *Major Speeches.* London: Stage 1, 1968.

————. *Speech to the United Nations.* New York: Fair Play for Cuba Committee, 1960.

Ch'en, Jerome, ed. *Mao.* Englewood Cliffs: Prentice Hall, 1969.

Congar, Ives. "Theology's Task after Vatican II." *Theology of Renewal.* Vol. 1. Montreal: Palm, 1968.

Cox, Harvey. *The Feast of Fools.* Cambridge, Massachusetts: Harvard University Press, 1969.

————. "The Marxist-Christian Dialogue: What Next?" *Marxism and Christianity.* Edited by Herbert Aptheker. New York: Humanities, 1968, pp. 15-28.

Cullmann, Oscar. *The State in the New Testament.* New York: Scribners, 1956.

Dodd, C. H. *The Johannine Epistles.* New York: Harper, 1946.

————. *The Parables of the Kingdom.* New York: Scribners, 1961.

Editorial Statement. *Socialist Revolution* 1, (January-February 1970) 3-11.

————. *Socialist Revolution* 1, (March-April 1970) 7-32.

Engels, Frederick. *Socialism: Utopian and Scientific.* New York: International, 1935.

————. *Anti-Dühring.* Moscow: Foreign Languages, 1954.

Evans, Donald. *The Logic of Self Involvement.* London: S.C.M., 1963.

Fetscher, Iring. *Karl Marx und der Marxismus.* Munchen: R. Piper, 1967.

Fuller, R. H. *The New Testament in Current Study.* New York: Scribners, 1962.

Glasson, T. F. *The Second Advent.* London: Epworth, 1963.

Gogarten, Friedrich. *Der Mensch zwischen Gott und Welt.* Stuttgart: Friedrich Vorwerk, 1958.

————. *Despair and Hope.* Philadelphia: Pilgrim, 1970.

Gottwald, Norman. *The Church Unbound.* Philadelphia: Lippincott, 1967.

————. "A Sociology of the Religion of Liberated Israel, 1250-1000 B.C." Unpublished class notes, Graduate Theological Union, Berkeley, California.

Guevara, Che. *Socialism and Man.* New York: Merit, 1968.

Hegel, G. W. F. *The Philosophy of History.* Trans. by J. Sibree. New York: Dover, 1956.

Huizinga, Johan. *Homo Ludens: A Study of the Play Element in Culture.* Boston: Beacon, 1955.

Johnson, Sherman. *Jesus in His Own Times.* London: A. and C. Black, 1958.

Johnstone, Monty. "Marx and Engels and the Concept of the Party." *The Socialist Register, 1967* (New York: Monthly Review Press), pp. 121-158.

Josephus. *Jewish Antiquities.* Loeb Classical Library. Cambridge, Massachusetts: Harvard University Press, 1965.

Käsemann, Ernst. *Essays on New Testament Themes.* London: S.C.M., 1960.

Kolakowski, Leszek. *Toward a Marxist Humanism.* New York: Grove, 1969.

Kümmel, Werner G. *Promise and Fulfillment.* London: S.C.M., 1957.

Küng, Hans. *The Church.* New York: Sheed and Ward, 1967.

Lenin, V. I. *Collected Works.* Vol. 21. Moscow: Progress, 1964.

————. *Collected Works.* Vol. 31. Moscow: Progress, 1966.

————. *Imperialism: The Highest Stage of Capitalism.* New York: International, 1939.

————. *"Left-Wing Communism," An Infantile Disorder.* New York: International, 1940.

————. *The Revolutionary Proletarian Party of a New Type.* Peking: Foreign Languages, 1960.

————. *Selected Works.* Moscow: Progress, 1963.

————. *State and Revolution.* New York: International, 1943.

————. *War and the Workers.* New York: International, 1940.

————. *What Is to Be Done?* New York: International, 1943.

Liebman, Marcel. *Le Leninisme et la Revolucion*. Paris: Editions du Seuil, 1970.

_____. "Lenin in 1905: A Revolution that Shook a Doctrine." *Monthly Review* 21 (April 1970) 57-75.

Ling, Trevor. *The Significance of Satan*. London: S.P.C.K., 1961.

Lukács, Georg. *Geschichte und Klassenbewußtsein*. Berlin: Malik, 1923.

Manson, T. W. *The Teaching of Jesus*. Cambridge: University Press, 1935.

Mao Tse-Tung. *Selected Readings from the Works of Mao Tse-Tung*. Peking: Foreign Languages, 1967.

Marcuse, Herbert. *Negations*. Boston: Beacon, 1969.

Marx, Karl. *Capital*. 3 Vols. New York: International, 1967.

_____. *Early Writings*. Trans. and ed. by T. B. Bottomore. New York: McGraw-Hill, 1964.

_____. *The Poverty of Philosophy*. New York: International, 1967.

_____. *Pre-Capitalist Economic Formations*. New York: International, 1966.

_____. *Wage-Labour and Capital*. New York: International, 1933.

Marx, Karl and Engels, Frederick. *The German Ideology*. New York: International, 1966.

_____. *Selected Correspondence*. New York: International, 1962.

_____. *Selected Works*. 2 Vols. Moscow: Foreign Languages, 1962.

May, Rollo. *Love and Will*. New York: Norton, 1969.

McCabe, Herbert. "The Priesthood and Revolution." *Commonweal* 88 (March 1, 1968) 261-265.

Mendenhall, George E. "The Hebrew Conquest of Palestine." *The Biblical Archaeologist* 25 (September 1962), 66-87.

Merleau-Ponty, Maurice. *Humanism and Terror*. Boston: Beacon, 1969.

Metz, Johannes. "Created Hope." *New Theology No. 5*. Edited by Martin E. Marty and Dean G. Peerman. New York: Macmillan, 1968.

_____. "The Return of J. B. Metz: An Interview." *New Book Review*, December 1968, pp. 10-13.

_____. *Theology of the World*. New York: Herder and Herder, 1969.

Moltmann, Jürgen. "Hoping and Planning." *Cross Currents* 18, (Summer 1968), 307-318.

_____. *The Theology of Hope*. New York: Harper and Row, 1967.

Muckenhirn, Maryellen, ed. *The Future as the Presence of Shared Hope*. New York: Sheed and Ward, 1968.

Niebuhr, H. Richard. "The Hidden Churches and the Churches in Sight." *Religion In Life* 15 (1946), 106-117.

_____. *The Meaning of Revelation*. New York: Macmillan, 1960.

_____. *Radical Monotheism and Western Culture*. New York: Harper, 1960.

Pedersen, Johns. *Israel: Its Life and Culture*. 2 Vols. London: Oxford University Press, 1926.

Perrin, Norman. *The Kingdom of God in the Teaching of ·Jesus*. Philadelphia: Westminster, 1963.

_____. *Rediscovering the Teaching of Jesus*. New York: Harper and Row, 1967.

Plato. *The Laws of Plato.* Trans. by A. E. Taylor. London: Dent & Sons, 1934.

Polanyi, Michael. *Personal Knowledge.* New York: Harper and Row, 1964.

Rahner, Hugo. *Man at Play.* London: Burns and Oates, 1965.

Rahner, Karl. "Theological Reflections on the Problem of Secularization." *Theological Renewal.* Vol. 1. Montreal: Palm, 1968, pp. 167-192.

Robinson, James M. *A New Quest of the Historical Jesus.* London: S.C.M., 1959.

————. *The Problem of History in Mark.* London: S.C.M., 1968.

Robinson, John A. T. *Jesus and His Coming.* London: S.C.M., 1957.

Ruether, Rosemary. *The Radical Kingdom.* New York: Harper and Row, 1970.

Sanders, Jack T. "The Question of the Relevance of Jesus for Ethics Today." *Journal of the American Academy of Religion* 38 (June 1970) 131-146.

Schnackenburg, Rudolf. *God's Rule and Kingdom.* New York: Herder and Herder, 1963.

Schram, Stuart. "The Party in Chinese Communist Ideology." *The China Quarterly,* No. 38. (April-June 1969) 1-26.

Schurmann, Franz. *Ideology and Organization in Communist China.* Berkeley: University of California Press, 1966.

Schweitzer, Albert. *The Quest of the Historical Jesus.* London: A. and C. Black, 1910.

Steward, David S. "Historicity and Empirical Method." Unpublished Paper, Graduate Theological Union, Berkeley, California.

Van Leeuwen, A. Th. *Christianity and World History.* London: Edinburgh House, 1964.

Watzlwick, Paul *et al. The Pragmatics of Human Communication.* New York: Norton, 1967.